ESCAPE FROM HELL

Other books by George F. Wieland

Changing Hospitals

Organization Theory and Design

Improving Health Care Management

Bessarabian Knight

Celtic Germans: The Rise and Fall of Ann Arbor's Swabians

Stubborn & Liking It: Einstein & Other Germans

ESCAPE FROM HELL:

GERMAN VOICES

George F. Wieland

ANN ARBOR, MICHIGAN

Copyright © 2017 George F. Wieland

All rights reserved. Except as permitted under the U. S. Copyright Act of 1976, no part of this publication may be reproduced, distributed, transmitted in any form or by any means, or stored in a database or retrieval system, without the prior written permission from the author, George F. Wieland at gwieland@umich.edu.

On the cover: Andrea Jakob, ready for *Fassnacht*

ISBN 13: 978-1537244723

ISBN 10: 1537244728

PREFACE

Many people have helped me over the years that it took to do the research for this book. I'm very grateful to all the people I interviewed, some of whom appear in this book and others who were helpful in confirming information or clearing up my misunderstandings. Many graciously took time to answer my questions.

The late Prof. Heinz Biesdorf of Cornell University and his wife, Ellen, entertained me over the years with stories about Germans. I was also encouraged by visits to Prof. Ulrich Planck at the Universität Hohenheim, as well as Prof. Martin Scharfe, Prof. Hermann Bausinger, and the late Prof. Utz Jeggle—all at the Universität Tübingen—and the late Dr. Paul Sauer, historian and head of the state archives in Stuttgart.

Michael Betzold copyedited my manuscript, trying to fix my Germanic syntax. Jack Lyon of the Editorium helped with the index. My readers over the years have been helpful not only in correcting drafts but also in providing encouragement: Dr. Barbara K. Petersen, Patience S. Wieland, Charlie Zakrajshek, David Lindemer, Dr. Elaine Hockman, and Sharon Kane Wieland. They are not responsible for the inevitable errors and infelicities that remain.

The University of Michigan and Ann Arbor District libraries obtained many books for me with interlibrary loans.

Finally, Nancy Shattuck of Wayne State University provided needed encouragement when I was overwhelmed with computer and publication problems.

CONTENTS

INTRODUCTION 1

1: POVERTY 5

2: THE STEPCHILD'S STORY 25

3: THE APPEAL OF THE NAZIS..43

4: 1930S JEWISH REFUGEES 55

5: MAX GIDEON: JEWISH FARMER 75

6: HOLOCAUST SURVIVORS 87

7: RICHARD FLEISCHER: SURVIVOR 107

8: WAR AND AFTERMATH 115

9: SONIA CIRESA: WARBRIDE 143

10: THE FLIGHT OF THE *VOLKSDEUTSCH* 157

11: GUNTHER LEILI'S STORY..167

12: THE CHILDREN OF THE IMMIGRANTS..........................173

13: WALTER LUIKART'S STORY 187

14: RUTH GOLDSTEIN'S STORY...195

15: CONCLUSIONS 201

REFERENCES 203

INDEX 209

THE AUTHOR 217

INTRODUCTION

This is the story of twentieth-century immigrants to America who were forced to escape from southwest Germany. I focus on the Swabians from that area because my own Swabian heritage helped me find respondents and helped me develop rapport with them. Swabia was also a microcosm of Germany, comprised of both rural and urban areas.

On the other hand, the mentality of the Swabians is somewhat distinctive. According to at least one observer, they are "Super Germans."[1] Other Germans seem to agree, characterizing them as more individualistic and more stubborn than the average German. These quirks of Swabian character will become evident in the stories here, but their reasons for fleeing Germany were similar to those of other Germans: poverty, Nazi abuse, and postwar desolation. (Superscript numbers in the text point to references that are found at the end of the book.)

In the 1920s, southwestern Germany, or Swabia, was very rural and very poor. Since at least the eighth century, Swabians had practiced divided inheritance: each son received an equal share of the family farm. By the twentieth century, many farms were only ten acres in size, forcing many people to flee to America. One typical immigrant told me, "I could have gotten a share of the farm by staying, but a quarter of the farm wasn't worth much." Others left because they were illegitimate children and would receive no inheritance at all.

Swabia mostly avoided the violence common during the 1920s between the Communists and Nazis in urbanized North Germany. Most people in the backwater of Swabia were not political. However, some Swabians shared the widespread feelings of shame and anger over the country's defeat in World War I. Hitler was able to capitalize on these feelings to get a grip on the German people.

Jews had a long history in Swabia. After their emancipation in the nineteenth century, they gradually moved from their villages to towns and cities. Thus, Albert Einstein's family moved from their ancestral village of Bad Buchau to the city of Ulm, where he was born in 1879. Jews took advantage of the growing economic opportunities open to all Germans. There were, for example, no quotas for Jews at universities as there were in America.

However, immediately upon taking power in 1933, the Nazis fired all Jews from government jobs. Many people with leftist leanings, including Jews, were arrested, so that politically aware Jews were the first of the Jewish escapees of the 1930s. Nazi abuse gradually escalated. One man came home from a business trip in 1935 to find that kids had pushed his wife and five-year-old son off the sidewalk and then threw stones through their window and almost killed the boy. They had put a rope around his neck, and when his mother said what they were doing was stupid, they responded that their teacher said they should play at "killing Jews."[1]

After the November 1938 Crystal Night pogrom, almost all Jews wanted to escape, but American quotas for German immigrants were full. During the fall of 1941, the Nazis decided they would kill all Jews still in Germany. Of the 1,050 forced from Stuttgart in the first of so-called "resettlement" programs in December of that year, only thirty survived. Tales of the camps and eventual escapes from the Holocaust are heartbreaking.

As World War II progressed, people on the home front experienced carpet-bombing by the Allies: indiscriminate bombing of cities. Later in the war even teenagers as young as fourteen years old were drafted. The end of the war in May, 1945 was known by Germans as "Time Zero." Many were homeless and with little fuel and food.

In addition, millions had to flee from German territory annexed by Poland and Russia. Other refugees were forced from long-standing German settlements in Eastern Europe. Some of these refugees were able to escape from their hard lives starting in the mid-1950s when America again began to accept German immigrants. Other Germans were not permitted to flee their homes in communist Hungary or Romania, and they escaped to America only twenty years after the war's end.

One such refugee recalled, "I couldn't really feel good in Germany. I wanted to have a place I could call my own. I wanted to have some land where I could be happy and plant things again. I'd go to any country to do it. Even to Australia or America."[2]

Life in America for the escapees was initially difficult. They had to learn a new language and discard many of their old habits. Even formerly well-to-do Jewish women had to become maids, housekeepers, or manual laborers. Men might have to start work as elevator operators. However, having escaped various versions of hell back home, the immigrants were very appreciative of America.

Most refugees retained some Swabian values, such as a claustrophobic reaction to any limits on individual and religious freedom and the distinctive Swabian conscientiousness, especially concerning frugality. Their children became more American. As one German refugee from Romania told me, his children will be "more modern than us." They might even have a "mixed marriage, marry an Italian or an American." But even if the children were to become like Americans, "they're going to manage better than the other Americans. They know how to work and save."

Swabia is today very different from the difficult times described by the twentieth-century escapees. Americans with a German heritage from nineteenth-century immigrants should be grateful to have avoided the awful poverty, political repression, and destruction of war suffered by many not so very long ago.

My own parents came from Germany in 1926. Curious as to what privations I had avoided by being born in America, I asked my parents about their early lives and how they came to America. I then talked to other German immigrants, including some of the many Jewish refugees who lived in and around New York City, where I grew up. In locating Jewish survivors, I was helped and encouraged by the late Walter Strauss, who gave me a copy of his book, *Signs of Life*, about Jewish refugees. My interviews took place from the late 1970s into the late 1980s, in time to collect many stories while the escapees were still alive.

To preserve privacy, I have given pseudonyms for a few interviewees.

Readers interested in learning more about Swabia and Swabian immigrants to America may wish to consult some of references in the endnotes, as well as my two earlier books: *Celtic Germans*, and *Stubborn & Liking It*.[1,2]

1:POVERTY

Swabia in the early twentieth century was still a mostly rural corner of Germany. A third of the people were peasants, and most suffered from grinding poverty.

Swabians have long had a distinctive culture which can be attributable to the earlier mixing of Germans with the original inhabitants of southwest Germany, the Celts. This mixing made the Swabian Germans shorter and darker than other Germans further north. More important were some acquired cultural influences, such as the sometimes excessive spiritual enthusiasm that would later conflict with the established Lutheran religion.

A second possible Celtic cultural influence is excessive individualism. For whatever reasons, the Swabians are extremely independent. This was reinforced by an inheritance practice unique among the Swabians, shared or divided inheritance, going back at least to the eighth century. Land was divided among all sons in the family. Everyone had his own realm, however small.[3]

Wartime

Many of the Swabian peasants who escaped to America in the 1920s had been young children during World War I. They had some war experience, not on Germany's Eastern Front or Western Front, but on the third front inside Germany. Because the Allies blocked shipments of food to Germany, the Kaiser's government had to use severe measures to ensure that people in the cities could eat.

Ernst Weber, from Schleissweiler, recalled, "Government

officials knew how many acres of wheat you planted, and they figured out how much grain you would get. You would be allowed to keep a certain amount for each person. If you had a poor harvest and you couldn't turn over to the government what you owed, you wouldn't have enough for yourself." Lena Schlimmeyer from Trailhof, a small hamlet of six families, recalled a neighbor who told the authorities that her family was holding back food, so police came with long forks and rods to poke through their hay. But the family's meager supply of meat was hidden under the woodpile, and the flour was in the attic. Lena's family was lucky, because by 1918 the authorities often searched the living quarters on farms.[4]

Germany had open plains to the east and west and so it was frequently subject to invasions. Only clever peasants could survive. Even though the Kaiser's government kept records of how many cattle and pigs each family owned, they missed the pig that Weber's neighbor raised inside the house! Another neighbor was able to spirit a pig into the woods while government agents first made the usual courtesy stop at the mayor's house. Peasants knew that in wartime those with power used force to take whatever they wanted.

The stresses of life made the Swabian peasants conservative. Their small plots of land didn't justify the risks of changing long-standing practices. Bob Wiesenmayer, from Kirchberg in the Neckar River valley, recalled how his family still followed a three-year rotation of crops used since the Middle Ages. Some peasants' tools—like the flail, simply two sticks joined together with a leather thong—dated back more than a thousand years. Wiesenmayer remembered, "To thresh the wheat, there were four of us together, two on one end of the pile of grain and two on the other end. We had to swing our flails just right, to hit the grain flat on the floor and not hit another flail."

The Wiesenmayer family farm was ten *Morgan* in size—what a peasant could plow in ten mornings—about seven acres. Such small farms were common in Swabia because of the generations of divided inheritance. This is why Swabia was so poor compared to the rest of Germany, and why so many peasants were forced to escape to America.

Conscientious

Besides spirituality and individualism, a third important Swabian trait is conscientiousness. Swabians are careful, tidy, hardworking, punctual, scrupulous, thrifty, perfectionistic, and well organized. Swabians had to be conscientious to survive on their small plots of land. They housed their cattle in barns and brought feed to them, rather than using the less efficient pasture system common in northern Germany. The conscientious culture of the Swabian peasants had also been fostered by nearly three centuries of religious courts that existed in even the small villages. These courts enforced the doctrine that individual possessions really belonged to God, and it was a duty to be efficient and frugal and to work hard to take care of God's things.

In *Celtic Germans*, I have reported twentieth-century survey data showing that Swabians are more religious, more individualistic, and more conscientious than other Germans. Swabian individualism is particularly distinctive. These traits colored how Swabians dealt with the stresses of living in Germany, escaping, and later adapting to America.

These peasants did not produce goods for markets. They were self-sufficient, and lived on what they raised themselves. Gottlieb Wiel, from a small village near Sulzbach in the Swabian Forest, came from a relatively large farm with fifteen acres under cultivation. Wiel recalled, "A farm family didn't shop often, and then just for soap, sugar, salt, and clothing that the family couldn't make. For flour, we took the grain to the mill across the creek. For oil, we raised poppies. Vinegar came from cider. We used beech tree leaves to stuff mattresses and as bedding for the animals. When we cut down trees for lumber, we chopped the branches up and used them to heat the house and the bake oven. The small branches from evergreen trees were also used for animal bedding." Even the energy to run the farm came from the farmers themselves. Machines were hand operated.

The farmers were careful with all their resources. After manure taken from the barn had lain a while in the fields, rain would wash out the straw, which would then be raked up and used for animal bedding a second time. A couple of times a year, the peasants used a special, tank-shaped wagon to transport cow urine from the barn to the fields. They filled pails and carefully poured the nutrient solution around each plant. Even the droppings from horses passing through the village would not escape attention. There was sure to be an old lady who scooped them off the street for her garden.

While the peasants weren't wealthy, they took pride in their independence and conscientiousness. In one story, the village pastor congratulates a peasant who had spent years improving a wasteland into a veritable Eden: "Now we see that all things are possible with God's help." The peasant's arch retort: "Well, you should have seen what it looked like when only God was working there."

Many jobs, such as sowing grain by hand, needed a special touch. But even seemingly simple tasks, like harvesting hay, required skills like knowing how to sharpen the scythe's blade to get out nicks and gouges. The woman riding on top of the hay wagon had to be able to pile hay carefully. The top of the hay stack had to be wider than the bottom, and a skillful overlapping arrangement kept the top-heavy pile from spilling.

Women

Women bore a great burden. The men made sure women did more than their share. Their hands were never idle, and they often did more than one thing at once, like knitting while cooking. Wiesenmayer recalled that his mother was the first one up in the morning to start the fire and to cook. To do laundry, she had to carry water fifty yards from the village spring, build a fire under a big pot, boil the clothes, wash them by rubbing, then wring each piece by hand. For simple things like washing a salad, she had to walk to the village spring. Wiesenmayer remembered, "She had no fun. Once my parents rode in a car, when my sister got married. My mother talked and talked about that."

But household matters were not the only tasks required of women. Most of the year, women worked another shift. After preparing, serving, and cleaning up from the main meal, the women would return to the fields to rake and turn the hay or load it onto the wagon. Wiel remembered, "Women would plant the potatoes, keep the beds clear of weeds, hill the dirt up against the potato plants, and later harvest them with the hoe." Women were also usually responsible for feeding the animals and cleaning the manure out of the barn.

Children also worked starting around age five, as go-fers or by performing simple tasks. Wiel recalled "My village used to sell fishing rights in the brook to rich people. As kids, we hit the water with branches to scare the fish so the rich people could net them. We only got a nickel. Rich people thought we did it for fun." Wiesenmayer remembered arriving home late one night after helping a neighbor. "My father was angry with me until I showed him the money I earned. Then it was all right."

Gene Wieland, from Bartenbach, grew up helping at his family's *Wirtschaft* or inn. When he was nine, his mother had to go to Stuttgart, so she told him how to cook a meal for twelve people, a pork roast with sauerkraut and potatoes. "She told me how to do it with the wood fire. At twelve o'clock I had to do something on the side. When I came back in the kitchen the potatoes were scorching. My father was home, and I was really scared. So I took the ones on the bottom out and put some cold water over the other ones and put them back so they steamed a little. Nobody said anything, and they all ate them." His parents, like many others, took advantage of their children. That's why he left for America. "I worked for my parents until I was twenty, and I was never paid." When he told his parents he was leaving, "what could they say but 'I understand'?"

Schooling

Formal schooling was a low priority. For children born in the first decade of the twentieth century, seven grades of school was the maximum. Even so, they were often shortchanged by the disruptions of World War I. The Kingdom of Württemberg, the core of Swabia, eventually mobilized 500,000 soldiers out of a population of 2,530,000, and 74,000 were killed. Because of the shortage of men, teachers were usually invalids from the army, and they often had to cover two villages, teaching on alternate days.

Nevertheless, school did have a major impact on the children. The aim was to teach not only basic skills like reading and arithmetic but also obedience. The teachers, as college-educated employees of the state, had to be addressed as "Honorable So-and-So."

Wieland recalled the brutality used to foster obedience. "The teacher would watch while I was writing composition to see if I left a comma out. Then he used his bamboo cane to hit my fingers. He would sometimes keep hitting kids until he couldn't lift his arm anymore. There was another kid who couldn't even write his name without making a mistake, so he got hit all the time.

"I was good in learning, so I wasn't hit for that, but for other things. Like the time a girl kept scratching between her legs while she walked to the front of the class. I was thirteen then, so of course I laughed. The teacher asked three times why I was laughing, but I couldn't tell him. So then I got it twice on the hands, and I was put in the last seat. I was second in the class before."

Louis Gruber from Bartenbach recalled how a mentally retarded girl was hit until she got a blister on her hands. Boys had to lie over a bench and get hit with a stick on their butt. "They had to pull their pants tight so it hurt more."

Even on visits to Germany, former students would make a point of avoiding the teacher. "I would cross the street so I wouldn't have to say Heil Hitler to him."

Religion

Obedience was also used to enforce religion in Swabia. At the start of the Protestant Reformation, the peasants had clashed with the authorities, claiming that they could speak directly to God and that priests should be elected, not imposed. The nobility killed thousands of peasants to put down the revolt, and the state adopted the new Lutheran religion, enforcing it with many laws and strict punishments for disobedience. Some rebelled by joining sects. They rejected the state religion in favor of their inner religious feelings and understandings of God and the spiritual. But the state permitted activities by sects only if they did not interfere with legally required attendance at Lutheran services.

Wiesenmayer recalled, "We were forced to go to church until we were fourteen, but even as adults we had pressure. When I invited friends to play cards on Sundays, my father would bring out a famous preacher's sermon book, and he'd tell us to listen just for a little while. One by one, we would slip out. I had some friends who belonged to a sect, the *Stundebrüder* ["hour-brethren"]. They had to go to the regular church with us in the morning but afternoons they went to a religious meeting at someone's house. They had lessons in the evenings, too."

Wiesenmayer rebelled against the religious pressure, but at the same time he couldn't help but absorb some religion. "My father said I should make up my own mind about joining the *Stundebrüder*. So, when I was fifteen, I read the Bible all the way through. It was just one horror story after another. Like David saw a beautiful woman and fell in love with her. He put her husband, a soldier, in the front line and got him killed. Then David was sorry, and he made love to that wife. What the hell kind of story is that? So I made up my own mind about how to be good. I believe in something, but not what's in the Bible." Almost everybody in Swabia had some spiritual, if not religious, feelings.

Louis Gruber recalled how when you passed the local pastor on the street you had to say "Herr Pfarrer" and tip your hat. "If not, you would hear from his higher-ups that you should be more friendly. You had to say *erwürdige* [esteemed sir]."

Wieland joined the Methodists. They were viewed as a sect, because parishioners paid for their minister in addition to the religious tax imposed by the state to finance Lutheranism. "Music drew me to it. A group of Methodist guys showed me how to play the trumpet, and I became good enough to play in a brass band with them. Sunday afternoons, there was preaching and good music."

Some children had parents who suggested they go to America. Gruber was one of seven boys and one girl. One boy died in the war. Gruber recalled that they might have only cider for meals when there was a bad harvest and no food. Gruber worked for three years in the sawmill, but he saw there was no future there for him. His mother said they were too many children, and they might seek their future in America. "There wasn't much work in Germany, and a lot of fellows our age left for America. Close to half of the families in our town had someone come over."

Gruber left in 1923, the year of Germany's terrible inflation. He went to Philadelphia because his neighbor, Gene Wieland, had gone to Philadelphia half a year earlier. An uncle there sponsored him. He got a job right away. "The company always hired people right off the boat because they were the best workers, but they didn't pay much, only fifty cents an hour." Four Gruber brothers eventually went to Philadelphia.

Apprenticeship

Ironically, some of the poorest children like Wiesenmayer got a better chance to make their way in the modern world than did the children living on bigger farms. The poor children might become lowly apprentices, but eventually they became skilled craftsmen.

"While I apprenticed, the Meister [master] felt he had to be demeaning, and I was brought up that you don't talk back. The Meister couldn't be too friendly. He had to act like he was the boss. Sometimes, if he had a layout for a piece of furniture, and I asked him a question, he'd be nasty and insulting. So, what the hell, I didn't ask him questions anymore. I did all the work by hand rather than by machine. The Meister didn't want to pay the electric bill. He told me I was the machine."

Wiesenmayer finished his apprenticeship in 1923. "One day I delivered a cabinet to a well-to-do lady, and she gave me a 100,000-mark tip. She told me to spend it right away. So at the end of the week I went to buy a train ticket. I was going to ride home for once, instead of walk. They laughed at me at the train station. The 100,000-mark bill was worth so little, I couldn't even buy a little roll at the baker." This was the time of Germany's terrible inflation when people lost all their savings. Gottlieb Wiel recalled how his parents had paid into an insurance policy for years, but it was eventually worthless.

The inflation caused much economic upheaval. Wiesenmayer recalled, "I quit working for the *Meister*, but I couldn't find a steady job. Eventually, I got work in the village quarry, breaking rocks into gravel, working with ten other young guys. Most had a trade like me, but they couldn't find a job. The village employed us for a couple of weeks, but my father was angry that I took welfare like that."

Wiesenmayer finally got a job near the city of Stuttgart, but was laid off when work slowed. At the next couple of jobs, the same thing happened; he was last hired, first to be laid off. The irregular work and the expenses of working made it hard to save any money. Wiesenmayer needed a bike to commute and a suit to wear, so he borrowed the money from neighbors. It was two years before he could pay off the debts.

Boys from larger farms usually couldn't train as apprentices. Wiel recalled, "When I finished the seventh grade, I had to work on the farm without any pay. The oldest boy would always do that until the next boy was big enough to replace him. Then the oldest could hire out to work on somebody else's farm, for money! I was twenty when I finally got my turn away from home so I could earn money." Even then, Wiel had to work on the family farm a couple of hours before he caught the train to his job in the morning and also work a couple of hours after he came home late in the afternoon.

Non-farm jobs were mainly brute labor in the extractive or agricultural industries. There was also work in the factories around Stuttgart, but for most peasants this was too distant. Instead, Wiel commuted an hour each way to the county seat. "My first job was in a tannery. The dried hides, fifty in a bundle, came from Brazil. We had to soak the hides in deep pits for a month. Then they were soaked in other pits with ground-up oak bark in the water. Throwing fifty pounds around was hard. You had to hold the hides on the two front legs, swing, and throw them so they landed flat. It was messy and hard."

Wiel was laid off and had to take a job at a brick factory shoveling clay all day long. "Another guy working there told me that people in my job only lasted a couple of weeks. I did get a sore back after a while, but I held on until I saved enough for my ticket to America."

Leisure was what you did when there was no possibility of work, which was rare. An anecdote tells of the Sunday afternoon walk, a common practice in Germany. For years, it was strictly illegal to work on the Sabbath. But you could walk and look over the farm. In the winter, a vintner might check if the rains had washed soil down from the upper terraces of the vineyard. Then he'd think, "As long as I'm going there, I might as well get a little work done..." and he would take a few large pockets full of manure for the vines on the top terraces.

Lena Schlimmeyer's father continually pressured her to work. She recalled how she dug some ground and made a little flower garden. But her father was upset when she would weed and care for the flowers. She wasn't doing "real work."

Turmoil

On the other hand, Wiesenmayer's farm was so small that it didn't require all his time. He eventually joined the *Turnverein* or Turners. It was an athletic and social club for men of all ages, where they would put on plays and skits, but the club broke up because of politics. "A lot of farmers were conservative, while those who worked in the factory were more 'left.' There was fighting in the club between the Nazis and the Communists."

Another immigrant recalled his experience with the Communists. "I worked at a factory, starting at seven o'clock, and at nine o'clock the union steward came along saying, 'Out, on a demonstration.' All of us walked out, they closed up the factory, and we all had to march around. There was a soap-box speaker in front of City Hall, and we stood there like dumb sheep and listened to him. Around three or so hours later, we went back to work. That was in 1921. We overdid it. The leaders of the union weren't Communist-inspired, but they were pushed by the Communists.

"We were in dreamland. All the money that was collected from us went to the head office in Berlin. Then the shop steward took a suitcase of money and went to Switzerland. We stood there holding the bag."

He recalled how the Communists gave orders in his small town. "One night they said that out of maybe sixty of us who were Communist-inclined, they would pick ten. We had to go to the city, because that night they were going to overthrow the government and kill the mayor, the city officials, the state troopers, and so on. When they came out with that, the guys all got goose bumps. They couldn't believe it was time for the revolution. When they gave the order to kill people, nobody was ready to do that.

"I came over in January 1924. The inflation was so bad that in December it went up every day. Everybody was broke. A friend's father had been in America since 1912, and he helped me come over. It cost over 325 American dollars to come over. I worked for nine years until I got everything paid off."

Wiesenmayer wasn't the only one who belonged to a club. Women were involved in clubs too. And that's where, like the men, they often displayed an earthy sense of humor. According to Paula, Gene Wieland's wife, "just because a lot of the Swabians are religious, doesn't mean we're prudes." She recalled how her club put on a play with the theme, "The Hairy Ape and the Saving of Crailsheim," a story with some historical basis. "Crailsheim was a walled city, and around 1400 or so it was surrounded by an army trying to starve them out. The people hit on a plan. The burgomaster's wife was very plump. They got her up on the city wall, where she lifted up her skirts and showed her fat ass. It was called the hairy ape, because she had these fat cheeks and lots of hair in between, but no nose, just like an ape looks. The enemy decided it was no use, the town must have plenty of food, and they left."

Young men and women were able to get together on Sunday afternoons or during evenings in the winter. This was tolerated by the parents, for the young people were, after all, searching for their life's workmate. Wiesenmayer dated only one girl seriously before escaping for America at age twenty. "You couldn't get too friendly with a girl. Otherwise the whole town would talk and say one of you is too good for the other." Townspeople would carefully assess how much property each would inherit.

Alcohol was one solution for dealing with the hard life of the peasants. A typical Swabian joke explains: A deacon was visiting sick people in the hospital when he spied an open bottle of schnapps at a patient's bedside. "I hope this is not the only consolation you can turn to in your sickness." Patient: "Don't worry, Herr Deacon, there are six more bottles in the cellar at home."

Wiesenmayer recalled, "When I was apprenticing, we used to have a few drinks in the evening and haul one of a farmer's cow-piss tanks up into a tree. Next morning we would wonder how the hell we did that."

Wieland recalled, "When I was six, I would go behind the bar in our *Wirtschaft* (inn) and have a glass of beer. All the *Schwaben* [Swabians] had some alcohol at a young age." He justified this by quoting the book of Timothy in the Bible, "Take a little alcohol for your stomach's sake." Gene added, "When I was ten or twelve, I did my schoolwork behind the bar, and I'd see the drunkards. They'd buy a round for others, and the others did the same. They'd start singing songs about how they weren't young any more, and soon it would be midnight."

Leaving

Because the Swabians practiced shared inheritance that reduced the size of farm properties, thoughts of leaving were part of the culture. When there were more than a couple of boys in the family, they would realize that inheriting a small fraction of the farm would be insufficient to make a living. It would be better to take the risk of leaving and going to America.

Some emigrants were illegitimate children who had no possibility of inheriting any land, or stepchildren afraid of being cut out of any inheritance, or they could be psychologically less attached to home and family. In Wiesenmayer's case, "my mother died, and I was closer to her than to my father, so I left."

People also left because they were limited by the problems and reputations of prior generations. Stigmatized families passed on their disadvantages to the children. Wiesenmayer remembered, "In Germany, what matters is that you come from a good family. When you grow up, everybody knows your family and your family's business. If something happens in your family, they know that for fifty years. Even if you are smart, they still think you are nothing. For example, there was a boy who wanted to marry a girl, and her parents turned him down. He committed suicide, and that was a black mark on the rest of the family."

In addition, an emigrant might want to escape family conflict. Swabians are notoriously stubborn. No one gives in easily. Close family members may not speak to each other for a lifetime, each waiting until the other apologizes. An oft-told Swabian story has a peasant on his deathbed calling for the burgomaster and the pastor. He had always been at odds with both, so they figured he was finally going to apologize and make amends. The peasant asked each to stand at one side of the bed and take a hand. Grabbing them both very firmly, he explained, "I want to die like Christ did, between two thieves." He died stubbornly insisting he was in the right.

Conflict between siblings is common in Swabia, given the usual practice of shared inheritance and the difficulty of creating equal shares. It seems to be human nature to feel your pieces of meadow or field or woodlot are not as good as your siblings' pieces. Wiesenmayer described his family's solution to the inheritance problem. When his mother died and his father decided to retire, they wrote the name of each tiny plot of ground onto a piece of paper and then drew the slips from a hat. Wiesenmayer told his brother to use his share while he was in America and just pay the taxes.

Of course, their farm was small, and no one was going to make a living from a tiny fraction of it, so the precise division hardly mattered. In the case of bigger farms, inheritance could be a very serious matter. There is a standard response in Swabia when someone remarks how well two siblings get along with each other:

"But have they inherited yet?"

Interpersonal conflict exacerbated by shared inheritance was important in triggering Wiel's leaving: "If I stayed, the family farm would be divided between my older brother, Fritz, and me, and neither of us would make a good living. Plus, Fritz was a hard guy to get along with. He always wanted to boss everybody. Once you're eighteen or so, you know what has to be done on the farm. It doesn't take much bossing. But Fritz would always have something to say. He would start an argument, and he would fight. He used to throw the pitchfork at me. How would it be to live in half of the same farmhouse with a guy like that?"

Lena Schlimmeyer's trigger for emigrating was her father always giving her a hard time. She was slight of build and unable to do the physically hard fieldwork that farmers expected of the women. But her father still wanted "work, work."

Many Swabians saw America as a way to escape their impoverished farms, and youths jumped at the opportunity. Ernst Weber heard his best friend, Henry Höfer, who was illegitimate, mention he was asking an uncle in Youngstown, Ohio, for boat fare. On the spur of the moment, Weber suggested that Höfer write for two tickets. Weber was one of thirteen children and had no chance of inheriting much.

The German peasants of the 1920s generally had little trouble getting into the United States, despite the stricter laws barring immigrants. The 1917 literacy test (in one's native language) was no problem, even for peasants. They'd had seven years of schooling. A 1921 law set annual quotas for the number of immigrants equal to 3 percent of the sending nation's foreign-born already in the United States, as listed in the Census of 1910. In 1924, the quotas were reduced to 2 percent of the 1890 census. Germans fared extremely well with these quotas because there were already so many Germans in America, more than any other ethnic group.

Beginning in the 1920s, prospective immigrants had to be screened for a visa at an American consulate. Priority was given to farmers. Because of divided inheritance, almost everyone in Swabia owned a little land, if only for part-time farming. They could all tell the American consul they were "farmers."

Swabians had still another advantage. At that time, there was no welfare for immigrants. Prospective immigrants had to find an

American who would guarantee to take care of them financially for five years or until they became an American citizen. Because many Swabians had earlier escaped to America, it was relatively easy for prospective immigrants to find an older relative or former village neighbor who would make this pledge. From 1923 to 1929, some 43,000 from Swabia alone escaped Germany for America.

A few immigrants thought they'd just work in America a few years, save a pile of money, and then return for a much better life in Germany. Wieland, for example, thought he'd return and start his own *Wirtschaft*. This wouldn't take long, he thought, because a friend had written, "You can take a broom out on Broad Street [in Philadelphia] and sweep up the money."

Women Escape

Women were eager to escape to jobs off the farm. Then they wouldn't have to labor in the fields in addition to their housework, and they were generally treated better and paid more. Lena Schlimmeyer left the family farm at eighteen to work as a maid for a minister in a nearby town. In Germany, the university-trained minister was a "big deal," so she was able to learn "finer things, fancier cooking." But they paid very little, and "they acted as if you should thank them for the chance to work there." So she escaped to America at age twenty-three.

First, Schlimmeyer worked for an aunt who had left in the 1890s for frontier Nebraska, but she earned only five dollars a month as a babysitter and household helper. Paying off her ship passage would have taken forever at that wage. Schlimmeyer then began a succession of maid's jobs. She moved to live with her brother in Ohio. Working for a bank president's family, "The father and the son each needed a fresh shirt every day, so the wife showed me how to iron. They were so nice to me even though I could hardly talk English."

After a year, Schlimmeyer decided to move to New York City to be near a girlfriend she had met on the boat to America. "I worked mostly for Jewish people. They had the money. The first lady was good to me, but I left because I wanted to make more money. Next, I worked for a Mrs. Weinstock, who was very nice. She always told me whatever I wanted to cook it would be good with them. That's what I liked, the freedom. She didn't stand over you and tell you what to do. She was a singer, very busy, and out all day."

Despite her employer's kindness, difficult situations could arise. "Mrs. Weinstock's husband was a lawyer and came home only in the evening. Sometimes, when he felt good, he would give me a nightgown or something. They like you when you're young. He was pretty old, but he chased after me. He came in my room once, and I was scared."

Schlimmeyer got another job, but the elevator operator told her, "Nobody stays a whole month there. The lady gets all her help for nothing. She makes it so hard that they leave without the pay." But Schlimmeyer was stubborn, "I got my pay. I had to wash walls, everything, but I stayed till payday." She finally went back to Mrs. Weinstock. "She always said I was like one of the family. That's how she made me feel good. When she had company, she flattered me at the table. She would say how this chocolate roll Lena made, nobody can make it like her."

There were other benefits on the job. "Sometimes, I took their girl to the movies, and they paid for it. I used to get at least one day a week off, either Saturday or Sunday, right after I made the breakfast. Then I'd go with my girlfriend to Yorkville, to 86th Street [Little Germany], to dance and talk. We called it the fish pond, where we used to fish for guys.

"Then I got married, and it was all different. People go their different ways. We moved to a cold-water flat in Jersey City. I was home with my kids until the younger one was eleven. Then I started work in a paper bag factory. I worked there for over twenty years, until I retired." This was often the pattern for female German immigrants, working as maids while they were single or childless, then becoming housewives raising the kids, and eventually returning to the workforce.

Ernst Weber's wife, Louise, came to America in 1923 as an eighteen-year-old. She recalled, "There was no future for young people at that time. You were on your own from fourteen or so. Whatever money you could earn, you would need for your clothes and expenses. I worked for a minister. I learned to cook there. They were so thrifty. I told my mother she should cook soup twice from the same soup bone, like they did. Before I left for America, I learned how to sew for a year, so I could make a living from it. Every day I walked an hour each way to another town for that."

Getting Ahead

Most of the men from Swabia lacked formal job training. But having worked as jacks-of-all-trades on their own farms, they had acquired significant skills. They could analyze any problem, tinker and try various remedies. Their problem-solving abilities enabled them to work at almost anything, so the tinkerers were able to find jobs even during the Great Depression. Gottlieb Wiel's first job in America was to put up a garage for his uncle. "It was the first time I'd done carpenter work. It had a hip roof with four parts, and I had to do a lot of measuring and cutting. Of course, in Germany, I had done a lot of fixing on the barn or the wagon, so the building came out all right."

In 1932, after a few years in Ohio working as a handyman in a factory, Wiel went to New York City and became an elevator operator in a Washington Heights apartment building. The superintendent of the building, a German, took him along when he moved to a larger building. Wiel was successively a doorman, elevator operator, garbage collector, and repairman. He excelled in repairs because he confronted problems with his can-do attitude: "One time the elevators broke down, and the super couldn't fix them. He called the company, but I got them going before they came."

For someone like Wiel, an independent Swabian, union membership was not attractive. All the workers in his apartment building belonged to the union except him. After a year, he joined, only because he was worried that the other workers might get nasty with him. He recalled, "I was getting more money than everybody else, but after I joined I got less. That's what can happen. You can make more on your own when it all depends on how good you are."

Wiel got his freedom back by becoming superintendent of his own small building, and later a bigger one. He had one or two men as helpers, but he did all the repairs. He liked being a building superintendent because he was on his own. "You've got no boss standing behind and pushing you." Wiel stayed on this job through much of the Great Depression. He felt he was kept on because he gave such good value with his skilled work. The owner never had to hire expensive workmen to do masonry, plumbing, or electrical repairs.

Wiel left the job after seven years because of problems getting along with the boss, not uncommon for these Swabians. He ran afoul of the owner's son, who had been given a free apartment in the building. Wiel refused him unwarranted special perks, such as a new stove destined for an unrented apartment. The son told his father that Wiel wasn't doing enough work. Wiel thought he'd rather get a factory job, put in his time working eight hours a day, and then be done with people bothering him.

Independence

Wiel moved his family out of the super's apartment to a two-room summer bungalow in New Jersey. He spent two months expanding the summer bungalow into a six-room house, doing everything including the plumbing and the electrical wiring and even installing a steam heating system. He then found a factory job easily enough, since World War II was on, and he worked there almost thirty years until retirement. He bought extra property and started a business on the side, growing evergreens like those in the forests of his homeland.

Such part-time farming was popular among Swabian immigrants. It gave them a feeling of independence. Wiesenmayer bought extra property where he lived in Buffalo. He grew a huge garden, including fruit trees and berry bushes, and he raised chickens. Some Swabian immigrants even raised pigs and cows. They did the farm work evenings and Saturdays. For animal feed, they cut grass with a scythe, just as they'd done in Swabia. Self-reliance in food was one way a factory worker could maintain feelings of independence.

Working as craftsmen also afforded many men a degree of independence. Their skills often made the immigrants the final arbiters of how a job should be done, and they took pride in the quality work they did. In retirement, Wiesenmayer would take pleasure from his earlier work. Whenever he saw a bank or store he'd worked on, he'd say to himself, "I made this, I made that." He recalled, "I used to get only a rough drawing, and then I'd have to use my own noodle to figure out the layouts and how to do things."

Other Swabians, such as Ernst Weber, were able, in time, to become entrepreneurs, the epitome of independence. Weber arrived in Youngstown, Ohio, and started doing manual labor in order to pay off the ship's passage. Three years later, opportunity came knocking. A dump truck was for sale by an English neighbor who, with his son, hauled road-building material and coal. But "the son was galloping around nights, and he couldn't get up in the morning. The father couldn't drive, so they didn't make a good living with the truck." Weber bought the truck. "The first load, I never forget. I never drove a truck before, and I couldn't back in. Then one day, a construction company sent me with fifty sacks of cement to where my old company was building a big garage. The owner remembered me. After that, he'd call and ask for the Dutchman, and I'd haul cement, sand, bricks, and plaster. We did everything with 'armstrong' loaders in those days. By hand."

Next, Weber heard that a man who had died had a contract with a steel company to dispose of their cinders. "The steel company had to have those cinders out every day. I started the next morning. Then I sold some cinders to a small shop making cinder blocks. The owner eventually rented me the place, and I used the cinders I got for free from the steel company. I had three guys working for me. In the end, I bought the place. All this time, my wife was at home taking the telephone orders."

Weber's friend, Henry Höfer, had his own successful hauling business, while a third friend hit the hauling jackpot, eventually selling out for a quarter of a million dollars. All three of them were Methodists imbued with the spirit of having a special, direct relationship to God. (In Swabia the Methodists were a "sect," not run by the government like the Lutherans and Catholics.) According to Weber, "Religion had a lot to do with how well we all did. You betcha!"

The wives of these Swabian entrepreneurs often had it hard. They didn't always accept their husband's excessive work ethic. Hilda Gruber, from the Palatine region of Germany, saw Swabian men as "slave-drivers." She said of her husband, Karl, "If you had given him a whip, he would have used it. I worked in our grocery store on the cash register and did the produce, but only from six to six. Later in the evening I did more work upstairs in our apartment, on the books or housework. But I told Karl I had a limit with the store: not after six."

Entrepreneurs would make good use of children, too, just like on the farm in Swabia. Hilda Gruber recalled, "Even on Friday evening, Karl and our daughter would be down there stocking shelves and getting ready for Saturday. When you work for yourselves, there is always something to do."

The German work ethic influenced political attitudes. Most of the 1920s immigrants agreed with Gruber's preference for the Republicans. "The Schwabs believe in free enterprise. They believe the guy who works earns. The guy who has got a factory should have that. The Democratic thing is more giveaway, more like Santa Claus. That system doesn't work too well with the Schwabs."

Unlimited Opportunities

The immigrants found almost unlimited job opportunities in America. In Germany, you needed a formal apprenticeship of several years and formal credentials to take up most occupations, as a carpenter, baker, or even a sales clerk. In America, all it took was a little on-the-job experience or just the ability to learn fast.

Wieland's first American job was at a slaughterhouse near Atlantic City. The boss had been told that Wieland was a butcher in the Old Country. The first morning the boss took him to a big table with hundreds of fresh hams, saying, "Now we bone them hams." In Germany, Wieland had helped the butcher with the killing, but he'd never boned a ham. So Gene asked the boss to show just how he wanted it done. Later, Wieland recalled, "I boned as good and quick as he did."

The slaughterhouse foreman often put Wieland on special work, and he bluffed his way through. When the man killing the pigs quit his job, the foreman asked Wieland if he wanted to do it. "I didn't like to kill, but he gave me more money. So I stood there while the pigs came by. I'd take a leg and 'zip, zip,' with the knife. The pigs jumped around, and I'd be covered with blood, killing up to 1,200 a day."

When Wieland developed rheumatism from going into the cold freezers during hot weather, he left. He eventually moved back to Philadelphia, because his girlfriend, Paula, had arrived there from Germany. He first worked as a cook for a chef and then went into business for himself. "But I went kaput. It was 1929 and 1930. I could have declared bankruptcy, but I didn't. I worked as a chef for different restaurants. I didn't think of going back to Germany like my sister did. You've got to make good. You can't go back otherwise."

Wieland married Paula and, with help from her brother, started in business again. "I bought a saloon and added American food and some German dishes, too. I hired people who I thought were good workers. And honest, that was the main thing. In my first business, I thought everybody was as honest as me, but they weren't. When you're open from eight a.m. to one a.m., you need good controls. In the new restaurant, I started in the morning and worked till supper. Then Paula was there after that. And I had a bartender I could trust. We checked the amounts and double-checked."

Retirement

Most of the immigrants continued to work even into their eighties despite being financially comfortable. They couldn't stop while still physically able. Work gave meaning to life. Weber, for example, took small hauling jobs that others didn't want to bother with. If someone had scrap lumber for the city landfill, Weber would sell some for recycling and keep the rest for firewood. He was reducing landfill expenses and being productive at the same time. Wiel continued to raise evergreen and azalea plants that were more robust than those sold by others. He took pains to instruct the buyers in choosing varieties wisely and properly caring for them. It was good to be productive, to put your knowledge and skills to use, and to make the world a better place to live, all in the service of personal freedom, and a little money.

Almost all of those who escaped Germany for a better life in America decided to stay. Wiesenmayer, the cabinetmaker, recalled, "I thought I'd go to America for just four years and make some money. But when I got here, the difference was like night and day. In America, I could have two eggs for breakfast. In Germany, I never had an egg. To get one, I had to be sick. And people over there would keep track of every goddamn egg. They would stick fingers up the hen's bottom to feel if the egg was still there. If it was gone, they'd check over at the neighbor's to see if the chicken laid it there. In America it was a different life!"

2: THE STEPCHILD'S STORY

Ferdl (Ferdinand) Bucher recalls his ninety years of a life that was never boring. Many of the 1920s peasant immigrants shared his background: a tyrannical father, cleverness in evading governmental laws, fanatical frugality, a craftsman's love of tinkering, spirituality outside of organized religion, and strong reasons to escape to America.

****

Catholic Swabia

When I was an altar boy, I drank the holy wine. I was tricky. During the service, my job was to pour the wine from the bottle into the golden cup. I poured real slow so there would be wine left over. The priest would lower the cup to make the wine come out of the bottle faster, but I just poured slow. There was usually leftover wine for me.

I was an altar boy from when I was ten until fourteen. The pay was 3.65 marks a year, a pfennig for every day [totaling less than a dollar for the year]. I got dressed up almost as fine as the priest.

During the holidays, there were four altar boys. We'd light the candles or give the incense to the priest. We also had to hand him the book for reading the Mass. He stood first on the left side of the altar, and then we took the book over to the right side where he would read more. Once, the younger altar boy didn't know when to do it. He looked over to us, behind the priest. We moved our eyebrows up, "Yes, yes." So he took the book away while the priest was still reading.

Afterwards the priest found out we were at fault, and he hit us with a stick. He was rough. Once he saw two of us talking in religion class at school, and we had to come up to the front and hold out our hands while he smacked them. The other kid screamed, but I thought, "I won't scream no matter how much it hurts."

In the spring, on Corpus Christi, we would parade through the fields with the priest. We walked in front, one carrying the crucifix, the others the incense and the holy water. Then the priest came, carrying the holy box with Christ's body, the *Abendmahl* [sacramental bread]. He walked under the *Himmel* [heaven], a fancy rug that four men would hold up at the corners with poles. People would follow behind, singing along with us. We stopped at altars decorated with flowers and birch tree branches. The priest would pray for good crops, no bad weather, no hailstorms. He'd sprinkle the holy water and bless the wheat.

People from the Protestant towns would wait just like people watch a parade in New York City. Their churches weren't like ours. In the Catholic Church, everything is fancy, not plain like in the Protestant churches.

The French

World War I broke out in 1914 when I was twelve. I saw plenty of French prisoners. Oh, they had it nice. Some were playing with the farmers' wives, and one wife had a baby from a Frenchman. I guess the husband forgave his wife when he came home, because he couldn't do anything about it. Later on, he'd say to us, "Here's my little Frenchman." He was a nice little boy.

Another French prisoner worked for our neighbor who had a saloon and also a still for brewing schnapps. Once the prisoner came back from threshing wheat, and he saw that I had a quart jar of schnapps, the first that came from the still. It's so strong you can't drink it. We used it for rubbing alcohol. But he didn't understand. He grabbed the jar. I pulled, and he pulled. Then I thought: before it breaks, I'll let him drink it. Five minutes later, he was knocked out. We had to call the barracks where he stayed, and they carried him away. I heard in some places they'd bury people like that in the manure pile, to take the heat out of them. Otherwise, they'd die.

The French prisoners weren't allowed to drink schnapps, but I gave it to them in exchange for chocolate or cookies. We didn't have anything like that. Everything was rationed during the war. But people in France sent good stuff, so the prisoners gave us treats, and we gave them schnapps.

They were people just like us. Nobody bothered the prisoners. It wasn't their fault. The school planted all that hate, saying that the French were different from us, how they wore red pants and had horns. Actually, when I saw those red pants and blue caps, I thought they were pretty nice uniforms. And when I met the French, I thought they were damn nice people, and easygoing too.

I'm still against teaching how some people are bad. I don't call that history, planting hate. They do that in America. They teach about the Germans and the Nazis. We should forget about the past and see what's coming in the future, not create hate. When it's war, it's war, and a soldier has to do his duty. But when there's no war, they're people, and you should be civil.

War

There were a lot of wars in our section of Germany. The French and Germans were always going back and forth. My mother told how a drunk French soldier wanted to shoot my great-grandfather. Our house was a *Wirtschaft* [inn] then. Another soldier pushed the drunk soldier's elbow, and the shot missed. The hole where the bullet went into the ceiling is still there.

The name of the next town, Hohnweiler, came from the Thirty Years' War [1618-1648]. It means place of shame. The French camped there a long time trying to take our castle on the hill. But the cannons couldn't break down the big walls. The castle defied them, and the French soldiers had to leave in disgrace.

I was sixteen years old at the end of World War I, and they called us up at seventeen. If you had to go, you had to go. It could be an opportunity if you survived. You would have learned a lot in different countries. You would be a different person. If you came back.

Many didn't come back. I remember when a neighbor got a telegram. The son was blown apart. There was nothing left of him. Others came back cripples, with one arm or one leg. If they were gassed, their skin was yellow. One lived and married, had a couple kids, and then died. Another didn't even get married because he was a weak man. He could hardly breathe.

After the war, Germany wasn't allowed to have an army, so I didn't have to put in my two years like I would have before the war. And because the Kaiser lost the war, he had to go. Our King Wilhelm of Württemberg had to go, too. The one that lost, lost everything.

War is crazy. It really affects everyone. I remember during and after the First World War how people would drink beer and start fights.

Strictness

My parents and relatives were strict. Once my mother saw me out sled riding with the other boys and girls, and it was six o'clock, after dark. She came and hit me with a big soup spoon. Another time, I was visiting my uncle looking at the comics in the newspaper from Stuttgart. I was just nine or ten, and we couldn't afford a newspaper at home. My uncle just ripped it out of my hands.

To parents, you were only "good" if you could work hard. My parents never took me in their arms or played with me. They never had a conversation with us kids. Usually they didn't even tell us what to do. We were trained. There was work from morning to night. Parents would take kids to the field in the baby carriage. At three years of age, you want to help, and maybe at five you do. Of course, when you get older, you don't always want to.

My parents didn't yell or hit. The man across the street did. He hit his kids, and his wife too. I remember one of the kids, he was fourteen, and I was eighteen at the time. He said, "When I'm as old as you, I'm going to beat him up." Another man beat his stepchildren. The girl was about eight, and he grabbed the clothes under her neck, picked her up, and threw her on the ground.

Poverty

Some people in my village were very poor. An old widow had just a couple of dollars from a pension. She had a bench in her house where she kept a chicken or two underneath, so she could sell an egg or two. Another poor woman went around asking when your birthday was. Then she'd come and congratulate you on your birthday. She got a piece of bread, a couple of apples, or an egg. That's how she survived.

Then there were some dirty, filthy people who dressed just like the gypsies did. I brought some lice home from school from one of the kids. The family had nothing. They lived in two rooms. The bedroom was for the mother, and the other room served as the living room, kitchen, and bedroom for the seven or eight kids. There was no man. He'd come once a year and make a new baby. She didn't want to marry. He was an alcoholic. She said, "If I marry him, I haven't got even a house no more."

The Jews we saw were peddlers, selling clothing or fabric. They'd also buy old things. Every year they'd bother my mother for one of the old zinc plates or bowls from when our house was a *Wirtschaft* a hundred years earlier. They also bought and sold animals. There was a nice Jew who would even put a cow in the barn for no money down, a cow already pregnant a few months. The Jews were nice to poor people. They'd let 'em pay when they had the money.

In my town, almost nobody had much money. Only if they owned a business, like the butcher shop and *Wirtschaft*. On the farm, we had money only in the fall, when we sold fruit, and a couple of times during the year, when we sold a pig or a steer. Most people were poor. If you owned one goat, then the ones who were also poor but had two goats wouldn't talk to you. That was from the beginning, from when you were born.

When I was a teenager, we used to take our musical instruments and play in other towns at the saloons. At one place, the owners had five daughters. But they wouldn't talk to us. They just served us. They knew our town had mostly poor people. We were not good enough to talk to.

Our town was poor because most people didn't have much property. But everybody owned an animal, if only a goat, for milk. You could keep a pig or goat even without land, because grass grows along the road, and kitchen wastes like potato peels made good feed. Some had a cow, too. Everyone also had a half-acre of land that they either owned or rented from the state. They planted mostly potatoes and wheat and a big vegetable garden.

Our Big Farm

My family had more property than other people, and we farmed full time. We had about thirty-five acres altogether, about thirty pieces scattered in other villages that were twenty or thirty minutes from where we lived. See, my father, really my stepfather, had land. After his wife died, he needed a mother for his children, so he married my mother, a widow. My real father died when I was very young, so my mother also had land that came from him. We were the biggest farm in our town. We had six or seven cows altogether in the barn.

My grandfather used to have two acres of *Weinberg* [vineyard], but then a disease [phylloxera] came and killed off most of the grapes. When I was growing up, we had only a quarter acre left. My stepfather didn't do any of the work in the *Weinberg*. He just drank the wine.

In place of most of the grapes, we planted fruit trees—apples, pears, plums, and peaches. We were the only ones that grew *Blut* [blood] peaches, all red inside. I used to fill the baby carriage with a hundred pounds and walk to the market a couple of hours away.

Alcohol

We also used the fruit to make *Moscht* [hard cider]. For months and months I picked apples. The good ones we sold, but the ones on the ground were for *Moscht*. Starting at three o'clock in the morning, my mother and I would grind up the apples, put them in the big tubs, and add water, 400 gallons or more. We left to work in the fields by 6 a.m., but at night, when it was too dark to work outside, we'd do more apples. After they fermented a week, we'd press out the cider and put it in barrels.

I also made schnapps from the fruit. I would grind up fruit not fit to sell in the market, put it in those big tubs, add water, and let it ferment. In the winter, I'd cook the fruit in a big boiler. Steam came out in tubes that ran through a tub of ice. I'd keep cooking the stuff until the alcohol coming out didn't burn anymore.

Government officials used to measure the big tubs. Then they'd give us a permit to distill a certain amount of time, say ten days. Tax was paid only on the amount they measured, so we'd hide some extra fruit. We were supposed to stop making schnapps at six p.m., but I didn't. Behind our house was a hill with trees and bushes, so nobody could see. And I didn't use a light. The officials never came to check at night, and nobody else could tell because there was smoke coming from all the houses in winter anyway. And it didn't smell much, only when I was changing over to a new batch of fermented juice. So I just kept the boiler going days and nights.

One time, the wagon maker across the way squealed. He used to drink with my father, and he was a drunk too. My father told him we had some plums hidden away. No one else knew. A few weeks later, we came home from the fields, and the tax officials were there. They wanted to see the schnapps we had on hand, but we didn't have any. My father drank it all up already. Then they went to the neighbors, but they didn't find any plum brandy there either. If we sold, it was to strangers, because the neighbors didn't have any money. Later, my father beat up the wagon maker.

Making cider and schnapps was in addition to the regular chores. Every day the animals had to be cared for—preparing feed, feeding them, and taking the manure out. Threshing the wheat was another chore. My mother, my sister, and me worked together, swinging the flails, one after the other. Then we raked the straw from the grain and tied it in bundles to use later. We had to crank a machine that blew the chaff and dust out of the grain. In the winter, important chores were pruning the fruit trees, cutting down the old or bad trees, and digging up the stumps to use for firewood.

Learning

I had to learn a lot of things when I was young. For a while, I worked at a tree nursery. I learned how to root quince cuttings and graft pears on and also how to make dwarf trees. At home I grafted pears on apple trees. Some things worked, some didn't. Well, if you never try, you never find out.

Then I learned about sauerkraut. Some people would use a big hardwood stamper on the shredded cabbage in the big tub, but the priest told me, "It's better with the feet." So for him I used my stinky feet. I would stamp until the cabbage juice came up over my ankle. Then, I'd add more salt and cabbage, and so on. The job could take a whole afternoon.

I always got extra jobs from the priest and the teacher, and I watched everybody. I learned there are different ways to do anything. Like the lye for *Laugebretzele* [big Swabian pretzels]. During the war, the bakers couldn't get any lye. So my father put wood ashes in the water. After the pretzels were proofed up [risen], they'd get dipped in the boiling water with lye. That's what makes them shiny. Then you put the pretzels on a special long, narrow peel (tool). See, a bread peel has cornmeal under the bread, and you can slide bread off into the oven. But the pretzels were wet, so you had to turn this special narrow peel over and dump them onto the oven stones.

I learned in the market, too. Once I had a whole baby carriage full of early pears. The tree grew from a seed, so they weren't real good. But they looked so nice and yellow. Some women were selling green pears. They looked like they weren't ripe, but they were really sweet. I decided to sell mine just a little cheaper. Everybody bought from me. In a half an hour I was done. The city people didn't know any better. They were looking for the nice color and cheaper.

When I was about sixteen or seventeen, my mother got the idea that in the winter I should learn from the basket maker. Afterwards, I went off to where my uncle lived, near Stuttgart, and got lots of jobs by the rich farmers. I worked in their living rooms. The young girls would sneak me cigarettes, and I didn't even smoke. I earned good money and all the food and drinks I wanted, when we hardly had enough to eat at home. I could have worked all year round, but I was needed on the farm. My father didn't work, my brother was young yet, and my sister didn't want to work in the fields. So I had to help my mother.

Sex

Another thing I learned about was sex. When a cow was in heat, I had to bring her to the next town where a guy had some bulls. Once, when I was about fourteen, I put a male rabbit and a female cat together. I thought I would get something with rabbit ears and a cat's tail, but each animal went in a different corner of the box. Nothing happened.

There was a girl in town, Hedwig, whose family was forced to leave Alsace after World War I. I liked to talk and dance with her at the *Wirtschaft* where she worked as a waitress. But she was not a girl for me. She was too rich. She probably wouldn't go out with me, and I never even had the nerve to ask her. She wanted to be something better than a farmer's wife. She was educated and dressed like a baroness, and I only had seven years of school. She married someone from another town who was somebody. Later on, they had their own business.

The town crier knew my father and wanted me to marry his daughter Margaret. I think that he sent her younger sister to hang out with my sister. Friends told me how certain parents thought their girls were right for me. One girl who came around already had a house because her parents were dead. But how can you love if you can't stand the girl?

There were some guys who bragged about sex—two brothers, for example. One was quite a bit older and got a girl in the city pregnant. His parents had to raise the child. When she got to be ten or eleven, the younger brother was then my age, fourteen. He told how he and his older brother, the father of the girl, both had sex with her, how it was a *"himmelische Gefühl"* [heavenly feeling]. After a while, it got around what was happening, and the police put the brothers in jail.

Of course, there were cases where couples married after the girl was long pregnant. One had the baby the day she married. But I was careful. I was with two girls, but both times I used protection.

A Stepchild

I left Germany because of my father's drinking. I was doing the work, and when something got sold, he'd take the money and go on a spree for two or three weeks. My mother had nothing to say. It wasn't a new thing with him. My mother never wanted to marry him. People told her about his drinking, but he said he was going to burn up his house if she wouldn't marry him, and she did.

See, my father, really my stepfather, had children that were older than me, and they'd all gone to America. So I was left to take care of the whole farm. I raised all the cattle and did all the fields. At fourteen, I was plowing, bringing the hay home, everything, while the father was sitting at home. Once in a while, he would work for a couple of hours. At haying time, my mother and I would get up at three in the morning. She'd tell him to come, and he would get up at eight o'clock and work with us. But we had to stop at eleven, when the grass was too dry to cut. So he worked only two or three hours altogether. I never saw him out in the wheat field or picking apples. The only thing he did was complain when we came home late from the fields and the cows were hollering to be fed. "What takes you so long? What I do in two hours takes you all day."

The other reason I left was a girl. She was good and honest, not fresh or lousy. I could have gotten nicer-looking ones, but I looked for the personality. I met her at a dance. She was living with a family in the next town and sewing clothes for them. When I saw her dressed nice and clean, not like the farmer girls, I figured we'd make a nice couple. When I visited her parents, I was more at home than I was at home.

Her older sister went to America first and, half a year later, she sent my girlfriend a ticket. After a year of postponing, the ticket was going to expire. My girlfriend told me that if I said she should stay, she would. But I said, "You go, and if you like it over there, I will come too."

When she got to America, she liked it. She wrote me, "*Wo es dir gut geht, dass ist deines Vaterland*" [Where things go well for you, that's your homeland]. Half a year later, I was there, too.

My half-brother was seven years younger than me. When I left, he was sixteen, so he could do the work then. I had stayed long enough. They couldn't say I left them helpless.

There was no living for two farmers on our land. If my brother would have learned a trade, I might have stayed and maybe gotten the farm. Or the other way round, if I had learned a trade, I might have stayed. Both of us had no trade. We were just two farmers with only one farm.

What burned me up was I never got anything. I did the work, I trained all the oxen, and then the father would sell them cheap in the saloon. Then he'd go drinking every day and play the big shot in the county seat where he used to live. He wouldn't come back till two or three o'clock in the morning.

My mother never had money even to buy sugar. When I made baskets or other things, I had to spend that money to buy sugar. When I sold fruit at the market, I gave the money to my mother. But she was as dumb as me. She gave it to the father, and he drank it up.

Once I told her that there was a guy who picked apples and then brought them into Stuttgart on his truck. I asked, "Why don't I sell half the apples to him before we get home?" "*Das darf man nit macha,*" she told me. "One can't do that." She was afraid. The husband was always the boss.

My mother even took my own money away. When I was eighteen, I wanted a raincoat to wear to church. I wrote my stepbrother, Hermann, in Philadelphia, that I worked the whole year and I didn't get anything. Can he send me money for a coat? I wasn't at home when the letter came, so my mother took the $20 out. "We need it for taxes."

My mother used to tell me, "We take nothing with us when we die." But there was no will saying that I get the part of the farm that belonged to my real father. After a while, I got wiser. Why should I keep working, when they want everything for themselves? I saw it coming, that everything goes to the younger ones from the second marriage.

Escaping

I had wanted to go to America since I was seventeen or eighteen. I wrote Hermann because he had a bakery in Philadelphia. He visited us in Germany a couple times. I asked if I might be able to work there a while, but my mother saw the letter and wrote them not to let me come. Hermann wrote me that I couldn't come without the parents' consent.

I never considered going someplace else in Germany. A lot of people from my town worked in Stuttgart. They took a room there during the week. Saturday evening they came home. On Monday, at three a.m., they would start out again. The wife stayed home and did the farm work and the housework. What kind of life was that?

When my girlfriend's sister sent the ticket, I found I could go to America right away, as a farmer. Otherwise, with no trade they wouldn't let me in for some time. So I got the papers in Stuttgart and more papers from the *Schultheiss* [village head]. In half a year, I had everything arranged.

I never said anything to my parents. I was over twenty-one. Then the *Schultheiss* told my father "I hear your son is going to America," and my father nearly fell on his ass. But he couldn't say anything. It was too late.

I packed my trunk with some clothes and a couple of prayer books. I had a suit made. It cost three months' money from grafting trees, basket making, different side jobs, and even from playing music. I told the tailor to make my suit like what visitors from America wore, but he made the pants for suspenders, not a belt, and he made the bottoms too narrow. Later, I sent the suit back to my brother, and the $45 shoes, too. In America, they could always tell a greenhorn from the clothes.

I called a taxi. "Goodbye, father. Goodbye, mother." My mother was crying, "I won't see you again" but I walked out, and that was that. It was December 1925.

My girlfriend's sister sent a first-class ticket, because she had to go through Ellis Island in 1923. She didn't want that for me. So it was a $360 ticket for the Andania of the Cunard Line. I ate things I'd never seen before. I also had $160 cash. When you got off the boat, they checked if you had money. Afterwards, I sent the borrowed money back.

My mother always wrote if I don't like it, I should come back. But I decided right away I would never go back. No matter how lousy it was, I wouldn't give them the satisfaction that I failed.

Soon, I was writing her how nice it was in America, working in bakeries where they had nice things like pastry horns filled with cream. I put a $5 bill in with every letter. She wrote not to send any more, because she knew I didn't have work during the Depression. But I always put something in. I never saw my mother after I left Germany. I got married and had children and never had the money to go to Germany before she died.

Waste in America

I'll never forget when I first came to New York City. All the stores had their garbage piled on the sidewalk. And in every block there was at least one garbage pile on fire. You never saw such a thing in Germany, not even on the farm. In Germany, everything was used, nothing wasted. No garbage collector there. The animals got anything people didn't eat. Human food wasn't wasted, either. People ate a lot of things Americans don't. We'd even eat the cartilage on the joints of the chicken bones. It tasted good. You just had to chew it longer. Butchers also ground it into the liverwurst.

Our newspapers never went in the garbage. If you were rich enough to get a newspaper once a week, you'd save it, cut it into squares, and use it [as toilet paper].

If America would be like that, there would be no government deficit. I think bad times are coming in America. Other countries take jobs away. We live too high. We waste things. Over in Germany, they fix things. Here, you see refrigerators or televisions on the curb if they don't work. People would rather throw something out than fix it.

The other night at the bakery where I work, I saw six new

aluminum plates in the garbage. The helpers ate some tarts, and there was only a little apple juice on the plates, no dents, but they threw them away. That's why some businesses go bankrupt. The plates cost maybe five cents each, and it would be all profit to take a minute and wash them off. That's what I did.

When I first started at the bakery, I saw the owner throw layer cakes in the garbage. He made too many to sell. That was when everything was made from real butter, so I took the cakes out. The garbage bag was new, and there was nothing wrong with the cakes. I ground them up and made pastry filling out of them. I was always careful with things.

Starting Out in America

I got my first job in America through an Austrian friend of my girlfriend's sister. He sponsored my coming over, sent the affidavit saying he'd be responsible for me. He tried to get me a job in New York City as a waiter like him. But I couldn't talk English. So, he got me a factory job where he lived, in New Jersey.

At the factory, I could only talk to one of the bosses, a Jew who knew German. I stood there like a damn fool. Later, I found out there was a *Landsmann* [countryman] from Stuttgart, and also a German-Russian who was a nice guy, but do you think any of them would talk German to me in the beginning?

The factory made explosives, gun cotton. It was dangerous, and it was unhealthy working there because of the heat and the dust in the air. The *Landsmann* put the cotton in one side of a machine, and it came out clean on my side. I had to put a certain weight in each barrel, whatever amount was written on the barrel. But the cotton came out so fast, like a snowstorm. I got further and further behind.

After a while, I got smart. I lost too much time weighing the cotton. The foreman only came once in a while, so I put some weighed barrels where he would check. I filled the other ones without weighing and brought them over real quick to the other building. They only made one thing in each building. If there was an explosion, the whole factory wouldn't go up at once.

After I was six months on the job, there was an explosion in the building where I had to bring the cotton. There they soaked the cotton in alcohol and ran it through wringers. Some of the wringers caught fire and then the whole building. A railroad car full of barrels went up, one after the other. Boom. Boom. Boom. Up 300 feet in the air.

Becoming a Baker

I went to New York City, to the employment agencies, and got a baking job. Most bakers were German or had help who talked German. If I knew English, I could have taken any job. That's why the Irish could be policeman or fireman: they read, they write, and they speak English right away. We couldn't do that. We had to be slaves for five or ten years.

They knew I was a greenhorn when I went into one of those job agencies and took my hat off. A German told me, "This is not the Old Country. Here, you don't take your hat off." After a while you learn the right ways. Like in Jersey, they asked me to chop wood on a Sunday. I never worked before on a Sunday, so I made believe I was sick and stayed inside. But with time, you learn.

I started as a baker's helper, down on Bleeker St. You clean the place and you watch what they do. You learn things little by little. Then they let you do this, then that. First, I had to wash the floor and the walls. I also had to carry the baby up four stories for the missus, so it could sleep. Next, I had to go down and wash the lunchroom dishes. Then I worked in the cellar where the bakery was. And they got all the money. That's why they called us "greenhorns." It was like in the South where they had the slaves doing all the dirty work.

Those were the days of the sweatshop. They tried to get as much out of workers as possible. There were no mixing machines then. You used to dump the flour and water into a big wooden box. Then you'd lay your two arms in there and turn 'em around like a paddle wheel, and the mixture gets tougher and tougher. You'd break off pieces and knead 'em together, squash 'em down, then break off new pieces, squash 'em, and so on. It was lousy work. And you looked all white from working in the cellars, no color in your skin. There was bad air, too, from all the gas fumes. Every once in a while, I'd come home after twelve hours in the bakery, and my wife would say, "What, you're home already?"

Marriage and a Family

At first, I stayed at a rooming house on Eight Avenue and 28th Street, in a small room with bedbugs. In 1928, I married my wife. We figured two could live as cheap as one. We rented an apartment in Brooklyn, and the wife and me and her sister lived there.

My wife and I loved each other. We were two partners who understood each other and worked together. She looked up to me—that I was the provider and I take care of her everything. I did the shopping. If one of our children needed a coat, I got it. She was often sick, so I did the cooking too.

Our first girl was born in 1929. Before that, my wife worked for a Jewish dressmaker from the Other Side [Europe], sewing dresses for rich people. It was always, "Hurry up, hurry up." When they know you're a greenhorn, they take advantage. You only get so much money, no matter how good you are or how much you work. Many times, the boss went out and bought her a sandwich, so she had to work through her lunchtime.

The job agencies were the real crooks. They took your money and then sent you out, but there was no job. You would have to be in the East River to find the address. They made money other ways, too. After I was at a job for a while, I would get a raise, from $20 to $25 a week. But then the agencies would call the bakery and say "I can get you a man for $20." The boss wouldn't ask if you'd work for less, he would just let you go. The agency earned a month's commission, and I had to look for another job and start at the bottom again.

Those days, you'd see piles of furniture on the sidewalk every few blocks. People couldn't pay the rent. There were jobs during the Depression, but there were too many people chasing after them. Winter was especially bad, when construction people couldn't work their regular jobs. We had a carpenter doing sweeping-up work in the bakery.

Working

We moved from Brooklyn to Jersey before World War II—me, the wife, and our two girls. I bought a one-room, unfinished bungalow, and I added a second room. Eventually, I built it into a whole house. I watched builders, I saw what tools they had and what they did with them, and then I got the tools and did the same thing. Sometimes I made mistakes, maybe cut a board too short, but they made mistakes too. I was careful, and I took a little longer. I did all kinds of different things, the house foundation, a dormer in the roof, brick steps, kitchen and bathroom tiling, the chimney.

I did this plus my job, as much as fifteen hours in the bakery and only three hours of sleep at night. Sometimes I fell asleep at the fryer. That was dangerous. I could have burned myself bad if a hand got in the fat along with the donuts. But I also had to do work on my house by myself. I could never save enough money to hire someone.

I wanted to go into the bakery business for myself, but the missus was always sick, starting even before I married her. She died at fifty. I didn't want to go into business without my wife, with just strangers. The help cheat and rob you. I saw it in the bakery. They take money out of the cash register, or they give the stuff away to friends, filling a bag up and just ringing a quarter.

Baking comes easy to me. After working three-and-a-half years, I was a foreman. I went from greenhorn to being in charge of trained bakers because I learned from mistakes. Those who can't make mistakes and then learn from them are the ones who can't get ahead. Baking is complicated, because dough is a living thing. I found out already at home that the dough will proof [rise] faster when it's rainy. Then you have to watch that it doesn't crust over and bake with a rough-looking face. If it rises too much, I make it over. I mix in new dough. That could turn out even better than new dough alone.

For the last twenty-five years now, I've worked for an Irishman. He didn't know much about baking when he came here. I've been with him from when he started. His sons are working for a few years now, but they still don't know how to do much. Whether it's carelessness or *Dummheit* [stupidity], I don't know. They only know how to follow a recipe.

But the recipes in books are not always right. Once, I got in a big argument with the boss. We were making French crumb cakes, and the book says put two inches of crumbs on top. We had a two-inch pan, and there was three-quarters of an inch of dough in there already. I told him, "not even Einstein could put two inches of crumbs on." After I while, I figured the book meant two ounces of crumbs.

Religion

I can't say I'm religious, but at least I'm not a Communist. I say my prayers when I go to bed and when I get up, also when I eat dinner.

When I was working nights, I couldn't go to church. When I moved to New Jersey, I had work clearing the trees on the property and building the house, for ten years and more. You have to come first. You need a home and you need money to pay taxes and to take care of your children. A few times when the bakery was closed I went with the missus to her Lutheran Church. It's almost the same as the Catholic Church, only the confession is out loud. Then they came around with a collection basket and held it under my nose with a couple of $5 bills in there. I didn't have $5, so I didn't go to church again.

I believe in something higher. One night Jesus came to me, holding out His hand to me. It was fifteen years ago or so, but when I sat up in bed and reached out to touch Him, He was gone.

Another time, I think God spoke to me. My second wife came back from a trip to Florida. I picked her up at the airport, and then I lay down around nine o'clock in the evening, because I had to sleep before work. Then I heard a loud voice tell me, "Count your money." I had $700 cash in a brown envelope to pay the taxes and other bills. When I got up at my regular time, at 10:30, and looked, I saw there was only $125 left. She told me she didn't take it, my grandchildren did. But no one else knew where the money was. A day later, she mentioned she was buying a house in Florida for $1,000 down.

The voice must have been God, because God sees everything and hears everything. I don't believe in everything they say in church, but some is true. God spoke to Moses and told him what to do, to kill his son. That must have happened, and the same for me. I don't hide my money now, my grandchildren come all the time, and nothing ever happens.

I was thinking about whether we go to Heaven, and I figure probably only like a ghost, just like Jesus came to me. Otherwise, where would all the people eat, where would they shit? It's impossible. There's so many people. In Germany we believed that the good people would come and visit us, the *verklärte* [transfigured] ones.

A really religious person is a good person. Like when the priest saw a man lying there by the road. He hurried on by, he wanted to go to church and look good. But another man came and helped, put oil on his feet, gave him money, and put him in a hotel. God looked on and saw that he was a good man. A good man helps other people. You should love your neighbor like yourself. The point is that in church God doesn't look at how good you dress, it's what you do.

In Germany, the law said children had to go to church. Adults didn't have to, and some didn't go, yet they were good people. A good person follows the Ten Commandments, loves his neighbors, and doesn't talk about other people when he's really worse than they are. He doesn't put them down or act better than them. He doesn't tell lies, steal things. You're good if you help the sick people or those that have nothing.

We learned those things in religion class in school. But here people don't learn religion in school. People will do anything as long as there is money in it. That's why there are drugs, for example.

I could never cheat anyone. But my own people cheated me. My mother died while the Second World War was on, and Hitler wouldn't let my part of the money come out. My half-brother used the money for lawyers and other things. He got the whole farm. He got punished. First his two children died of a disease. Next his wife died, and then he died at fifty-seven. Strange people got the property and the money. But here I am, almost ninety years old, still working at the bakery and earning money. That's why God lets me live so long. God made it up to me.

3: THE APPEAL OF THE NAZIS

Although Swabia was spared most of Germany's terrible violence during the 1920s, a Swabian working in the Rhineland saw it firsthand. Hermann Fischer was trained as a toolmaker, and he had gotten a job in an armaments factory there during World War I. After Germany surrendered, the French occupied much of the Rhineland, and tensions festered. The French harassed and humiliated the Germans and even attempted to annex a part of Germany. In 1923, after Germany failed to deliver some war reparations, the French invaded and occupied the Ruhr, Germany's industrial heartland east of the Rhine.

Fischer had seen fighting all along, gangs of young Germans taunting French soldiers and roughing up those with German girls. The French responded with collective punishments, punishing Germans in general. The Germans called a general strike in response to the French occupation of the Ruhr, and at least 130 Germans died. Fischer heard that French machine guns killed many, so that year, 1923, Fischer decided he'd had enough, and he left for America.

The crisis helped right-wing nationalistic groups gain popular support. This was especially true in Munich, which had become quite reactionary after temporary Communist rule had been put down. A former Austrian corporal, Adolf Hitler, had been in the city since 1919. Soon uniformed members of his Nazi, or National Socialist Workers Party, paraded in the streets, publically heaping abuse on Jews and leftists.

In September 1923, the German government called off its resistance against the French occupation of the Ruhr. This triggered attempts by both the Right and the Left to take over Germany. Communists struck in Hamburg, Saxony, and Thuringia, and the Nazis in Munich and other parts of Bavaria. Hitler proclaimed a *Putsch*, or coup, in a Munich beer hall. The next day, his marchers were blocked by the Bavarian police, who killed sixteen and ended the coup.

Hitler's public trial for treason allowed him, for the first time, to make his views known across the nation. Hitler received a light sentence and served only nine months. During his confinement, he wrote *Mein Kampf* (My Struggle), detailing his plans for Germany. Such leniency for right-wing criminals was common. Judges saw the Nazis as conservative supporters of an order they could live with. The Left, on the other hand, wanted to turn the world, including the privileged judiciary, upside down.

Extreme Solutions

The social, political, and economic disorder in Germany in the 1920s encouraged extremist views. The middle-of-the-road Social Democratic governments had been ineffective. People gravitated towards the Nazi or the Communist forms of enforced order.

The Versailles Treaty contributed to the growth of extremism in Germany. The Social Democrats had signed the treaty accepting the guilt of Germany for World War I, enormous war reparations, and the loss of substantial territory including Alsace and West Prussia as well as all German colonies. The treaty was an enormous humiliation for the Germans. Many Germans felt great anger and shame about Germany's defeat and subsequent diminished status.[5-7]

In the search for an explanation, many Germans accepted the right-wing claim that the German army had been stabbed in the back by Social Democrats, Bolsheviks, and especially the Jews, a number of whom held important positions in the new Weimar Republic. Physical violence and assassinations, particularly against left-leaning Jews, became common.

As the disorder in Germany increased, voters in the early 1930s increasingly supported the Nazis. Hitler had formed a coalition with the conservative Nationalist Party that controlled a string of newspapers and popular photo magazines as well as movie houses that showed Nazi newsreels.

In the 1930 election, there were four and a half million new young voters, many of whom found the Nazi vision inspiring. The Nazis received 6,409,600 votes, eight times more than in 1928, and suddenly became the second-largest party in the Reichstag or parliament.[8]

Before the next election in 1932, a banking collapse and the beginning of the Great Depression led to 30 percent unemployment. The Nazis expanded their brown-shirted Storm Troopers to 600,000 strong and battled leftists in the streets. Nazi parades and election rallies dazzled the German people. The 1932 elections doubled the Nazi seats in parliament.

Nazis in Control

The military and the industrialists who controlled the country had to recognize the strength of the Nazi party and make a deal with Hitler. President Hindenburg was convinced that a leftist coup was imminent, so on January 30, 1933, Hitler became chancellor. In Berlin, complete strangers embraced each other on the streets with relief, "At last we are saved."[9]

Hitler appointed henchman Hermann Goering as Prussian Minister of the Interior, thus controlling the police in two-thirds of Germany. Four weeks later, the Reichstag building was burned, allegedly part of an attempted Communist coup. Hitler had elderly President Hindenburg sign an emergency proclamation suspending most civil liberties: habeas corpus, freedom of the press, the secrecy of the telephone and mails, and the freedom to assemble and organize. In Prussia some 10,000 leftist opponents of the regime were arrested and imprisoned. Elections were called, and the Nazis and their conservative allies gained a 52 percent majority. Three weeks later, in March 1933, Hitler was able to get the Reichstag to pass an enabling act giving the government power to decree laws without a vote in parliament. Hitler now had absolute, dictatorial power.

At this time, in 1933, the Nazi Party was approximately two million strong. Germany became a one-party state, since all other parties were banned or dissolved. Some Germans subsequently joined the Nazi Party out of opportunism, but membership never exceeded eight million. It was not really the Nazi Party that was so loved by Germans, but Hitler, who acted through government officials. Hitler was the strong leader Germans wanted to soothe their fears.

Hitler and the Nazis appealed more to secular voters than to religious traditionalists, more to Prussians than to the Catholics in the Rhineland and Bavaria or the deeply religious Protestant Swabians in the south.

Nazis in America

Swabian peasants were generally not excited about politics, and their attitudes in America were similar, as Ernst Weber in Youngstown, Ohio, recalled. "I could see that this Hitler idea could not work, and I told people so, but they always called me *dumme Schwab* [dumb Swabian]. Some men who had served in the German army in the First World War formed a club after they came to America. They were 'Heil Hitler!' all the time. They just wouldn't keep quiet about it. They were watched and eventually lost their jobs in the steel plant."

As for American politics, many Swabians were like Gottlieb Wiel in New York City, busy working. "A guy wanted to give me a job as party block captain. But I told him no. I wouldn't like trying to persuade people. I'd have to go to meetings, too. Most of the *Schwaben* I know say politicians are all no good."

The Nazis' organization in the United States, the German-American Bund, had a peak membership of about 25,000, mainly immigrants. This was a very small proportion of the 1.25 million German-born in America or the total of some twenty-five million German Americans. But the Bund was highly vocal, and every member had to swear allegiance to Hitler. Some Americans were fearful because they knew that the Nazis had started in Germany with only a small handful of members.

Many German Americans were wary of the Bund. Membership was drawn mainly from young disaffected lower-middle-class artisans. Many had experienced poverty and hunger in Germany and had been active in right-wing politics. Many were in fact from the same youth cohort attracted to the Nazi Party in Germany.[10,11]

The Bund was most prominent on the East Coast, where there were many immigrants who were still German citizens. The Bund established quasi-military camps in New Jersey and on Long Island. The climax of its influence was a February 1939 rally in New York's Madison Square Garden that 20,000 attended.

Walter Hockele was curious about the Bund. He had come from Pforzheim, Baden, with his family as a five-year-old in 1926. "Friends drove us up to the Bund's Camp Nordland in North Jersey. My father's reaction? '*Quatsch*'[drivel]. I even had a hard time getting him to let me be a Boy Scout because of their uniforms, so you can imagine what he thought of all the Bund guys with their uniforms. I never got a toy gun for the same reason. My father was so disgusted by World War I."

Eventually, the House Un-American Activities Committee investigated, and the Bund's leaders were imprisoned. When the United States later entered World War II, the Bund became illegal.

An American in Nazi Germany

Hockele had a more extended encounter with the Nazis starting in January 1939. His father paid for the seventeen-year-old to travel to his German grandparents and learn the tool-and-die business. At the trade school he saw "maps with red for all the parts of the world that were German, a lot of Africa where Germany used to have colonies and parts of Russia where the Volga Germans lived. Germany wanted to get more *Lebensraum*, more living space. It was craziness!"

He saw many military parades. "May 1st [Mayday] was a Nazi holiday with a huge parade, and I didn't take my hat off or raise my arm in the 'Heil Hitler' salute that all Germans had to give. One woman looked and looked at me, so I finally whipped out my passport to show her I was an American."

Hockele was even invited to become a member of the elite Nazi guard. "A guy came to the school saying he was looking for tall, blond men like me for the SS [*Schutzstaffel*]. He told me, 'You are of German blood.' My answer was, 'No, I am an American.' I saw how the Germans thought everything President Roosevelt was doing was wrong, and the same for Stalin. They even had cartoons showing Roosevelt as a Jew with a big, curled nose."

He remembered, "In June of 1939, the political tone changed. We saw German language films from Russia, how Bismarck had wanted good relations with the Russians because they had all the raw materials. Russia and Germany together could conquer the world. The newsreels showed how the Russians had wide-gauge railroad tracks and the Germans standard-gauge, so shipments of heavy machinery had to be unloaded from German trains, loaded back onto Russian trains, and the reverse for the grain shipments coming from Russia to Germany." Hockele was witnessing the rapprochement which would lead to the Nazi-Soviet Non-Aggression Pact of August 1939.

At the end of August, Hockele was sent home from work to listen to a 2 p.m. radio speech by Hitler. "He said the Poles had been shooting at Germany, so Germany will shoot back. Germany had made an overture to Poland about building an autobahn to East Prussia across Polish territory, but they refused. Early the next morning, September 1, 1939, Germany invaded Poland."

After that, his parents sent a ticket so he could come back to America. "I took along a letter from an old Jewish man, a scrap metal dealer in Pforzheim. There used to be some eight hundred Jews in the city and two temples. The letter was for his grandson in America. The family had left, but the grandfather couldn't get out of Germany. I don't know if he got out. When I later left from Genoa on the S.S. Manhattan, there was a whole section on board that was kosher, because there were a lot of Jews on board. But that was almost the last ship to leave from there to America."

The hard times of the Great Depression in America kept many German immigrants from returning to visit their homeland and families. However, a few were so fed up with America and so attracted by the good economic conditions during the 1930s created by Hitler that they sold everything and returned to Germany. Psychological reasons could also play some role in returning to Germany. Gene Wieland in Philadelphia recalled that his sister went back because, "She didn't have it so nice in America. She was the oldest of us, and she was always used to being the boss."

Most of the 1920s immigrants had come from small farming villages. Everybody knew everybody else. It would have been hard to go back because people would say, "He couldn't make it in America."

Most immigrants, however, didn't reject America. Like Wiesenmayer's two eggs in America compared to no eggs in Germany, the difference for a peasant was clear. A formerly impoverished immigrant recalled visiting his Black Forest hometown. "They wanted 'Heil Hitlers' from me, but I just told them I didn't understand. Then the mayor of my town suggested I stay in Germany. I asked him what work I should do. 'Oh, the same thing you did before.' Then I told him that they had enough slaves and they didn't need me." Rejecting Nazi Germany, however, didn't guarantee American acceptance. During World War II, his bakery windows were smeared with tar swastikas.

Attacks on German Americans

An official campaign against German Americans began secretly in peacetime. In 1936, J. Edgar Hoover of the FBI started a five-year plan to list all individuals who might be security risks, ordering agents to gather information "regardless of the source from which this information is received."

After war broke out in Europe, President Roosevelt created the Emergency Detention Program. The FBI produced a secret Custodial Detention Index listing everyone to be apprehended and interned if America became involved in the war, as well as others "who should be watched carefully."[12]

The F.B.I. investigated some 78,000 accusations in 1939. Many were as flimsy as the woman who turned in the German-born man delivering her laundry, telling authorities, "He could only be whistling because he was happy about Hitler's successes." Even anonymous denunciations could end up on a dossier that would follow a person everywhere in the United States. To assemble the list of security risks, the Justice Department used membership rosters for German-American organizations, subscribers to German-language newspapers, and names of people attending German cultural festivals. Even eminent anti-Nazis such as Albert Einstein came under suspicion by the FBI.

The Alien Registration Act of 1940 required all aliens age fourteen and older to be photographed and fingerprinted. In October 1941, aliens had to give a detailed accounting of all their assets if their combined value was over one thousand dollars. Even Jewish refugees from Germany had to comply.

The FBI was a problem for some German Americans during the war. Gene Wieland was visited at his restaurant in Philadelphia every week. He was buying meat on the black market for his restaurant, but the FBI never asked anything about that. They were interested in Nazis. They would visit the American Legion down the street. He had given the Legion the profit from one night, so they said he was "OK." "It was competitors who gave me the main trouble with the FBI. They wanted to get me out of business. I belonged to five German Clubs, like singing clubs. The FBI even investigated my brother-in-law who had helped me open my restaurant. They wanted to know where the money came from."

Ernst Mauser in Philadelphia had similar problems with the police department. His wife's parents lived with them. "They would invite people over to have a couple of beers, and there would be more cars parked outside in the street. So the neighbors called the police and said there were Hitler parties in our house on Saturday nights. The police captain was always nice. The third time he said we don't want to, but we have to come when they call. He said my record was clear, and I didn't have anything to worry about. I was a citizen and classified 4F [a deferment from the draft], and the neighbors didn't like that."

Louis Gruber recalled when a FBI agent visited, he looked for ties to Germany. "He wanted to take the picture of my brother from when he was in the army. I told him he couldn't take it, it belonged to me, and he left it." Gruber was a citizen and an upstanding owner of a grocery store. He had a relative in North Dakota who wasn't so lucky. "He was a Mennonite conscientious objector and said he would only defend the country against enemies on our own shore. He wound up in an internment camp.

An American Internment Camp

On December 8, 1941, Hoover sent to the Immigration and Naturalization Service a list of 636 German aliens, 1,393 American citizens sympathetic to Germany, and 1,694 persons of German descent with unknown citizenship. Over a thousand were arrested immediately, even before Germany's declaration of war against America on December 11. American citizens outnumbered German citizens, because Hoover saw the citizens as more dangerous, more easily blending with other Americans.

Eventually nearly 11,000 Germans and German Americans were sent to the internment camps. Some were Nazi sympathizers or agents or German seamen caught in U.S. ports, all of whom could be interned under international law. But many more were simply guilty of being German-born aliens or Americans with German ancestry. Many were wives or children, often citizens, who "volunteered" for custody because they could not survive without the family assets frozen by the government.[13, 14]

The legal status of the internees was ambiguous. They were not part of the relocation program, nor were they criminals or prisoners of war. They weren't allowed to have a lawyer. Attorney General Francis Biddle remarked that the exclusion of lawyers, "greatly expedited action, saved time, and put the procedure on a prompt and common-sense basis." Many internees never did find out the charges against them, even after their release, which for some came as late as August 1948.[12]

Gunther Graeber was one of those interned by the FBI. His father, Theo Graeber. aged twenty-nine and, his wife Emmy, twenty-two, were living in Elizabeth, New Jersey, with young Gunther and his brother, Werner. Theo was a master tool-and-die craftsman who had come from Swabia in 1935; Emmy arrived in 1937. Gunther said their Polish landlord had "tremendous anti-German feelings" and called the FBI, claiming his German tenants were signaling the U-boats that were torpedoing ships off the Jersey shore. The FBI came and took his father away and interrogated him. The family then moved to Bayonne, where Theo worked in a classified job that required security clearance, but even there the FBI continued to harass and question him.

Gunther remembered, "We were finally uprooted, put on a Coast Guard cutter in Jersey City, and taken to Ellis Island. We could bring only what we quickly packed in suitcases." His mother and father were the first "enemy aliens" to arrive with children. "A woman imprisoned there had a husband who was an Irish lawyer, and he tried to help us, and so did the local Catholic bishop." But no one could help, and the family was sent to a former women's prison in Seagoville, Texas. A year and a half later, they were sent to nearby Crystal City to a detention camp for thousands of Japanese and German internees, where there were barbed wire and continual surveillance.

Gunther's father eventually volunteered for a prisoner exchange program allowing the family to return to Germany. In January 1945, they were put on a neutral Swedish ship that landed them in the south of France. Under heavy American security they traveled up the Rhone Valley to neutral Switzerland and then to Swabia.

Gunther recalled when his family arrived, "Times were pretty grim in Germany in the last month of the war." The family didn't even qualify as refugees, like other Germans coming from Eastern Europe. Refugees from America were unheard of. "We really should have stayed in the United States. My father was a hard-headed man. He felt he was being seriously wronged. That's why he returned to Germany. He felt the United States didn't have to get involved in the war. It was a war between Germany and other countries. He would never let himself be inducted to fight against Germany. He was outspoken and stubborn and that's what got him into trouble. Also, you know there was a real craze at that time in New Jersey about submarines. People saw them everywhere."[15]

Gunther had a younger brother, Teddy. "He was born crippled, with spina bifida, because during an unannounced nighttime FBI visit, my mother fainted and fell down the stairs. She gave birth prematurely at seven months. Teddy's legs were paralyzed, and he was in the hospital almost all the time. He died in 1948 in Germany from pneumonia and other things."

Gunther's parents, embittered, never returned to America. But Gunther and Werner, decided to take up the option they had, at age eighteen, to become American citizens. They had help from an American uncle who had immigrated in 1927, He, too, had been subject to FBI interrogations during the war, but he was a citizen and was spared imprisonment. The uncle visited several times after the war and convinced the boys to forget the trauma they and their family had suffered, that life would be better in America.

German Americans were fortunate to avoid the ethnic cleansing suffered by Japanese Americans on the West Coast. The Japanese clearly suffered from Americans' racial prejudice and from their inability to assimilate as easily as the Germans.

Importance of Hitler

Most of the 1920s Swabian immigrants to the United States deny having had any interest in the Nazis. But behind such denials there could well be sympathy and support, especially for Hitler.

Many immigrants could repeat positive things that relatives in Germany wrote in letters. Lena Schlimmeyer emphasized that "Hitler built the autobahns." This helped peasants market what they raised. Gottlieb Wiel heard how Hitler straightened out the Murr River so that low-lying fields no longer flooded. Others would argue that Hitler put unemployed young people to work, the same as what President Roosevelt was doing with the Civilian Conservation Corps and Works Public Administration in America.

Besides Hitler's many material achievements, some immigrants would admit that he brought order and pride to German society. Bob Wiesenmayer recalled, "When I was still in Germany, the system wasn't working. People had to choose between Communism or the Nazis. People eventually chose the Nazis, because they didn't want to be dominated by the Russians."

Wiesenmayer, like many Germans, could emphasize how Hitler capitalized on the Germans' sense of victimization, of being unfairly viewed as starting World War I. Hitler also cleverly played upon the Germans' great insecurities about Communism, and he continually emphasized Communism as the real threat to Germany.

Hitler's campaign against the Jews could also appeal to some of the immigrants to America. These immigrants had left Germany before Hitler came to power, but some carried the same hatreds later expressed by the Nazis. Wiesenmayer insisted, "In every country the Jews build a state within a state. They stick together. They want to control the world, and they get control of communications, factories, and stores. We saw that especially during the First World War. Nobody had the guts to go into every farmer's barn and find out how many cows the farmer had. The government employed the Jews. They would say, 'Alright, the government takes this one.' The farmers hated them for that. Not only for that, but especially for that."

In the final analysis, there is no simple way to characterize the stance toward the Nazis held by the 1920s immigrants. They could sympathize with Germany, because they still had family ties. They could also empathize because they had grown up with the same feelings as those left behind—feelings of shame and resentment about Germany's defeat and postwar treatment as well as insecurities that later became a fear of Communism and a hatred of Jews.

But besides being German in these ways, the immigrants did differ from those left behind in Germany because they had actively rejected German life for one or more reasons. It could have been simply the lack of economic opportunities, but also the rejection of stifling traditions. Historians recognize that Hitler and the Nazis created a true social revolution, one as momentous as that launched by Napoleon over a century earlier.[16]

Wiesenmayer praised the Nazi destruction of the traditional hierarchical relations that still existed when he left Germany. "I was glad when Hitler got rid of the system where some people could look down on others. After all, we were all the same people in Germany. Friends wrote me that the factory owner had to march with the floor-sweeper. Before I came over, important people still looked down on others. You had to lift your hat to the *Herrenstand* [gentry].

"Let's say the truth, Hitler did good. He just didn't do it for the Jews."

4: 1930s JEWISH REFUGEES

In Nazi ideology, Germans were an Aryan super-race. But the race was being sullied by mixing with a Jewish race considered to be inferior. Jews were marrying Gentiles and also having sex with Gentiles outside of marriage.

An Illegal Affair

By the 1920s, Jews had assimilated in Germany. Starting at age thirteen in 1925, unbeknownst to her mother, Lotte Cahn had an affair with a German Gentile named Max.

Like most Jewish children in the small villages and towns of Swabia, Cahn played with Gentile children in her town of Riedlingen. They were separated only during religion classes in school. When the Catholic bishop visited Riedlingen, he gave the children religious pins. Her mother said nothing when she wore it for several months. Cahn recalled, "When I was growing up, the Jews and the Gentiles lived together happily. We went to their church, and they came to our temple."

As an elderly woman in Florida, Cahn prefaced her personal account by confiding to me, "I never told this to anyone before." Most Germans are very private about their intimate relationships.

In 1935, the Nazis made sexual contacts between Jews and Aryans illegal. But Cahn became pregnant by Max. She told her family she was going to visit her great aunt, but instead biked to Lindau on Lake Constance, then to Bregenz in Austria, and finally over the Swiss border to get an abortion.

In a small Swiss town, Cahn told a woman on the street that she had pain and didn't know what to do. That's how she found an abortionist. At the doctor's office, she started crying. "I told him how my mother would throw me out. I was so frightened. He did it and didn't charge me a penny!"

When Cahn's father died, she took over his bicycle route wholesaling cigars. Her lover Max lived along her route, and one night while staying with him she had a premonition. She woke up around 5 a.m. and told him, "I feel something. I'm afraid. I had better leave now." He didn't want her to go because it was still dark, but she left anyway. "Nothing could have kept me there."

She biked to the next town and caught the train. But at the next stop the conductor called out, "Lotte, come to the phone. It's urgent." It was Max, and he told her that her uncle had sent the Gestapo to his home. "They know everything about us," he told her. They threatened to send him to the concentration camp.

When Cahn arrived home, she faced her crying mother and her hypocritical uncle, who was also involved with a Gentile. She told him if he turned her in, she would tell of his crime, too. Cahn didn't say a word to her uncle for two years, even while eating at the same table with him. Then he got sick. When he was near death, Cahn's mother told her to apologize. She refused.

A neighbor's affair ended more tragically. A Jewish man who lived across the street also had a Gentile girlfriend, Maria. She wasn't permitted to see her lover and was forced to marry somebody else. She committed suicide.

Cahn's illegal relationship was not prosecuted after she moved to the big city of Stuttgart. Her lover continued to visit her until she left Germany in 1938 at age twenty-six. She had wanted to go to America even as a little girl, because she was unhappy at home. Max's cousin, once the maid for Cahn's family, had left for America and had gotten an immigration number for Cahn in 1928. She sent it to Cahn, but it was canceled because of the Great Depression in America.

When Cahn escaped in 1938, it was just in the nick of time. "Later [1941] the Nazis took our house and everything and put my mother and my younger sister and all the other Jews in town into one big room with no beds, no nothing. My mother had a little kitten which she liked, and she took it along, but when they saw that kitten, they killed it. After four weeks, they sent them to Riga [Latvia]." Most of the Jews sent there died or were murdered, including Cahn's mother and younger sister.

Jewish History in Swabia

Most Jews in Swabia were thoroughly accepted because Jewish families had long mingled with the peasants in small rural villages or towns. Most of the Jews living in Swabian cities were only a generation removed from this rural life.

Jewish settlers had arrived in the villages around the end of the fifteenth century, when the Duchy of Württemberg, like England and Spain, expelled all Jews. The refugees went only as far as the tiny independent rural principalities near the borders of Württemberg. In some places they comprised half of a village's population. Most were peddlers earning their money from peasants in other territories and passing on much of their earnings to their rulers and protectors in the form of exorbitant taxes.[17, 18]

Until the beginning of the nineteenth century, Jews were considered foreigners. But Napoleon became convinced that Jews were individuals of a different religion, not members of another nationality, and should be considered ordinary citizens. When Napoleon combined the minor Swabian principalities into an expanded Kingdom of Württemberg, his egalitarian ideals remained in force even after he was defeated and Württemberg freed of his control. Over the next half-century, Württemberg gradually granted Jews the same rights as other citizens.

As it had done earlier when Protestantism emerged, Württemberg imposed its own rules on Judaism. Rabbis became state employees. They had to be university trained and had to preach sermons, there had to be music during services, and Jewish textbooks were required to be similar to the state-mandated Christian catechisms. The state even laid down specific rules of behavior during Jewish services. Jews had to be orderly, with no one individually praying directly to God, as had been common before.

The plan was that differences between Jews and Gentiles should be reduced and Jews would become more like other Swabian citizens. In 1864 a chief rabbi wrote how Swabia had come to be the Promised Land: "...we view Württemberg, which, according to its location, fertility, wise government and harmony between different religious groups is equal to the former Palestine, as our fatherland, and love it as much as our fathers loved theirs..."[19]

As late as 1925, 36 percent of the Jews in Württemberg were still living in villages of less than 2,000 people.[20] Most of these rural Jews had assimilated to Swabian life through generations of living in peasant villages, and they were accepted by the Gentiles. Most Orthodox Jews did follow kosher practice and strictly observed the Sabbath, but otherwise they followed Swabian peasant customs.

The situation of most Jews in Germany was very different from Jews in Eastern Europe, where Jews maintained a separate society from Gentiles, including dressing differently, and rabbinical study was the highest, most prestigious education. In contrast, Jews in Swabia lived among Gentiles, dressed like them, and like their peasant neighbors they mostly disdained book learning. Swabian Jews didn't emphasize rabbinical learning. They were considered to be devout if they respected their parents and followed the ethical standards of the community. If Jews moved to a large city such as Stuttgart, they often gave up most religious observance. Urban Jews were almost indistinguishable from their Gentile neighbors.

The Jewish refugee emigrants of the 1930s were a broad cross-section of the Jewish community, not just the malcontent or black sheep, as was often the case with the peasant immigrants of the 1920s. In the first year under the Nazis, 1933, many socialists and communists fled, Jews as well as Gentiles, after Hitler arrested and jailed some prominent leftists. The Swabian playwright Bertolt Brecht narrowly escaped because he was in a medical clinic the night of the sudden dragnet. Albert Einstein, the most eminent Swabian Jew, was out of the country and decided he wouldn't return with Hitler in power.

Frank Herz, an Early Escapee

Frank Herz was just one generation removed from the countryside. His mother had come from a small town, Hechingen, where she had a Jewish school education. His father had grown up in the city of Heilbronn and had a public school education. Both had been Orthodox. However, during the horrors of World War I, his mother decided, "If God lets this happen, there can't be much to it [the Jewish religion]."

According to Herz, the urban Jews of Heilbronn were not very religious. People would go to the synagogue only on the high holy days. Some didn't go at all. "I didn't. I declared myself a Jew, because Jews had been persecuted at one time, and I didn't want to give the impression I was running away. But I had nothing to do with the religion."

Herz recalled that when he was growing up in the 1920s, the Jewish community was becoming more and more German. "The majority of your friends might be Jewish, but you would have non-Jewish friends, too." There was some intermarriage, but Jews still tended to marry Jews, though not primarily because of religion. "I felt I knew the Jewish mentality better, and a non-Jewish girl might not always understand me."

Perhaps half of all Jewish marriages in the urban areas of Germany were with Gentiles.[21] If Hitler hadn't come to power, the Jews and Gentiles might have blended completely after a couple more generations. In Swabia the intermarriage rate was only a little lower.[22]

Herz remembers how the Nazis were visible even before they took power. The *Sturmabteilung*, Nazi Storm Troopers or Brown Shirts, marched around in uniforms, as did the Communists in their own uniforms. The *Reichsbanner* were also anti-Nazi, but not as radical as the Communists. They were Social Democrats and marched in black, red, and gold uniforms, the colors of the democratic Weimar Republic founded after World War I. The *Stahlhelm* (Steel-Helmet), a nationalistic organization of former veterans, also marched. "Everybody marched. But we didn't have fighting in Swabia like there was in Berlin. I don't remember anything in Heilbronn or in Tübingen [Herz's university town], maybe because the Swabians were always so slow in catching on to anything."

The conflict in the streets ended after January 30, 1933, when Hitler was appointed chancellor. With the communists eliminated, the March 1933 election gave the Nazis and their nationalist partners a majority in the government. The Nazi Storm Troopers were then fully legal.

Herz was serving the third year of his clerkship in a law firm. One day the Nazis came "officially" and trashed his law office. "They didn't kill or beat up anyone, but it was still a shock, the physical disorder. I didn't go back to the office again."

Herz and his family were more psychologically prepared than other Jews. His mother's uncle had been a Social Democrat, the leading party in opposition to the Nazis during the Weimar

Republic. This uncle had long warned that if the Nazis ever came to power, the family should be prepared to move. However, Herz's father had a very good ready-to-wear and dry goods business with a big following among the peasants from the villages surrounding Heilbronn. The business was almost sixty years old, and customers told him, "You don't have to go." He had a good reputation and let people buy on credit, and they liked him for that. He was not eager to leave Germany.

Fortunately, Herz's mother acted. She was in Switzerland in January 1933. After Hitler took power, she wrote her husband, "Well, it's okay if you want to stay in Germany without me. I'm not coming back." The Nazi Storm Troopers' boycotts of Jewish businesses at the beginning of April helped convince Herz's father to leave.

Herz was only twenty-five when the Nazis took power. He still needed to take the bar exam, but the Nazis immediately passed a law that Jews would not be allowed to take it.

Herz found it easy to emigrate because he was a loner, independent minded like so many other people in Swabia. When he settled in France, he also made a point of distancing himself from other refugees. His father had been an apprentice in a Paris export firm as a young man and had connections there. But Herz didn't want to stay in Paris because there were so many other émigrés. "I wanted to be independent. I wanted to look forward. They all looked back. They remembered all the things they had in Germany."

Records for Baden-Württemberg in southwestern Germany show 7 percent of the Jewish population decided to escape in 1933—about the same proportion for Germany as a whole.[23]

The Jewish Commitment to Germany

After the initial shock of Hitler's coming to power, many Jews who were not politically aware felt that they were in no danger. In 1934, no significant anti-Jewish legislation was passed, and only 4 percent of the Jews in Baden-Württemberg emigrated. Most Jews did not want to leave their homes. In 1935, only another 3 percent did, despite the Nazi determination to get Jews out of Germany.

But Nazi pressures increased. The 1935 Nuremberg Laws carefully defined and labeled all Jews, exemplifying Germans' great love of rules and dislike of ambiguity. Extremely detailed legal definitions specified who was of Jewish blood according to the numbers of ancestors who had connections to the Jewish religion. And the mixing of Jewish and Aryan blood through sexual relations was forbidden.

The mounting official discrimination still couldn't drive out all the Jews. They had advanced economically and in status and had developed intrinsic motivations to belong to Germany. They didn't need extrinsic rewards. Over time, an emotional commitment can develop out of such partial reinforcements. People persist.[24] They will even endure punishments. As some German Jews told me, "We were dyed-in-the-wool Germans."

Germans develop strong commitments. German Jews, like their Gentile neighbors, were not opportunistic or flexible. They were deliberate, even stubborn. Despite the escalating Nazi abuse, only 7 percent of Swabia's Jewish community felt the need to escape in 1936 and another 7 percent in 1937. Despite the passage of five years, only a little more than a quarter of Swabia's Jews had left in the years since Hitler's taking power.

Early in 1938 the German government took a census of all Jewish property worth more than $2000 and began "compulsory Aryanization." Jews were forced to sell their properties and businesses to Gentiles at depressed prices.

A Child's Experiences

Ray Rothschild recalled for me how his family hung on for five years under Hitler. His father had grown up in a small Black Forest village and became a horse trader traveling to France and Belgium. After the advent of the automobile, he entered the oil and soap business in Stuttgart.

Ray was ten and living in Stuttgart when Hitler took power. "You know how kids can be; they busted the spokes on my bike, let air out of the tires." Soon Jews were no longer allowed to attend public schools with Gentiles. They had to attend segregated Jewish schools. An exception was made if a father was a World War I veteran. Ray's father brought his military records to the school director so his son could remain in the *Gymnasium*, the elite high school.

Ray Rothschild continued to observe religious holidays and

Sabbath services, and in school he still had religion class. "Despite all the hatred of the Jews, the Nazis made sure the cantor or rabbi came to give us religious instruction." However, Ray soon found his freedom curtailed. In the beginning, most of his friends were non-Jewish. "We were totally integrated. Suddenly I couldn't go to the swimming pool any more with them. So I developed Jewish friends."

Nazi law also prevented most Aryans from working in Jewish homes, and the Rothschild family had to fire their housemaid, a peasant girl. "The Nazis were afraid of sexual contact, *Rassenschande* [race defilement]." The law did permit a maid who was older than thirty-five years to stay if she was a long-term employee. A new employee had to be over forty-five."

Ray's father took a trip abroad to scout out alternatives. Relatives had already moved to Argentina and Brazil, but a visit convinced him that there was too much anti-Semitism in South America. In 1938, the family escaped to the United States.

Rural Jews

It was harder for the Jews in the rural towns to leave. They were well integrated into their communities and had relatives and friends nearby. They were accepted by Gentile townspeople. Also, they were usually poorer than urban Jews, and their main assets, a house and land, were not easily converted into the cash needed to escape.

Else Fuerst was a young widow in the town of Rexingen. She recalled why many Jews didn't leave. "The people who went to Palestine needed 1,000 English pounds. Old people like my Aunt Betty weren't well and didn't want to go. She thought she could live out her life at home, that she wouldn't be bothered by the Nazis because she didn't work or have a business."

Some Jews remained in Nazi Germany because of uncertainty and fear of the unknown. Fuerst recalled, "People were afraid to leave. Even though I had my brothers, my mother, my son, and my niece with me, I still wouldn't have minded if the boat to America never came." She had always been sheltered. She was married at nineteen, and after her husband died in an accident her family took care of her. "I never had a job or travelled." It was a big change when she escaped with her family to America in 1938.

Switzerland

If they could, Jewish parents might send their children abroad. One such child, Gretl Marx Temes, was fourteen when she became aware of the changes in Germany. Suddenly her friends, all Gentiles, turned away from her. Temes recalled for me mass demonstrations in her small town of Buttenhausen when the Nazis came to power. "On the hills we would see fires where townspeople gathered to sing hymns. It was mass hypnosis."[25] Suddenly girls started wearing the uniforms of the Bund deutsche Mädchen, the Hitler Youth for girls.

Fortunately Temes had family in Switzerland, and an uncle welcomed her in April 1934. Her parents remained in Germany, hoping to endure. Temes returned home for summer vacations in 1935 and 1936. Then her parents felt she shouldn't visit any more, saying, "We don't know if you can get out of Germany again."

After her last year of regular school in Switzerland, Temes went to a finishing school there to learn cooking, sewing, cleaning, and handicrafts. She recalled how a teacher told her that if she remembered only half of what she was taught, she'd do well in America. "I thought she was bragging, but time proved her right. In America, I worked twenty-three years as a designer of children's sportswear."

Temes recalled that neutral Switzerland did not live up to its humanitarian reputation.[26] The Austrian parents of the man she later married were turned back at the border by the Swiss and sent to their eventual deaths. And far from being generous to the refugees, the Swiss provided only housing. Money for food and clothing came from American Jews. "The Swiss are afraid somebody will be taking something away from them. The people are very cold, very selfish."

Nor has Temes forgotten how difficult life was for the German refugees. She worked with children eight to fifteen years old who were housed in a hotel in the mountains. The children would be allowed an hour or two for walking and exercise. "But it was like the military. A soldier guarded in front and one in back. Where would the children have run?" The director walked around with a loaded pistol on his belt, and when Temes asked him why he said, "You can never tell. They might do something." Recalled Temes, "He was ready to shoot the children if they tried to run."

Jewish Commitment to Germany Is Broken

The event that overcame any remaining Jewish reluctance to leaving Germany was the destruction of the synagogues and Jewish businesses during what came to be known as *Kristallnacht* or Crystal Night, November 10, 1938.

In October, the Nazis had deported Jews with Polish nationality residing in Germany. When Herschel Grynszpan, a native of Hanover, received a letter that described the harrowing arrest and deportation of his parents to the no-man's land between Germany and Poland, he took revenge, assassinating the third secretary at the German Embassy in Paris. The Nazis used this as a pretext for the Crystal Night destruction.

The American Consul General in Stuttgart reported to Washington how "practically every synagogue...was set on fire by well-disciplined and apparently well-equipped young men in civilian clothes...Bibles, prayer books, and other sacred things were thrown into the flames...the fire brigades confined their activities to preventing the flames from spreading..." Henry Stern, a fourteen-year-old at the time, saw "a huge crowd of people standing there, and I remember clearly that there was complete silence."[27]

The Nazis also attacked Jewish stores in Stuttgart, smashing the windows, destroying furnishings, and throwing merchandise into the street, the broken glass making a "Crystal Night," as the Nazis termed it. The police just looked on.

The consul estimated that some 80 percent of the non-Jewish population seemed to disagree with the violence. "Many people, in fact, are hanging their heads with shame. On the other hand, possibly 20 percent of the population has shown satisfaction." A later report from the consul indicated that a few non-Jews had been arrested for expressing disgust over the violence, and the Gentile population now feared speaking out in opposition.

The simultaneous arrest of almost all Jewish males during Crystal Night was arguably even more traumatic than the physical destruction of synagogues and stores. One of the most basic German values, ingrained in every child, Jewish and Gentile, was respect for the authority of the police. To be arrested was one of the most shocking blows an individual could suffer.

Arnold Blum was sixteen at the time of Crystal Night. His

parents had come from small rural towns, but he had grown up in Stuttgart. His early schooling was at a Catholic school. "I was okay with it because my mother had gone to a Catholic school, too." He was quite accustomed to standing quietly while other students prayed. Like many Jews, he was assimilated enough to be comfortable with the different customs of the majority.

His ordeal began with a nighttime knock on the door by the Gestapo. The Gestapo's reputation was apparently not bad everywhere. According to Joseph Weinberg, a Jewish resident of Stuttgart, "...always the SS [*Schutzstaffel*] were the bad people. The Gestapo more or less just did their job. That was in Stuttgart. I know the Swabians were much more lenient than further north in Prussia and Hessen. They were more anti-Jewish there than in Stuttgart. I must say that the situation in Stuttgart wasn't so bad. They just obeyed orders."[28] Apparently the Gestapo didn't go out of their way to harass Jews, but orders were orders, and during Crystal Night the order was to arrest Jews."

The Gestapo arrested Blum and his uncle and brought them, like Jews from all over Stuttgart, to the city's central police station, there to be jammed into a single cell. Blum felt "strange" crowded up against Stuttgart's eminent professors and doctors, as well as the fathers and grandfathers of his friends. There was an overpowering smell from the "toilet," a pail in the corner.

The Concentration Camp

Eventually they were bussed over the autobahn to the concentration camp at Dachau, used originally just for leftist opponents of the Nazis. Stiff from the three-hour trip, some of the elderly got out of the buses too slowly, earning them a beating by SS men in black uniforms.

Blum was somewhat hesitant about describing his concentration experience. Talking about it had been strictly forbidden by the Nazis. Upon arrival in Dachau, the Jewish men were marched past a ten-foot-high electrified fence and onto the central drill field. They had to stand at attention for hours in the cold and dark, and some of the men were humiliated when they wet their pants.

Finally they were marched to the barracks for newcomers. The political prisoner who was in charge kindly gave the oldest men, aged ninety-two and ninety-six, his straw bed. But the others were so crowded together that even sleeping on their sides they didn't have enough room. Blum slept on top of others' legs.

The next morning, the Jews encountered one of many humiliating tactics used by the SS. Shoes lined up the night before were mixed into a huge pile. Blum recalled, "I got two shoes that were different sizes, and both were too small for me." Next, the Jews were "processed," humiliated by having all their hair shorn, their clothing taken away, and their bodies hosed down by guards. The striped prisoner's uniforms had Stars of David on them and fit as poorly as their shoes. They were fingerprinted and photographed. The whole process was dehumanizing. They were told, "From now on, you will use only your number, not your name."

The daily routine included standing at attention for hours, both in the morning and evening. They were counted again and again. Sick prisoners had to be carried to their places. So were the bodies of the elderly who had died at night. The rest of the morning was filled with calisthenics and the afternoons with marching, all accompanied by insults and blows from the SS or the criminals placed in charge of the prisoners.

The first food came some sixty hours after the arrest and featured blood sausages and pork, both forbidden by the Jewish religion. Some of the rural Orthodox Jews preferred starving rather than transgressing by eating. Blum was nauseated by the food. "I'd always eaten kosher food till then."

Blum was released after only a week and a half. His mother had contacted distant American relatives who had sent an affidavit that they would financially support him. She took the affidavit to the U.S. Consulate, which supplied a letter indicating that a visa would shortly be issued. She then brought the letter to the Gestapo. It was just what they wanted. The Dachau experience was calculated to speed remaining Jews out of Germany. However, many suffered for weeks, even months, until they were released.

Panic

Almost all of the Jewish population now felt that the Nazis were dead serious. Jews who'd had the foresight to get visas from America or other countries escaped from Germany in droves. In 1938, 13 percent of the Jewish community in Baden-Württemberg left, and 16 percent escaped in the year after Crystal Night. For the first time in five years, the U.S. quota for German immigrants was filled, preventing more from escaping to America.

A few Jews were still reluctant to leave Germany, including some proverbially stubborn Swabians. Temes recalled that her parents had Swiss visas, but her father was convinced that the abuse of Jews would last only another year. He would often say, "The soup always cools off after cooking." Her father was "one of those typical Germans where everything had to be done right." He wanted to sell his houses legally. Even after a six-week stay in Dachau, he still wouldn't leave Germany.

Her parents went to Stuttgart for some dental work, and as they were ready to head home for the Sabbath her father asked, "What train are we taking?" Her mother's response: "We're not going home, I have the tickets and the visas for Switzerland. I'm not going to stay here and witness another May Day [the Nazi holiday]!"

Not all of her family survived. Her grandmother and aunt couldn't escape and committed suicide by taking sleeping pills.

As the 1930s drew to a close, Jews encountered many barriers to leaving Germany. Getting a visa was difficult. In part because of Goebbels' negative propaganda about the Jews, most countries didn't want Jews. And the American immigration quota was woefully small compared to the many who now wanted to escape. Escape became harder after World War II started in September 1939, when Jews could no longer leave Germany by way of enemy countries like France or England.

Few of Baden-Württemberg's Jewish community that still remained got out in 1940 and 1941. Altogether, by late 1941 almost two-thirds of the 10,000 Jews living in Baden-Württemberg in 1933 had been able to escape, mostly to the United States. The deportations to Eastern Europe began at the end of 1941. By 1945, of the remaining one-third, only 616 had survived the Holocaust by surviving the camps, going underground, or, in the case of a few so-called "privileged" Jews married to Gentiles, getting some support from Württemberg's Archbishop Wurm.[23, 29, 30]

Starting Over in America

The long tradition of immigration from Swabia to America meant that many Jews already had relatives living there. However, the

American immigration law of 1882 requiring a financial sponsor was strictly enforced during the Great Depression. However, even unrelated people could supply affidavits as long as they were willing to pledge their wealth to support the newcomers. Carl Laemmle, a Hollywood film mogul, gave affidavits of support for 300 families.[31]

Once in America, the refugees were faced with immense physical and psychological difficulties. The majority had been forced out of Germany, rather than choosing to leave, and most were unable to bring any assets out.

Some immigrants found they could continue to speak their native language. Herz's father and a friend from Laupheim had a little store in Jamaica on Long Island, and they were able to speak to customers in Swabian.

Else Fuerst maintained her Swabian mentality in America. Her second husband was a Berliner, and she was amazed that he and his family cared so much about opera and shows. "In Swabia we didn't play. When we had free time, we were sitting with knitting or embroidery." Her grandmother always told her that when she went to bed at night she should think how she had spent her time that day. "You were not supposed to waste your time. You carry this with you all your life."

Some refugees encountered overt anti-Semitism common in America at the time. Those who moved to Jewish neighborhoods in New York City found anti-German prejudice. Ruth Temes remembered, "We didn't speak Yiddish, so they looked at us and said, 'You are a German!'"

The immigrants usually had to take unskilled jobs when they came to America. Fuerst was lucky enough to make use of her homemaker's skills in New York City. She knitted shawls that were sold with hats. "We had to make the shawl overnight and next morning bring it to the hat shop. Customers paid a lot of money, and if they ordered it today, it should have come yesterday already." Many of the women worked as housemaids. According to Fuerst, "Nobody felt bad about this. Even the educated ones had to do that in the beginning."[32]

Some refugees like Fuerst's brother took up chicken farming in New Jersey.[33] She recalled that with a little money you could buy a six-acre farm and some chickens. "It wasn't so much farming because you bought the grain to feed the chickens and you just produced the eggs." Fuerst eventually went to live on her brother's farm where she met her second husband, a feed salesman.

Even once-wealthy emigrants were forced to start out in much the same fashion. Until 1937, Germans could transfer up to $2,000 out of the country if they paid a tax of 50 percent. But so-called "large capitalists" had to pay taxes of 95 percent. By 1938, the transfer of any German money was taxed at high rates.

Ray Rothschild recalled how his family and others outsmarted the Nazis by taking an expensive Leica camera. In the late 1930s, they cost about $650. Upon arriving in America, Rothschild had to sign a paper that he wouldn't sell the camera for two years. "But nobody checked. That's typically American. It's hard to check in a free society."

In addition, Rothschild's father had planned ahead and bought a Swiss insurance policy payable in American dollars and was thus able to transfer a small amount of his savings out of Germany. He still had to find a job. He was forty-nine years old, didn't speak English, and wasn't used to physical work. He didn't want to lose the few dollars he had, so he bought a chicken farm.

Becoming American Soldiers

During World War II, a number of young Swabian refugees returned to Germany as American soldiers to fight against their former countrymen. Their knowledge of the language and culture of Germany was invaluable. Herz gathered military intelligence from captured German soldiers. "The Germans are so exact that each soldier carried a detailed service history with him, the *Soldbuch*, from which we were able to reconstruct training systems and the structure of the army. Americans wouldn't do anything that dumb."

Arnold Blum found himself facing Germans in battle. "After we took a German prisoner on patrol, I spotted a minefield. The German admitted he helped put them in, so we took cover while he disarmed one of the mines." Finally he yelled, "Got it now." Blum and another soldier had taken just one step when a blinding explosion blew them onto the snow. "The German prisoner got most of it. My buddy was hit by shrapnel through the ankle. Me, I had shrapnel through the left thigh."

Blum's buddy reacted, yelling, "That sonofabitch did it on purpose. I'm going to plug him." Blum slapped the barrel of his buddy's rifle into the snow as the German cried out, "Don't shoot. I've got four children at home." Blum figured maybe he'd gotten the trip wire disconnected, but probably there were other wires he didn't see.

Later, Blum wondered why he'd kept a German soldier from getting killed. He thought it had to do with his Jewish upbringing. The Talmud says, "He who saves one life saves the whole world. He who takes one life kills the whole world."

Marrying a German

Ray Rothschild lived and worked on his father's chicken farm until he graduated from high school. In 1943, he borrowed $87 to start classes at New York University. "I worked days and went to school at night. I didn't have any life socially, in college or otherwise." Then he was drafted, and he eventually became an officer with the Civil Affairs Division in Belgium and France. "Our job was to keep civilians out of the army's hair." Near the war's end, he was stationed in Nuremberg, handling the military government for two counties.

German resident Lisa was twenty in the spring of 1945 and an avid reader of Nazi publications. She recalled how at that point in the occupation she had a choice of either shoveling debris or doing work for the Americans. "I was a good German, so I chose shoveling, not working for the enemy. But the Americans finally sent for me."

She recalled that Rothschild would address her very formally, "Fräulein this, Fräulein that." The war was still on. He was a hard guy to work for. "Other American officers gave you chocolates, but not him. He was the head officer and only twenty-one years old." There was no fraternization, no socializing between Germans and Americans—but they fell in love.

Ray's father in America was shocked and wrote him, "Don't ever marry a German girl." Ray recalled that his father's brother and sister-in-law and his mother's parents, her brother, and two cousins had apparently been exterminated in death camps. "At that time, the Germans didn't believe such things existed, and people in the US weren't sure, although they suspected."

Lisa realized she had been taken in by all the Nazi propaganda about the evil Jews, and Rothschild saw that she was the perfect woman for him. After Ray was discharged from the army, he stayed in Germany working for the War Crimes Commission. Then his father became very ill, and he had to take a boat home to be with him. By October 1946, he had papers for Lisa to emigrate as a war bride. American policy had changed within a year from non-fraternization to allow fiancées to come over exempt from the immigration quota. They were married in April 1947, proof that the Nazis were wrong and Jews and Gentiles in Germany were not really very different at all.

Visits to Germany

Many Jewish refugees returned to visit friends in Germany. A few like Ruth Temes went because of the curiosity of their children. "I never had an urge to go back to Germany, but my son wanted to see where I was born and lived." She just wanted to visit the Jewish cemetery, pay her respects, and leave. After arriving in Buttenhausen, she was worried about getting the rental car up the steep hillside to the cemetery. "We stopped at a mechanic's shop. It was our old next-door neighbor, and he recognized me right away, after thirty years. He was very nice, and he arranged a get-together with the people I had known."

Some Americans asked Ruth, "How could you have done that, met with those Germans?" Her answer was that they were only kids in the bad times. "They felt a lot of fear, that's why they did what they did. Children were trained to inform on their families and on each other."

Ray Rothschild felt similarly. "We visit Germany every year, mainly to pick up a new Mercedes. A lot of my Jewish friends would never drive a German car, but how can you penalize the current generation for what happened then?"

Herz and his wife vacationed in the Black Forest. He was pleased to rediscover a little bit of his childhood in Germany. "I spoke Swabian from the first day to the last, and people were so happy with it. It was like coming home for me." He didn't feel it was right to have a grudge against modern Germans on account of Hitler. "It was an aberration in German history. I don't see any precedent. It's one of those things that happen, that shouldn't happen, but do. People just went crazy."

Ruth Temes emphasized that some Germans hadn't given in to

hate during the Nazi times. She recalled a man in Riedlingen, a Jehovah's Witness, who would travel by motorcycle every Saturday to Frankfurt and bring back food for Jewish people in hiding. He was willing to go to prison along with the Jews. She admitted, "He was an exception, having such courage."

She continued, "Sometimes I feel like my father did about what happened to him during World War I. It was a closed book." But she made sure that her children saw television shows about the Holocaust so they could know what she went through. "You can forgive, but you should not forget."

The Question of Religion

Herz was independent minded in Swabia and continued to be so in America. Like some other individualistic Swabians, he has always believed that political organizations, including Jewish-American political organizations and even the state of Israel itself, are not useful. "We are Americans, and Judaism should be a religion, not a nationality. Zionism takes something away. Judaism should be available to every human being. You don't have to be a member of the Jewish community to learn about the good from the Jewish teachings. It's something universal."

Could something like the Nazis happen here? "Of course, things happen like swastikas on synagogues, but there are always nuts around. In this country, there are a very small number of nuts, and they are completely under control."

Arnold Blum gives another view of religion. He was extremely critical of organized religion. He recalled hearing in early 1945 about the millions of Jews killed in the death camps in the East. "I'd been brought up to believe in an all-knowing and all-powerful God, but after that I saw him as a despicable creature. I wouldn't go near a house of worship. I'd even cross the street, not to pass near one." He doesn't deny the existence of God. "But it was a God that could not use the million and a half children killed in the Holocaust."

Blum is also like so many others from Swabia in his strong religious egalitarianism, believing that no religion is better than any other. "I've found there are many religions, and they include art, literature, music. They all deal with the basic questions—who am I, where did the world come from, and where are we going? When it comes down to it, people are more similar than different."

He had no use for the idea that Jews are a chosen people. "If Jews are chosen to be periodically clobbered, then I don't prefer to be chosen." Blum likened this idea to people's need for prayer. "Imagine being God and listening to the contradictory praying. One team prays they win, and the other team prays they win, too. People need prayer more than God needs it, and it's people who need to feel specially chosen, too."

He wondered how some people could be better than others, when all are little spots on the planet. "Even the big headline makers will wind up just a collection of dust. To think of yourself as more than other people is an illusion."

Still Swabian in America

Blum's emphasis on personal humility is often seen in other Swabians, and it's the opposite of the traditional stereotypical German.

Ray Rothschild also emphasized his Swabian values and character in America. From all appearances he was a stereotypical wealthy Jewish businessman, co-owner and president of a large chemical firm and owner of a real estate empire of more than a thousand apartments. But despite being a multi-millionaire, he still lived in an ordinary tract home. He believed in "having it, but not showing it," like his former Swabian neighbors who embraced the ideal of living modestly. He didn't flaunt his wealth to show his status.

Rothschild remained very much the person he was in Germany. "You only pass through life once, so you have got to use every minute. I eliminate details." Like so many other Swabians, he worshiped efficiency and hated waste.

Another of his traits was willingness to forego immediate returns for the sake of long-term benefits. Under New York City's rent control, when he gave a tenant a new refrigerator, he could take the cost, divide it by forty months, and add that to the monthly rent. "That was a good deal, because I got back 30 percent a year on my money. But my employees worried about laying out the cash and that it took so long to get the money back." Rothschild knew that putting in those refrigerators was an investment. "It's saving money. Most people in America don't want to invest or save, they want to spend."

Rothschild was brought up to help other people in need. Every week his mother gave him five marks to take to a poor woman. However, his generosity stopped in America when he saw welfare programs taking away the incentive to work. He saw people move into apartments and then give up their jobs so they could collect rent subsidies. And he also saw the money from welfare checks "spent on alcohol or clothing, and then the landlord had to sue to get his money. I'm a caring person, but the welfare system is wrong. I always believed in working hard."

When he went to college, Rothschild carried twenty credits while he worked fifty hours a week in a delicatessen. "I always had ambition. My parents always told me, *"Gib mal Mühe"* [make an effort, take pains]. I still go by it." Rothschild vacationed in Germany, but only for two weeks, so he wouldn't neglect his work. "I even work Saturdays and Sundays, so two weeks is a big vacation for me."

Swabians tend to be conservative when it comes to finances, and so is Rothschild. He made his money carefully, avoiding get-rich-quick schemes. Like so many Germans, he worried about risks. He confided, "I'm more pessimistic than optimistic about the world and the future. I have my investments spread around, like my father's Swiss life insurance payable in U.S. dollars. That was all the money he was able to take out of Germany. I've also got gold coins put away."

The Nazis hated America and its progressive ideas, so it's ironic that forcing Jews like Albert Einstein to leave made such an enormous contribution to the American war effort. The Jews in Germany would have never left for America otherwise, for they were committed Germans, happy to live in a country that, until the Nazis took power, gave them many opportunities.

5: MAX GIDEON: JEWISH FARMER

Max Gideon (1916-1998) tells how the Jews in smaller Swabian villages like Baisingen were closely integrated with the Gentile peasants. In 1930 some 22 percent of the Jews in Württemberg still lived on the land like the Gentile peasants.[18] Gideon tells how local Nazis started as juvenile delinquents, but they soon had the authority of the state behind them. People hadn't paid enough attention to politics.

****

Most Jews in our area owned farmland. My family had milk cows and a manure pile in the back of our house just like every other farmer. I was a *Saubauer* [dirty old farmer]. My wife, too. She used to garden, cut the hay, and work on the hay wagons.

I wanted to be a farmer here in America, but my wife wouldn't go with me. There were Jewish farmers in New Jersey. But they weren't real farmers; they just had some chickens. A farmer like we were in Swabia, with a little bit of everything, that wouldn't pay over here in America. They couldn't make a real living in Swabia either. One or two family members always worked in the city, in a shoe factory or whatever, and brought cash home. The only farm crop that brought in real money was hops [for beer]. Otherwise, you mostly raised stuff for yourself.

I had no relatives who were 100 percent farmers; they did other things, too. One uncle ran a combination hotel, restaurant, and tavern. My other uncle was a cattle dealer. In Swabia, the villages are about a mile or two apart, and he used to visit maybe twenty-five of them. In those villages, when somebody got married, they went to my uncle, and he'd sell them two or three head of cattle. They could pay them off over time. He helped them by giving them credit.

So what did it mean? Nothing! The poor guy died in a concentration camp and his wife, too, and so did his mother and my grandmother. That's what hurts. Not that those [German] people in the villages actually did it. But I have to blame them, I don't know nobody else to blame. That's what happened. It's heartbreaking.

Of course, there were bad Jewish people, too. My father wouldn't even say "hello" to one cattle dealer, he was such a crook. The man was bad, and his father was worse. They were swindlers. When they weighed an animal, they'd push the scale with a stick. You don't do that!

Hitler and the Nazis said, "All the Jews are no good." If one day a Jew happened accidentally to shortchange you for a nickel, right away you'd say to yourself, "Oh, I know a cattle dealer who swindles, so this Jew must be a swindler, too."

Young Nazis

We didn't know anything about Nazis until 1930 or so, but we knew the people who would become Nazis. When they were ten or twelve years old, they stood out already. They were the kind of guys who were always out to hurt somebody, to steal something. They were known; others kept away from them. The police had a record of those guys.

My wife remembers them, too. When she walked from school and saw them coming, she went in the other direction. Everybody knew they would try to hurt people, even girls. Their minds were sick. Once Hitler got in power, whatever they thought they could get away with, they did. Nobody could stop them. They had Hitler behind them. By that time, it was too late for the decent people to stand up and say this was not right.

Later on, the schoolteachers were replaced. We got one who was a real Nazi. I wasn't there anymore, but I heard how he told the other teachers and the principal to do whatever the Party wanted "or I will report you."

There were a lot of young people involved in the Nazis, and the older ones had to fall in behind. The young people had power that they never had before.

My father was a real German. He said, "This is only a temporary thing. It will pass. I fought for this country. What can they do to me?" He was a soldier with a lot of honors.

Germany encouraged the Jews before the Nazis. Kaiser Wilhelm asked the Jews to come and stimulate business. Many came from Poland and Russia, where things were bad. Then Germany turned around and started to take away whatever the Jews had.

In Württemberg, the Jews had long roots. My folks go way back. Only my great-grandfather came from somewhere else, and that was only as far away as Alsace. In our small towns, I didn't know of any Jews who didn't have a father or grandfather from the local area.

There was no anti-Semitism to speak of in Germany in the years just before Hitler. You saw the people fighting alongside each other in the First World War.

Why did the people attack the Jews, even though they did so much for Germany? Well, when you're down, you're looking for something to eat. In the villages, we had our food, but in the cities in bad times, people think, "Why should that guy eat, when I got nothing?" If he happens to be a Jew, then the hell with Jews. In good times, nothing like that would happen. That's what helped Hitler establish himself. People didn't think about what he had in mind. It was too late when he had a grip on them.

Good Germans

I went back to my hometown of Baisingen after the war, because I was in the American Army. The mayor was a very close friend of my father. He was the only one I visited.

There were some large farms by us, eight or ten miles in diameter sometimes. One owner was a "von," a baron, and we were friends. There was another one who had a castle along the Neckar River. I know darn well these people weren't anti-Semites or Nazis. They were high officers in the First World War, and they wanted no part of the Nazis. Eventually, they went along, because they had to. Otherwise, they would have lost their prestige and everything.

Some good people in our town helped us. One warned my father that the Nazis were going to arrest all the men after Crystal Night and send them to concentration camps. My father had already made plans to go to Cuba, but it wasn't time yet for the boat to sail. So my father just put his things in a bundle and took off. Someone hid him in Hamburg till the boat was ready.

There were other good people, too. One family sold cattle to my father for his butcher business, and they'd drink beer together afterwards. That was the custom when you do business like that. Another friendly family ran a brewery, and still another one cared for the bulls—ran a stud service. The farmers were all close, too. You'd never be afraid to ask if there was ever something you needed. They'd never refuse you.

The Jewish and Gentile communities were integrated—in the singing society, the war veterans club, and the soccer club. Just the religious organizations were separate.

We did have separate Jewish schools, but we went together for some schooling, too. Athletics was together, and one afternoon a week, the nuns would teach all the girls how to knit, crochet, and do handiwork. We went to the Jewish school until we were thirteen years old. After the seventh grade, we'd leave the town and go to a higher school elsewhere. That would be mixed, like the business school where I went.

The houses in our town were integrated, too. The only exception was around the corner from us, a dead-end street. The temple was back there, and there were four Jewish families and one non-Jewish family living on that street.

If, If, If

My town of Baisingen had about 1,200 people. The townspeople as a whole were good people, but just misled. They were grateful for getting something from the Nazis, but by the time they realized that you don't get something for nothing, it was too late.

The Germans are good people if they get the right man to lead them. If Hitler had been a good man, Germany would be the top country in the world.

If a German sees a uniform, forget about everything else. That's it. That's what helped Hitler. In Baisingen, there were maybe five or six fellows—over here we call them bums—who didn't want to work, and then they got some shiny boots and nice uniforms. That's all it took.

People were intelligent in Germany, but I don't care if you're smart or college-educated, if you're hungry, you'll believe anything that will bring hope.

The Nazi Storm Troopers boycotted Jewish stores in 1932. That was before Hitler got in. They put a uniformed Nazi in front of the leather shop in Horb where I worked, "This is a Jewish outfit, do not buy." That was the Storm Trooper's job. They loved that. They could hit somebody over the head and not get punished for it. Slowly the shop was forced out of business. When a person bought from us, the Nazis would do something to him, beat him up. Or if he had any kind of business dealings with others, the Nazis would say, "That man buys from a Jew," and they'd try to hurt his business.

That's why I say that all it takes is a leader in Germany. Otherwise, they are the nicest people you want to meet, and they are trustful and smart. I'd like to have all those businesspeople and craftsmen come over here and show people in America how to do a job. They'd run rings around them. They know their jobs. Everything is done 100 percent.

It's just that the German people didn't spend time with politics. They just didn't feel like it. Then they got told, "Too bad if you don't like what's happening; there's a gun in front of you now." So what do you do? You're not going to argue with a gun. In 1931, the Nazis started carrying guns as part of their uniform.

Because Baisingen was so small, we didn't have the boycott there. They didn't come to my father's butcher shop. Anyway, mostly Jewish people bought from him; it was mostly a kosher butcher shop. We also had some little grocery stores and a tailor in town, but mostly Jewish people bought from them, so the Nazis wouldn't have achieved anything with a boycott. Jewish people would have gone there at night when nobody could see them.

The last time the Jews were allowed to vote, every Jew voted for Hitler. Because the Nazis knew everything. They'd pull out the paper ballot from the box, and they'd go to the voter's home and shoot him if he hadn't voted for the Nazis. That's how Hitler got in. I wasn't old enough to vote, but I know that's what older people did. They got told in the temple. And by 1930, Hitler was big already, because everybody was scared. "Why should I put my neck out?" Hindenburg brought Hitler into the government in order to keep his own big name, but Hindenburg was just a cardboard box.

Hitler had smart people under him. But you don't have to be smart to be rude. It's always easy to be rude. But they made use of everything. They had Nazi propaganda newspapers reporting, "That

Jew did this, this Jew did that."

Propaganda

The Nazi propaganda got so bad that a son would tell on his parents when they did something wrong. In school they taught, "Hitler is your father, your mother. Your parents at home are just there to bring you into the world. If they do something wrong, you tell us!"

The Nazis also said things like we killed children to make matzos. And people believed that, despite blood is the worst thing for a Jewish person to eat. We are not allowed to eat blood because blood is life.

The way the non-Jews reacted to us, it broke my heart. While I was still an apprentice, I had a friend; his father had a big tailor shop. He was an epileptic. We were very good friends for years, and there was never any sign of Nazi ideas. One day we were going to get together, and he just passed me by on the street. That hurt. Maybe he had no choice. If he really believed all the propaganda, he would have tried to needle me first. He probably knew what he was doing to me was wrong, but still it hurt.

Soon, we didn't have many chances to talk with non-Jewish people. We still had feelings for them, but we didn't want to get them in trouble. So we tried to do everything out of sight. Instead of seeing someone on the street and thinking, "I'll go over and talk business," I'd think, "No, I'll see him at night."

In Swabia, this didn't happen until 1934 or 1935. In other places, like Prussia or Hessen, they had it in 1930 or 1931 already. The Swabians were way more against the Nazis than the people up north. But in the end, it came out the same way, everywhere in Germany. Not like in Denmark, where even the king put on a yellow star to show how he was against the Nazis. Nobody organized to help us in Germany.

Escape

I always had in mind to go and see the world. I was supposed to work in Argentina for a businessman from Baisingen. But my father said, "No, no. We have a good country here. You don't have to go anyplace."

Well, you don't run out on your father. You listen! That's the way you were brought up. Whatever your father and mother said, that's what you did. You're not going to be a black sheep.

But my brother was killed by the Nazis in 1936. Then my father said, "Get out, get out."

Within four weeks, I was in America. It was early 1937, and I was twenty years old. Up to then, I hadn't been very far from home. Going to Stuttgart was a once-a-year thing; you prepared months for that fifty-mile trip.

Then my parents, and my sister and her family, altogether thirty-three families from Baisingen, got together and bought a piece of land in Israel where Swabians were settling, Shave Zion.

The girl that I would marry also got out. She's ten years younger than me. I met her when she was born. The first Saturday after a baby is born there is a special feast. The baby's in the cradle, and the rabbi prays with all the young children up to ten or twelve years old. Each child gets a bag of cookies or candy. Well, everybody left except me, and I looked in at the baby. Then the mother came and said, "When she's a thousand weeks old, you can have her." And she did become my wife. Of course, we didn't get married till after the war. She came over in 1939, at age twelve, just a month before Germany invaded Poland.

Because there were four small children in her family and the youngest was two years old, it took a lot of affidavits to show they wouldn't become a burden to the American government. Her father got away even earlier, before Crystal Night. He was a cattle dealer, so he wasn't tied down to working at a shop. And they didn't wait to sell their house. They just left, and somebody else just took it over. Your house didn't make any difference. You'd rather give up everything. Some were too hungry, and they lost their lives.

Jews Were Germans

People wonder why the German Jews didn't leave in 1933 as soon as the Nazis got in. But in Germany, it was a little different than in Poland or Russia. It took hundreds of years to change the way people lived in Germany, but eventually the Jews were mixed in. We were Germans. That's the way you were brought up. We thought, "This is a Frenchman—shoot him; we are Germans!"

The only difference between us and other Germans was in religion. We were Orthodox. The non-Jewish people were used to us. For example, they might see you and ask, "How come you're not home? It's Saturday." They knew we followed the law about observing the Sabbath. We followed the dietary laws, too.

I would say ninety-five percent of the Jews in our town were Orthodox and observed the Sabbath. The exceptions were the big businessmen or salesmen who traveled and the kids who went away to school. But the cattle dealers would be home every Saturday.

Yiddish

In Stuttgart, there were all kinds of different nationalities. Like Pietz, one of the biggest department stores, they were Polish, and they stuck together just like in America, where people will go to a Polish or to an Italian church. They spoke Yiddish or Polish, and they stuck together. In our town, nobody could speak Yiddish. But you listen to it, and it's easy to understand because when you mix a little Hebrew and German together, it becomes Yiddish.

In New York City, down around Delancey Street, ninety percent or more of the Jews were from Eastern Europe. After about 1850, there were big pogroms going on in Poland and Russia, so they headed west to Germany and then America.

When the Russian and Polish Jews were mistreated, we German Jews did not help them enough, just like the American Jews didn't do enough for us when Hitler came in. And the Eastern European Jews can't forget that. Even though they helped us, they let us know, "You didn't do the same for us." There is a little bit of bad feeling, not much today anymore, just with the older people.

We were friends with a neighbor here in America, and he didn't miss a minute to say to me, *Yegges, Yegges* [German Jews]. He was a Russian Jew and had a bad time when he had to travel through Germany to go to America. We didn't help enough, because we German Jews used to look down on them. They weren't dressed like we were. They had black hats and long black jackets.

There's no split between German Jews and Eastern European Jews in the younger generation. My daughter married a fellow whose folks came from Russia. My other daughter is single yet, but her job is helping the Russian Jews who come to America.

People my age, that's the problem. We stick together. Our closest friends are all German Jews, but I do play pinochle with two fellows, and they're not German, but it's hard, because my English is half Swabian.

Starting Out in America

My first job in America was roasting coffee on 8th Street [in New York City] the day after I came. Then I worked for an uncle of mine in a box factory for about ten years. In between, I was in the Army, in World War II, an interpreter for a construction battalion.

Then another cousin and I started in the meat business. Most of the people I know started their own business when they came over. I had small children then, but that didn't make a difference. If you want to go into business for yourself, you take a chance.

I supplied meat to restaurants. I never apprenticed as a butcher, but I learned it at home from my father. Eventually, we couldn't do much butchering in Baisingen because kosher killing was forbidden by the Nazis. Stupid people like my father took chances and did it anyway, in the dark.

That's why I say some of the Germans weren't so bad. There had to be a health inspection in order to sell meat, and the inspector could tell easily if an animal was killed kosher. There's no blood in the veins. The inspector knew that, but he came and he went. He could have turned us in if he wanted to.

But the Nazis passed lots of other laws, anything to make it difficult for the Jews. See, they couldn't start saying the Protestants can't do this or that. They were too big. The Nazis had to start with the Jewish people. It's easy to go after a minority that's small.

Appreciation

We immigrants appreciate more what we have, because everything was taken from us. When we came to this country, we had nothing. I assure you that 99 percent of the people like us who fled Germany are more American than other people. We appreciate this country because we've seen the other side.

We immigrants are different from people born here. I can't talk like my neighbors, they're very nice people, but when they say, "This is no good, that is no good," I tell them, "I don't care what they charge me in tax, I'm a free man. You people don't know what free means." That makes them think a little bit.

I feel I'm American. This is my home. But I might have ended up in Israel. I'm 100 percent behind Israel. You don't have to be a

Zionist, and we're not Zionists. I'm an American and America comes first, but a homeland for people like me means quite a bit.

I've been to Israel twice, once in 1946 to see my parents while they were still living, and again six years ago. I could have lived in Israel, but this is my home. I always think of Roosevelt. He made a difference by letting me come here. At that time, it was so hard for the Jews to go anywhere. I say "thank you" to the American people, but he's the one that put my name on the list. I'll go to Israel to visit, but I'll gladly come home again. Both of my children have been to Israel, too, but neither would want to live there.

Maintaining the Religion

We moved from New York City to Bergenfield, New Jersey, because of the religious community here. I wanted the kids to go to Hebrew school. We're Conservative Jews.

I think most people who experienced persecution like we did are interested in keeping up the traditions. There are exceptions, like one particular family. The father was in a concentration camp, and he does not believe in anything: "If there were a God, he wouldn't have let it happen." He's a weak man. He's the only one I know who reacted that way.

Bad things happen, and you cannot get an answer why. If somebody believes in God, these things are easier to take. You have something to fall back on.

We didn't give our children a choice about religion. Just like they had to go to public school, they had to go to Hebrew school. It is just one hour a day after school, and it covers the history and religion. And it doesn't stop at bar mitzvah. There is Hebrew high school, too. And in New York City, there is Yeshiva University.

Our kids went through Hebrew high school. Our older daughter lives in another town, and her family joined the temple there. The younger daughter has no reason to join a temple, because on holidays she comes over here and goes to temple with us.

My granddaughters look forward to the traditions during the holidays. When my daughter tells the grandchildren they're coming here for the holidays, they'll say, "Oh, we're going to have matzo balls, too?" There are certain things they associate with the holidays.

I thank God my kids listen to me. I'm proud of them, because they know the background. Some people say they want to shield the children from these things, but you can't do that.

Our two girls are American. They did study German in school so they could understand what we were saying. We spoke German at home if we didn't want them to understand. But after they took German, they still couldn't understand us, because we speak the Swabian dialect.

Still Swabian

I think the girls are like the Swabians in some ways. They are careful with money, because we trained them that way. Neither one believes in credit cards. If we don't have the money to spend on something, we don't buy it. And they are both hardworking girls.

They're independent and thickheaded, too. You find that in Swabia and here, too. That's our family sickness. The children can be very pigheaded. The father is, so why shouldn't they be? We have our own ideas. We brought that with us from Germany.

They're independent in other ways. They're professionals. One girl is a physical therapist and does work that is very independent. The other is doing social work, and she is very independent in mentality. Maybe that's why she's not married yet, and she's almost thirty. Anyway, in both their jobs, they are the boss. It's their knowledge that's important.

My girls are not German; we didn't bring them up that way. But we didn't bring them up the opposite, either. Don't forget, there are more good things over there than bad things. The girls know all about it. They can make their own minds up. We told them the people in Germany are nice, but Nazism was like a snowball; and when something like that comes up, you have to stop it early on. You can't ignore it.

That's the difference between Germany and here. We are more aware here. We didn't know anything when I was a kid. What did we know about politics? Why should we know the mayor's name from the next town? When we were worried, it was, "I hope we get ice, so we can go ice skating." And for our parents, there wasn't much talk about politics either, unless it was just our own community. They didn't know what kind of political parties Germany had. That was the problem. We just didn't know.

6: HOLOCAUST SURVIVORS

One of the most shocking things about the Holocaust was that Germany was a modern nation that should have outgrown the primitive hatreds of less advanced nations. In places like Romania or Russia, people harbored an intense hostility towards Jews, but Germany was a law-abiding nation. The anti-Semitic feelings were muted by laws protecting the rights of citizens, whatever their religion. How could such a nation have killed millions of Jews?[34]

Where Did The Hatred Come From?
Racism has beset many nations in recent history. Earlier in the twentieth century there was the genocide of the Armenians by the Turks. Indonesia killed and expelled the Chinese, Uganda slaughtered and displaced East Indians, and Nigeria had a genocide of the Biafrans. More recently, there has been the systematic Hutu killing of the Tutsi in Rwanda and the Serbian killing of Bosnians in the former Yugoslavia. The tragic list goes on.

Murder on a massive scale hasn't always been fueled simply by racial hatred. In the 1930s, millions died when Stalin engineered famine in the Ukraine. In the late 1960s and 1970s, millions more died in state-ordered purges in China and Cambodia for the crimes of wearing eyeglasses, reading books, or belonging to the bourgeoisie.

Humans may carry a genetic predisposition to define "in" and "out" groups as part of a primitive survival strategy. Perhaps early humans who banded together and supported the in-group while ignoring, or killing the out-group, were better able to survive than those who did not differentiate between in- and out-groups. Those who did not favor their own kind may not have had the resources to survive and mate and pass on their genes. They died out. But those who discriminated were able to survive and pass on their genes to successive generations. To us.

The Holocaust of six million Jews is unique because it was aimed at the annihilation of the Jews, not just a genocide in which large numbers of Jews were to be killed. Thus, the Germans did not just try to convert Jews into Germans, but eliminate them. In contrast, while some three million non-Jewish Poles were killed by the Germans, 90 percent survived. Some Poles who looked Aryan were accepted into the German community. The Germans sought dominance over the Poles. In contrast, during the same time, three million Jews living in Poland were annihilated, 90-95 percent of the Jewish population. The aim was to eliminate the Jewish community entirely. In this sense, the Holocaust was unique.[35]

Jews in Germany had blended into society. They were more assimilated than the Jews of America in the 1920s and 1930s. Many studied at universities, while in America there were quotas that limited the number of Jews. German Jews found it easier than American Jews to enter professions like medicine and law.[21]

Part of the process leading to the Holocaust was the reversal of this assimilation. The Nazis used laws, regulations, and propaganda to make Jews again an outcast group.

Hitler and his charisma was a driving force behind the Nazi anti-Semitism. Few other top Nazi leaders were anti-Semites before 1925. Sometime during late 1941, it was Hitler who apparently decided that Germany would no longer seek to drive the Jews out of Europe but instead murder them. The German invasion of the Soviet Union was bogging down, so Jews could not be deported to new German lands there. The slaughter of Russian Jews in that invasion could serve as a model.

By October 1941, the new Nazi policy was finalized, with an order by Heinrich Himmler, head of the SS, prohibiting Jewish emigration. Around that time, construction was begun on some death camps in Poland. At the end of November, invitations were sent out for a highest-level planning conference to be held at Wannsee, near Berlin, where the Final Solution for dealing with the

Jews was formulated. They would be murdered. It was the beginning of the Holocaust.

Legality

An important part of German culture and personality is respect for laws and authority. The Nazi government took great pains to use laws to eliminate Jews.

The Holocaust featured bureaucratic procedures. The Soviets and other autocratic nations made enemies "disappear." The Germans kept meticulous records of deportations and murders.

The German aptitude for technical and bureaucratic excellence and obedience ensured the efficient implementation of mass murder. A commandant at Auschwitz, Rudolf Hoess, wrote in his autobiography, "I had been brought up by my parents to be respectful and obedient towards all grown-up people...It was constantly impressed upon me in forceful terms that I must obey promptly the wishes and commands of my parents, teachers, priests, etc., and indeed of all grown-up people, including servants, and that nothing must distract me from this duty. Whatever they said was always right."[36]

Hoess continued, "These basic principles on which I was brought up became part of my flesh and blood. I can still clearly remember how my father, who on account of his fervent Catholicism was a determined opponent of the Reich Government and its policy, never ceased to remind his friends that, however strong one's opposition might be, the laws and decrees of the State had to be obeyed unconditionally."

A law enacted at the beginning of 1939 required that Jews add to their given name either Israel or Sara to make sure no Jew could pass for Gentile and evade persecution. This was a key step because most Jews had assimilated. Many looked like Aryans despite Nazi propaganda to the contrary. In Eastern Europe, many Jews were easily identified from their black kaftans and side curls. In Germany, Jews eventually had to wear a yellow Jewish star to distinguish them.

The Jews were further restricted and separated from other Germans at the start of World War II in September 1939. New laws required Jews observe a special curfew from eight or nine in the evening until six in the morning. They were prohibited from using public air-raid shelters and legally required to build their own.

Scarce foods such as chocolate and coffee were forbidden them.

In 1940, many Jews were forced to move from their homes. Jews and non-Jews could not live in the same buildings. Additional laws forced Jews out of major towns and cities, to make them *Judenfrei*, free of Jews. They were concentrated in small rural villages such as Buchau, Laupheim, Haigerloch, and Buttenhausen, where earlier many Jews had lived. In 1941, Jews were essentially forbidden to leave their town or village; they needed special permission to use public transportation.

A Few Survivors

Few Swabian Jews can report on the years of 1940 and 1941 before they were deported to the East. Victor Marx was born in 1903 in Baisingen. He grew up in the university town of Tübingen, where his father was a cattle dealer. Marx's younger brother, like many leftists, escaped from Germany in June 1933. He managed to survive the war, living underground in France and then in Switzerland. Marx's widowed mother also got out but was later caught in the German occupation of France, and in 1942 sent to Auschwitz.

In September 1938, Marx was no longer permitted to work as an independent textile merchant. After Tübingen was emptied of Jews, he got a job as a gardener in Stuttgart. His wife, Marga, worked in the household of a Jewish family. They had a daughter Ruth, born in 1933, who "was a real sunshine for the entire family." She was sent to live with her grandmother in France.

On Crystal Night, Marx fled Stuttgart to stay with friends living outside the city, but he was arrested a few days later and sent to Welzheim, a small concentration camp. After release in January 1939, he was able to work for a construction firm. It had a contract from the Nazis to clean up the wreckage of the Stuttgart synagogue destroyed on Crystal Night. The two years he worked "were very hard years, but they were a good teacher for me; without them I wouldn't have survived the concentration camps."

During 1940 and 1941, Hannelore Kahn was living in Stuttgart with her parents. She later recalled, "When most of our friends and relatives had a chance to leave Germany, my parents and I stayed behind, as our affidavits for the United States were not enough to get a visa. In 1941 we were forced to wear the *Judenstern*, a yellow

Star of David with Hebrew-like letters spelling out *Jude* [Jew]. This had to be worn on the left side of your clothing for everybody to see." As a sociologist has shown, those European nations that did a more thorough job of labeling their Jews as different also did a more effective job of killing Jews in the Holocaust.[37]

At this time, "we also had to buy all groceries, vegetables, fruit, and the small portion of meats, at one store. Our ration cards had small J's printed all over to make it impossible to redeem them somewhere else. Shopping time was restricted. All over Stuttgart's butcher shops there was no pork available; only the Jewish store had mainly pork for sale. Since we had no other choice, we bought it and exchanged it later with Gentile friends. Life was made harder and harder for us." She survived the camps, but her parents didn't.

In September 1941, the Gestapo informed Victor Marx that he and his wife would have to leave Stuttgart, to help make it "clean of Jews," and go to Haigerloch, one of the traditional rural Jewish towns. There they lived with their daughter Ruth, who had returned from France. They furnished their apartment "quite comfortably," expecting that they would be able to stay there until the end of the war. Marx worked as a laborer for a moving firm and later as a mason's helper.

The Legal Framework

Two months later, towards the end of November 1941, the Marx family got an order that they would be deported from Germany. Each person was permitted two suitcases, totaling 100 pounds, plus a knapsack. They had to sign over their remaining possessions to the state. All identification cards, passports, and other papers, as well as money and valuables, were taken away.

Many Germans subsequently claimed they didn't know that the Jews would be killed. Marx himself was not aware of the impending Holocaust. Of the transport, he recalled, "we had no idea where we were going." He added, "the treatment was good." Their railcars were sealed, but from time to time two people were allowed out to get water. Their guards were *Landjäger* (militia), one of whom hailed from Tübingen and tried to help Marx, "but understandably he had no such possibility." According to Marx, the militia were astonished at the reception given the Jews on their arrival at a camp near Riga, Latvia. Each SS man greeting them had a cane in his hand, and "we thought they were wounded." But then the SS started using the canes to beat the prisoners.

Of 1,050 Jews then deported from Württemberg to Riga, only thirty survived. Other transports followed—twelve in all, to places like Lublin in Poland and Theresienstadt in Czechoslovakia. Of the total of 2,500 Jews deported from Württemberg, 180 survived. A number of these survived only because the Nazis planned to use their labor before killing them. Josef Mengele and other Nazi doctors would make their notorious selections, where the old and the very young were sent to their immediate deaths—as were mothers of children, since those distraught over the deaths of their children would not be good workers. Young and physically strong Jews were spared as long as quotas of killed Jews could be met. Those with both extraordinary stamina and luck would live to tell of the Holocaust.

Horrors in the East

The camp near Riga was Jungfernhof, one of many small and little-known concentration camps established in Eastern Europe by the Nazis.[38] All the men were crammed into a barn with wooden bunks layered eight high. There was so little room above each bunk that they had to slide in sideways. The women and children had similar quarters. The buildings had only partial roofs, and the doors could not be closed. Wind, rain, and snow came in. During the winter of their arrival, temperatures often dropped to minus forty degrees. There were no proper sanitary facilities.

Rations were scanty. Typical meals were bread and thin malt coffee, except for the midday dinner, a watery soup of peas, potatoes, and grits. Once in a while they would get a fish-head soup and, twice a week, a half-ounce of margarine and an ounce-and-a-half of horse meat. Many people quickly died from the combination of cold and malnutrition.

Another of the Swabian Jews at Jungfernhof, Harry Kahn, born in 1911 in Baisingen, reported that every morning the camp commander, Seckt, would ask how many had died. After being told the number, he would respond, "much too few." Every few days, Seckt would order the barn completely emptied for an inspection. Those too weak to get up he shot. Victor Marx saw a mountain of some 800 bodies that couldn't be buried because the ground was frozen. The living were made to work and "died like flies." The commandant carried a stick and used it to beat people.

One March day, three months after they arrived, Victor Marx's wife, Marga, and their seven-year-old daughter, Ruth, were loaded onto a truck with others to be sent to Dünamünd. Supposedly there were hospitals, schools, and comfortable houses there. Marx begged the camp commander to be sent along with his wife and daughter. But he had to stay behind, presumably because he was capable of work. He never saw them again. This was only the beginning of Marx's ordeal of over three years in six different concentration camps.

Two Survivors

Ruth Lang and Sol Lemberger were also sent to Jungfernhof. With some difficulty they told me of their experiences.

Sol, one of a cattle dealer's four sons, was born in 1923 and was still a child when anti-Jewish laws began to affect his family. He recalled, "I went to a Jewish elementary school in Rexingen. When I was fourteen [in 1937], there was no more school. Other people went to Horb, to the *Realschule* [high school], but Jewish people weren't permitted to go anymore. So from fourteen on, I worked for my father."

Nazi laws soon made it impossible for Lemberger's father to continue as a cattle dealer. "From 1939, Jewish people were forced to work essentially only in agriculture for Gentiles. My father had to. It was working in the fields or whatever the farmer did himself, nothing more or less than what he did. I did it, too."

Lemberger recalled that "the farmers I worked for were very nice. They knew me, everybody knew everybody. The people in our town of Rexingen were used to living with Jewish people for 100 years. The only problem was that people were afraid. I worked for a man we had known all our lives. This man had a neighbor who was not a native of the town, and they did not get along. Our friend was always afraid to give me food or anything. He had to bring things to someplace else, and I picked them up there. He was afraid that his neighbor would see."

Today Lemberger is philosophical about why some Germans became virulent Nazis: "A farmer usually is a peaceful man. He's got his own worries, to work his fields and to survive the weather.

So he was not looking for any adventures. He had his full day. Only the guy who didn't work all day, he was not tired in the evening, the hoodlums in the night and those who do holdups" became Nazis, he maintained

Lemberger was sixteen when Germany invaded Poland. Living conditions deteriorated for civilians throughout Germany, but especially for Jews. "After the war started, there was rationing for everybody, and for the Jewish people, even worse rationing. But we worked for farmers, so we got a little bit more. If you worked for a farmer, you told him not to pay with money, but with flour and potatoes, so you could survive."

He added, "Jews in our area were small businesspeople. They were satisfied with their livelihood. A lot had traditional businesses; the father had run the business before them. They did not want to leave. It was only when they were forced to. In the little places like where we lived, the people were nice. Our parents wanted to hang on. They would say that maybe it will get better and nobody was bothering me personally."

Lemberger recalled that after Crystal Night and the sending of fathers to Dachau, "then Jews knew what time it was. And those who lived in the big cities, they knew long before we did what the Nazis meant."

Lemberger's family tried to get out after Crystal Night, like other Swabian Jews still living in the small towns. They tried to go to America. "People went to the consulate in Stuttgart and got a number, but it was just too late. The quota for immigrants from Germany was very minimal. America could have saved 200,000 Jews from Germany. Nothing was done like when the Hungarian revolution happened [in 1956] and America passed a special law to take in refugees." Lemberger continued, "Also, my parents had four children, and we did not have any relative who would give us an affidavit saying that they would support us. Who would sponsor a family with four children?"

His parents wanted the family to go to Palestine, but "the British made it very hard; there was a quota, and it took time to be processed. We sent all our belongings, our furniture and household things, shipped in a box big as a room. But we didn't make it ourselves. That was in 1938, but by 1939, Germany and Britain were at war, and we couldn't go anymore. Single people were smuggled through Romania and the Black Sea, but not families.

"Resettlement"

"On the 29th of November in 1941, when I was eighteen years old, they took us away from home to be deported for resettlement. A girl who worked in Stuttgart said we were being sent to the East, and it was going to be nice. People always want to believe the best. We hoped there would be a certain place where nobody bothers us. We were optimistic. They let us take along some things, a stove, sewing machine, and other things for resettling, and clothes, too. So it did seem like resettling. Anyway, you had no choice."

Lemberger went to the camp at Jungfernhof. "It was a farm with lots of big farm buildings. But there was no work, and there was so much snow. You had snow from December until April, the same snow, on top and on top and on top. I came from the Black Forest where you have snow, but I never saw snow like that."

He recalled, "In March, they lined up everyone in front of the barracks, and they shipped out two or three thousand. They sent them away in trucks, including my younger brothers and my parents. The trucks took people away all day long. I saw the trucks go out, maybe ten trucks. Dünamund is twenty-six miles away. In snow, it will take three or four hours to go and come back, but the trucks came back in an hour. Sooner or later, you figured maybe no one got to Dünamund."

Later, he found out what happened. "When we were finished harvesting, our commander loaned us and his horses to a Latvian farmer to work. From the farmer I learned the Nazis had gone to a woods and shot the children, some women, and the older people. The rest had to work in factories all around Riga."

Riga's Ghetto

Ruth Lang was on the same transport from Stuttgart to Jungfernhof. She was born in 1925 in Süssen, near Göppingen, and was sixteen at the time of the deportation. Her father and mother were in their mid-forties.

"When I was in Jungfernhof, they took 200 of us young girls to the ghetto in Riga," Lang remembered. The Latvian Jews in the ghetto had been killed to make room for German Jews. "I went because they said we would work in factories and in houses. They also told us that our parents would follow. My mother told me to go because it would be much better than working out in the fields and the cold weather. But that was the last I saw my parents."

In the ghetto, "I had to work at a job, and during the winter I also had to shovel snow on the streets of Riga. One day, they told us they needed to ship so many people from the ghetto to the same place where transports were going from Jungfernhof. Of course, we wanted to go, because our parents were being transported there." Lang and two other girls decided to go with the transport, so they skipped work that morning and packed everything they owned into their knapsacks.

But the girls were frustrated. "All of a sudden the police came. In the ghetto, they had three kinds of police: the Jewish police, the SS, and the Latvian police. It was the Jewish police. They told us, 'You know, girls, we have a surprise for you; you cannot go.' Of course, we carried on, how we wanted to see our parents, how we missed our parents. We made a struggle, but the police insisted we couldn't go and they pushed us into an attic. They knew that if we went, it was the end for us."

Lang considers, "I imagine they took sick people, elderly people, because if there is a quota, you have to fill the quota. The Nazis would have taken us even though we could work. They didn't care, as long as the quota was filled. But the police knew better, so they kept us and they sent others. That's how we knew when our parents died. It was the day of the transports to Dünamünd, March 26th, 1942."

Survival in the Camps

Life in the camps was a constant struggle to stay alive. Sol Lemberger explained, "It was a systematic way of destroying people. At Jungfernhof, people had no work in the beginning. So what did people do? You were not supposed to be in the barracks, but you did not know where to go. So people would take a garbage can, put some wood in, make a fire, and warm themselves. Sekt was the commandant; and when he saw four, five, or six people standing there warming themselves, he shot them. The Nazis just destroyed people. There was no compassion. People were in the way. The SS didn't have any work for them, and they didn't want to feed them for nothing."

Seckt and the SS were not the only ones feared in the camp. "We had criminals as well as Jews in the camp," recalled Lemberger. "They were called 'Capos.' They had been in prison in Germany, and all of a sudden they were put in charge of us. They made things really rough.

"How did people survive? First, you couldn't be a loner; you had to have friends. Alone you couldn't survive. One took care of the other, in food, in everything. You're not alone. And it's practical. It's cold in the night, and you sleep together; you have an extra blanket."

Lemberger also remembered another time, "In the fall of 1944, when we were in Buchenwald [concentration camp], we weren't allowed to sleep in the barracks. We slept in the open with barbed wire around. We were five boys, and each had a blanket. We put a couple of blankets on the ground, and the other three on top of us, and that's how we kept warm. Alone you couldn't do that. Also alone, somebody else might take your blanket away.

"It had to do with luck, too. But mostly young people survived, because they could take it more than the older ones. A young person has more strength and maybe more willpower. You always thought, 'Maybe tomorrow, maybe tomorrow.' You didn't give up."

Survival also had to do with work. "I was two and a half years at Jungfernhof, working in the fields. Once you had a harvest, you had something to eat, whether it was legal or not. If you harvested potatoes or carrots, you can eat one; they don't have so many guards they can see everything. We ate the potatoes raw."

Lemberger's prior work experience helped him survive. "When we were young, we were used to work. We worked at home, and we helped on the farm. Also, after the war started, we didn't have so much to eat in Germany. We were not spoiled. Starving was not sudden for us. That had something to do with surviving." Ruth Lang also had done physical work at a factory.

Lang felt being able to work at the camps was psychologically beneficial. "If you sit all day long, you can lose your mind. If you have to work, you forget, because you have to watch what you're doing. They always had plenty of work for us. The Germans didn't keep people who didn't work. Then they would eliminate you."

She added, "I think our religious background gave strength and hope. And also, later on, I remember we met English soldiers. They were POWs. We were marching from Poland back to Germany, and they were going the other way. They saw us, and they said in English, 'Soon out, soon out.'

"So you knew that it's soon over. The only problem is, do you survive till it's over? There was no food. The Germans didn't have anything themselves. Lots of people died in the last few days. A lot died after liberation because they were too weak, and sometimes they died even when they got some food, when they ate too much too suddenly. People died in lots of ways. In camp I met my former teacher from Göppingen, and he ran away when the Russians were coming closer in 1945. The Russians called out to him to halt. He ran, and they shot him. He didn't know it was the Russians.

"Yes, it was luck in a lot of cases, and you had to have the will; you had to have the strength. Religion helped, and you had to have other people and friendship, a lot of friendship. I was so very close with my friends."

But still, each day in the camp took its toll. Lemberger remembered, "It was hard for people to keep up their hopes in the camps. You get to the point that in Germany is called *stur* [in a trance]. You don't care anymore."

Later, it was different. "In June, 1944, I was helping build a barracks, and the foreman of this project was a German but not an SS man. He was an experienced carpenter drafted to work for *Organisation Todt* [an engineering and construction firm], and we were his helpers. The camp commandant came and told us that the Americans had landed in Normandy, but they were beaten back and they were all corpses there. The commandant probably reported what he heard on the radio. After the commandant left, we asked our boss what happened. He said they were not all corpses, and they were coming to Germany! This carpenter was sick and tired of the war. That gave us a little bit of hope."

Eventually, Lemberger was shipped from Latvia to the Stutthof camp near Danzig, then Buchenwald, and then to "a place in Thuringia where they made gasoline out of coal. This plant was bombed all the time by the Americans. The minute the air raid was over, we had to build it up again, thousands of us. And when the Americans came close in 1945, the Germans sent us further back.

Freedom

"We ended up in Theresienstadt [concentration camp in Czechoslovakia], where we were liberated. After a few weeks, we were able to travel on a special bus that the Czech government had sent to Stuttgart to pick up some of their own citizens who had been forcibly taken to Germany. The trip took only two days. Otherwise it would have taken us five weeks of walking, and we didn't have the strength for that anymore."

Lang's escape to freedom was harrowing. "In Riga [in the ghetto], I worked for a company called AEG, something like a German General Electric. I was trained, and I had to make parts for airplanes. Later on, I worked on a machine to make cables. In 1944, when the Russians came closer to Latvia, the Germans put us on a boat to Danzig, where there was another concentration camp [Stutthof]. Then an officer said he'd get us out because we were needed for work. They shipped twenty-five of us girls to Poland to work. Then the Russians came closer to Poland, and we had to march back to Germany." On their way, they heard the Russian artillery.

"One day on the march it got dark, and three of us girls hid from the SS guards. After they passed on, we ran across the fields of high snow. We went to a farm, but they were afraid to let us in. Then we went to another house where we saw a light. A woman opened the door, and we asked if we could stay. Then we saw there were German soldiers in there. Our luck was that we had civilian coats over the striped prisoner clothes with numbers. We also spoke German, so they thought we were *Volksdeutsch* [ethnic Germans] running away from the Russians. The woman told us that they already had a lot of people staying, and they couldn't take us. We left and went to a different farmhouse, where the woman let us stay in the barn."

After a few days, the girls were liberated near Bromberg by the Russians. "But we were afraid of the Russians, too, because we couldn't speak Russian or Polish. So we got together with another girl who came from Poland. Three days later, other girls from Bromberg joined us. We were eight girls altogether. When I went out with them, I never spoke German. I was afraid to. When the Russians asked why I didn't speak, the girls answered that I was deaf or dumb.

"I was in Poland for several months while the war was still on. I worked for the Polish in the kitchens of an officers' club. Then, when we heard that the trains were going through to Berlin, we found a few Polish Jewish soldiers who wanted to look for their families. So we had a few men along. The Russians gave us a hard time when we tried to get from East Berlin to West Berlin. They asked why we would want to go there, but we said we were looking for our families." After two tries, the Russians let them through.

Horror at Home

"We were happy that we were free, but we didn't know what we would find at home. I stayed in Stuttgart for a few days, because there were no trains, and nobody had cars." Lang finally returned to her hometown with the help of Americans, "soldiers who were born in Germany and left for America before the war and then joined the American Army.

"So I went to Süssen, where I was born. I stayed there only a few weeks. I didn't want to stay there with the Germans. There was a family in our house; but the town found them another place. Of course, there weren't any Nazis in the town. After the war, nobody was a Nazi, right? But you didn't come back with your parents. So you had the feeling of hate."

Townspeople came and told her they had a piece of her family's furniture. "Another one had two dishes, another person had something else, and so on. They said my mother gave them away. I told them if my mother gave something away, they should keep it. I didn't want anything."

Lemberger also recalled the terrible experience of returning home. "My town of Rexingen used to have nearly 300 Jewish people. When I came back, it was only myself and one woman, the mother of my friend. Before the war, some had emigrated to Israel or to America, but we were the only survivors from those sent to the camps. You can imagine how when you walk in the town, you know every house and every stone, but the people you grew up with are all gone. It is a terrible feeling."

Lang felt the same. "You can't imagine what it does to you when you come back, and you know every place. You spent sixteen years as a child growing up there. In the background, you always see your parents. Everything comes back to you. It's very hard to live with, very hard. So who wants to live there? Who likes people like that? Even if your neighbors were nice to you, and they were to us, it's not enough. It just does not work, because you are full of hate. You're only a human being."

Lang added, "Time is a healer. On the other hand, I am finished with Germany. It is also true that there is a generation that had nothing to do with it. When I think about it, I know these Germans were not born then and they had nothing to do with it, so it is not their fault. And yet, it's the country."

In a displaced persons camp in Stuttgart, Lang met Lemberger, who had known her parents before the Holocaust. Both began thinking of leaving Germany for America. Lemberger remembered some of the soldiers they met in the camp. "There were some Jewish boys who were in the Army, and they played the big shots. We thought they must be big men in America. Then Max Gideon [Chapter 5] came. He was a soldier, too, and we told him that we wanted to go to America."

Gideon's answer surprised them: "America is not an easy country; it's very hard. Don't look what those big shots do, because when they go back, they won't even find a job!" Lemberger recalled, "There was one big shot who drove a Jeep, smoked cigarettes, and gave us chocolate and everything. He told us to come up to their room in Stuttgart, and they had wine for breakfast. We thought they lived like kings, but they were just soldiers showing off."

Lang recalled, "After I got to America, one of those big-shot soldiers used to come to a store where I worked in order to sell Fuller brushes. I bought from him, because he was nice to me when he was a soldier, but he was looking for a job just like I was looking for one! Max told me the facts, that in America, I'd make a living, but I shouldn't get illusions."

In America

Despite the hardships that Lemberger and Lang expected they'd face in America, they were determined to leave Germany as soon as they could. Lang first stayed in New Jersey with one of her brothers who had escaped from Germany in 1940. "I was so lonely. My brothers did not ask me any questions. They did not want to hurt me. They wanted to wait until I would open up and talk to them, but I wanted to be asked. So I asked my brother if he would drive me to New York City, where I saw Sol Lemberger and other friends. You can understand why we survivors came together. But we didn't talk about it. We just wanted to see each other. That was enough."

Lang found work in New Jersey as a housemaid for a doctor with two small children. There she was able to learn English. "Sol and I got married in 1947. We moved to New York City, where he learned the butcher trade, and I worked in a factory doing sewing. After we got married, we weren't so lonely. All our friends came to our apartment on Saturday nights. I think most of the other survivors reacted the way we did. They wanted to see each other. We are still very close.

"I have been in America so long that I don't feel German any more. I feel I belong here. I worked myself up, and I have a good life. I am not poor, I do fine. So I'm happy here, I'm satisfied. I'm American."

Sol and Ruth's children were born in New York City. "We lived in Washington Heights, in what was called the Fourth Reich [where many German Jewish refugees lived].[39] You didn't need English there. They all spoke German. We couldn't understand that. We wanted to learn the language spoken here."

A tenacious attitude seems to have helped the Lembergers adapt to the United States, the same attitude that helped them survive four years in the camps. Ruth says, "I think the experience did make us stronger. Those who survived were mentally strong, with willpower."

Lemberger explained, "In New York, we met a man from Hessen, very demanding. He felt that his relatives owed him something because he was in the concentration camps and they were not. He would say it was unfair that he had to go through all those things. I personally did not feel that! It wasn't my aunt's fault, or my grandfather's, or my cousin's, that I was in the camps and they were here in America. When we came to America, we didn't have anybody to fall back on; we were all by ourselves. But we felt we can do it on our own. We didn't blame anybody."

Maintaining the Religion

Some adjustments to American life were difficult, however. Lemberger explained, "We were always religious, but more so when we came to America. I was lucky because in the beginning I lived in

New York City with my grandfather, a very religious man who came out with the last boat in 1941.

"When you came out of the camps you could have decided not to be religious, because in the camps, you couldn't practice your religion. I was offered a job to work on Saturday [the Sabbath], but I did not take the job. Today, it's easier; you have a forty-hour week, and most places don't work on Saturday."

It was rare to get time off for all Jewish holy days. Lemberger recalled, "Ruth worked sewing blouses, and the boss, a Jewish man, said he could understand New Year's. And Yom Kippur, he didn't work that day either. But Sukkoth, which comes a week later, he worked and didn't observe that day. He told her that if she took that day off she shouldn't come back to work the next day."

She did take Sukkoth off but still kept her job. Sol explained, "If your religion is important to you, you have to be ready to sacrifice for it. The friends we have, they aren't necessarily Orthodox, but they keep the holidays. I think it has something to do with their upbringing. In Germany, at least in the smaller towns, we were all religious."

The Lemberger children continued as Orthodox Jews. Both sons became rabbis. Lemberger noted, "I think the experience in the camps made us even more religious than we were before. To have the religious feeling, you have to have the knowledge of the Laws, so we learned more as we started our new life here, and the children did, too. The children became even more knowledgeable, really scholars."

Still, it was difficult to watch the two sons grow up. Ruth recalled, "Our boys went to Israel right after high school to study, and it took quite a while for me to adjust. Our parents didn't get out of Germany, and I was always afraid my sons would stay in Israel."

Ruth approvingly pointed out how her sons and their wives had been born and raised in America, where being independent is important. "They have to live their own lives. Otherwise, they will not grow up, and they will have a very hard time."

Reflections

Sol Lemberger looked back at his youth, first just struggling to survive in the camps, and then starting out all over again in a new country. "Our problem was that we were never teenagers. We were children, and then suddenly, in the camps, we were grownups. We had to learn very quick, because we were without parents. Maybe that pushed us to be independent, and we are stubborn Schwabs, too."

He sees other traces of his German upbringing in himself and in his children. "German parents are strict. Things have to be in a certain order. German Jews have this also. Children have to listen. My older son is the same way as me. I was never so strict with my sons that I gave an order like a sergeant. But there is one certain thing we are strict about in the store. We have a reputation as the cleanest butcher store in Baltimore. My children are the same way, very orderly and also neat and clean."

Of course, Ruth and Sol will never forget the Holocaust. Ruth emphasized, "It will be with us the rest of our lives. All the time, things come back."

She remembered when the Germans put her and others from the Riga ghetto onto a ship for Danzig. "They gave us a couple of slices of bread, but a very religious lady told us, 'Tonight is Yom Kippur. You're not going to eat.' This is the highest holiday when you are not supposed to eat. We young girls were hungry, and we insisted we were going to eat. But nobody did eat. We were all seasick. All night and through the whole next day, nobody wanted to eat. Now, when Yom Kippur comes around, I think of that."

While the Lembergers remember the camps, "it's seldom that we say anything to people who do not understand. We don't talk to American people about it." Sol agreed, "You can't picture it. What's the use to tell them the story? Maybe these days, when people see films or read, they ask. Then I explain. But I don't go deep. The Holocaust stories on television bring out some points but not the real things. A stranger doesn't get the true picture."

Nor was it something they were anxious to discuss with their sons. Ruth remembered, "Our children never talked about the Holocaust. They had children of other survivors in their school classes, too, but they didn't talk about it. They said they were not interested." She added, "I never go to synagogue or other places when there's anything about the camps, and with the children we just never went into it."

Sol explained, "It left its mark on everybody. The other day, I heard about a man who cannot sign his name if somebody else watches. It left the same kind of mark on us. For instance, there's the prayer in the synagogue every year on the day of my father's death. I know the prayer by heart, but in public, I'm very nervous. Ruth is too. We are not public speakers. I'm conscious that I should do well, but the pressure makes me nervous."[40]

7: RICHARD FLEISCHER: SURVIVOR

Richard Fleischer gives a different account of how he was affected by the Holocaust. His more urbane and secular Jewish background, together with his being the self-confessed black sheep of the family, give him a self-assured demeanor.

****

My father thought Hitler was an aberration, and my father was also one of those stubborn Swabians. Because he had an Iron Cross and so much money, he thought we'd be OK. My mother was concerned about other things, about taking care of her family and keeping up her appearance. When my father realized the Nazis were serious, he started to get American affidavits. But it was too late. The United States was not eager to take Jews. Our number would have admitted us in 1946 or 1948.

For a while the Nazis forced Jewish children to go to separate Jewish schools, but in 1941, my school had to close. My father got me a job with a friend, a vegetable and flower grower. It was physically hard work. That ended six months later, on December 1, 1941, when I was deported from Germany. I was only fourteen, an innocent child.

Legality
The Germans were very astute. At Killesberg near Stuttgart they made us sign off on our German citizenship, took our passports, and made us stateless. The Germans were very legalistic about everything. I knew a Jewish lady married to a German man. He was

put in jail and told to divorce her. He wouldn't, and she wouldn't. The Germans worked on it and worked on it, but the couple never gave in. That's how she survived. She was the only Jew who survived in her town.

At Killesberg, they told us "resettlement." Everything was low key, but when we arrived at the station in Latvia, there was typical German hollering. When hollered at, people can't think, they follow orders better, and that's just what we did. We walked to the camp, Jungfernhof, a huge estate that once belonged to a Baltic German. When the Russians earlier took over Latvia, they turned the estate into an aerodrome. They had constructed a landing strip out of hexagonal concrete pieces about six feet across. Our job in the spring would be to break those up and bring the land back into production.

Every day after we arrived, we took luggage that was crammed into train cars and carried it to a warehouse—luggage from Vienna, the Rhineland, all over Germany. People never came for it. We called the storage place Siberia, it was so far from the camp.

Unpredictable Camps

Camps had different standards. I think it depended on the man in charge. One was quite considerate and the next man, not.

Our foremen were Jewish, and they varied, too. Some were good, but authority went to others' heads. Our foreman screamed a lot but didn't do anything bad. He made like he kicked us. He acted with authority, and that was enough to satisfy the Germans.

Even the commandant of the camp wasn't consistently cruel. Some girls got pregnant; he took them to the hospital in his personal car for abortions. Sexual intercourse was a no-no, and he could have shot them, but he brought them back alive.

It was unpredictable. Things would be OK, and then, every so often, the SS would come and mete out punishment.

Because of the physical conditions in the camp, people died left and right. They were pampered people used to typical middle-class life, but it was brutal in the camp. The Germans didn't have to shoot people. Most died of natural causes.

My neighbor had a thermos of coffee, and it was so cold that it was frozen by midnight. People died, and the bodies piled up. In February, they had engineers blow up some of the frozen bodies, so they could be buried.

Survival depended on what kind of scrounger you were. Some people wouldn't do that. In our barracks, we slept on wooden shelves, eight tiers high. I made a nice bed with lots of scrounged blankets and a sleeping bag. As for food, what they served us was lousy, but in "Siberia" I scrounged chocolate, condensed milk, and other stuff.

Working

Our commandant was German, but the guards were Latvians who had joined the SS. In the winter I worked for them. I cleaned boots, got wood, and took care of the fires. Every time there was a transport, the Latvians told me not to show up. There would be bedlam, and I escaped.

Then we were assigned to regular jobs. We grew farm produce and took care of a dairy herd and chickens. We built barracks. I was at Jungfernhof for two years. Next, I was sent into the ghetto in Riga as part of a work detail cleaning out a factory building for four weeks. There was rationing and no scrounging. Then we were sent to Kaiserswald, a small camp, for two weeks.

Next, three of us prisoners were sent to take care of an SS officer's house on the seacoast. The officer was seldom there. We got anything we wanted from the two guards. It was sort of one-on-one there. I always figured, an individual could talk with another individual. If you were in a herd, you couldn't. We took care of the outside of the house, kept the driveway clean, and cut the grass. It was the summer of 1943. Then it was back to Kaiserswald, where we relaxed for the winter.

Next spring, they put me on a detail to build an artillery range. We cut a seven-mile-by-300-yard swath of forest. It was a very small camp, about 200 people, run by *Organisation Todt*, and it was humane.

Then they speeded up the work. They brought in a whole bunch of Hungarian women and made them work like men. One day, we heard cannons in the distance. The Russians were coming. Two hundred prisoners were organized into a transport. The guards didn't count us or take care as we walked along. They were scared of the Russians. I escaped into the forest, but after three weeks, Latvians spotted me and took me to jail.

After four weeks, they took me by car to the docks and handed me over to the SS. I figured Germany was in bad shape and needed me to work there. In normal times they would have shot me for running away.

I boarded a boat recently built in Sweden. It could outrun the Russian submarines. There were fifteen ships in our convoy, and after three days we arrived in the port of Gdynia.

We were transported by train to Stutthof. There I smelled the crematorium odor for the first time. I didn't know what it was. Somebody told me. I worked at Schichau where submarines were assembled. There were 40,000 people working twelve hours a day, seven days a week. I was on a construction crew, building concrete and tile shelters.

Death March

In February or March, the Russians came closer, and the Germans marched us out of camp. It was a real death march: no food, no water. At night, they would shelter us in churches. If you ducked into a ditch while marching, you were shot. If you stole a turnip along the way, you were shot. If you lagged behind because of the horrible weather, you were shot.

One night we stayed at a small concentration camp. Our commandant wouldn't let us go further, because there was typhus in the camp. So we stayed. There was no food, but every morning we were marched out to build tank traps. People died like flies. My weight got down to eighty pounds, and I'm not small. I'm five foot six-and-a-half inches tall. My normal weight was 165 pounds. When you're starved, you get lethargic. You can't think straight. You can't do anything. You can't even go to the bathroom. It was an effort to put one foot in front of the other.

The Russians finally came. Then we broke into the storeroom and gorged ourselves and got sick. Doctors came and put us in a makeshift hospital. There, many people died—from gorging, the malnutrition, and the shock.

The Russians took German women from the surrounding area, Pomerania, outside of Stettin, and made them personally responsible for our care. If one of us died, the woman was shot. I may have been in the hospital for five or six weeks. I was in a stupor, and I didn't know what was happening. It was peaceful, so peaceful. No pain, just drifting, like I was drugged. Every so often, a big, fat Russian doctor asked how I felt.

I was saved. I had a will to live. In camp, if someone didn't have the will to live anymore, you could see it. The lice would get hold of them. They were dirty, and they didn't take care of themselves. People couldn't take it anymore. They gave up.

Going Home

After the war was over, the Polish gave me papers so I could go home. I was feeling my oats, and I stopped at Berlin, Magdeburg, and a lot of small places. I would go to each town hall, show my identity card, and get a ration card. I had money, too. When I started out, I found thousands of Reichsmarks in a farmhouse. The Russians hadn't taken them, maybe because they thought German money wasn't good anymore. So I had enough money to enjoy myself.

I stayed with nice ladies. There were hardly any young men left in Germany. In a town, there might be only six men who were not cripples or old, while there'd be 150 women.

The Germans went back to dancing, to the theater, to the cultural aspects of life, and I had a terrific time. If I liked a place and the lady, I'd stay two or three weeks. I didn't get home to Göppingen until October. I wasn't in any hurry. My parents were dead. Besides, this was the first time in my whole life I was able to enjoy myself.

In Göppingen, I went to the police, and I asked whether there were any Jewish people left. Just one lady. I knew her, and she took care of me like a mother. I stayed one week. Then, an American showed up, a friend of my father's. She worked for the military government and helped me get to America.

My older brother left Germany in 1938 for England. When the war started, he was interred as a German national and deported to Canada. He got out of the Canadian POW camps in 1944 and moved to Toronto. After I got to America, I went to visit him. I spent a week at a Canadian resort hotel, where I met my wife.

Ann didn't care for me at first, she thought I was too assertive, but we exchanged addresses and wrote. Then I sent her ten pounds of chocolate. That made her see what a nice guy I am!

Back to Göppingen

I've been back to Göppingen many times. I have lots of friends there. I mean, I have lots where I could hold a grudge. For example, in 1938, my grandparents were forced to sell their business to a German who came back from America. He bought it for ten percent of what it was worth. And my parents lost everything. They were transported to Theresienstadt and killed there.

In order to get reparations from the German government, I would have to get papers and prove things were sold under duress. You either prove it was just so, or it didn't happen. It's very Germanic. I think I'm like that in some ways, too.

After the war, I saw drawings on a woman's wall, drawings that used to belong to my family. I said, "They're mine," and she gave them to me. All the other things, like our house and so on, I didn't care about. I'm not materialistic. I'm alive. That's the main thing.

On our visits, Ann and I see friends of the family and neighbors. A lot of them didn't know what was going on. Others didn't do anything, I guess, because of fear. You know, in Göppingen, it was imported thugs who burned the synagogue.

I remember when the Nazis restricted Jews from having certain foods, our nursemaid would sneak in with those things. After the war broke out, she brought some butter, even though the Germans got only a quarter-pound ration of butter.

About the Germans

I have no animosity towards the German people. The ones who were really bad to us were the Ukrainians and the Polish. Oh, sure, there were sadistic Germans, but a lot were forced to do things they didn't want to do in order to survive. We have a close friend, and her brother volunteered for the SS. She told us it was good that he got killed; their father wouldn't have let him in the house if he came back.

I have no problem driving a German car. In 1960 I went over to get my first Mercedes. Oh, there are Jews who won't buy German things, but I think those people who didn't live through the Holocaust are more anti-German than the ones who did. You know, the generation before me would have intermarried with Germans, that's how they felt about Germans. Hitler changed that. Before Hitler, every Jewish guy, with his convertible and everything, was sleeping with six non-Jewish girls for every Jewish girl.

I'm not religious. My father was not religious either, although my mother's family was. I don't like organized religion, whatever kind it is, Catholic, Protestant, or Jewish. The Protestants look down their noses at the Catholics and the Catholics at the Protestants, and so on. I do believe in God.

Ann was willing to convert to Judaism, but I said no, I would never ask anyone to change their religion, and I would never change mine. I went through too much for it.

In America, someone hired me to do tiling work. Then, in 1957, I started my own business. It's well paying, you can see what you've done, and you meet all kinds of people. I work half time now.

Maybe it helped me cope that I don't get upset often, and if I do, I get over it fast. I don't hold a grudge.

Every so often, I get a nightmare. Ann wakes me up and tells me, but I can't recall anything. But now, more than earlier, I chew things over. I relive certain things, generally the good things. Even in a camp, there were good times.

From my experiences I came to the conclusion that the SS men were different in a group than as individuals. In a group, an SS man couldn't show weakness or kindness. He wouldn't survive. But one-to-one, or even two-to-two, they could show their true faces, whatever they were, sadistic or kind.

I have to say I was never in a camp where they absolutely exterminated everybody. I was lucky not to be sent to that kind of camp. That's part of why I survived. Luck. And in some camps, there were caring people, and in others not. Also, I was young and looked healthy when selections were made.

Probably my independent attitudes helped, too. I was the black sheep of my family. I rebelled against the family. I wasn't obedient. I was always a loner. My sisters and brother wouldn't have survived the camps. They didn't have the will, or they were too particular about things.

The first time I went back to Germany, I was apprehensive. But after I saw a few people, I said to them, "I can't hold a grudge against you."

8: WAR AND AFTERMATH

America didn't want any German immigrants after fighting two wars against Germany. When regular immigration from Germany was allowed to resume in the 1950s, most older Germans had again become settled in their lives. Most of those who came to America then were young children or teenagers during the Nazi era.

Hitler Youths

After Hitler and the Nazis came to power in 1933, they merged existing youth groups into the *Hitler Jugend* (Hitler Youth) for boys fourteen to eighteen and the *Jungvolk* (Young People) for ages ten to thirteen. Girls had parallel organizations. By 1935, 60 percent of all young people belonged. In 1936, membership became compulsory. The Nazis used these organizations for indoctrination and to prepare boys to become solders.[41] The vast majority of youths obeyed the commands and regulations of the Hitler Youth.[30]

Rudy Schmidt, a postwar immigrant from Schwäbisch Gmünd, recalled political sessions as well as war games. According to Schmidt, "You would have a little red band on your wrist and the other guys blue bands. Your goal was to take over a certain area and take prisoners. You'd have to wrestle the guy down or punch him out and take his wristband."

In 1921, Schmidt's parents had left Swabia for Madison, Wisconsin, and two sons were born there. After the father died, Schmidt's pregnant mother returned to live with her parents in Germany, where Schmidt was born in 1926. His mother and the two older brothers eventually returned to America in the mid-1930s. In 1939, when he was twelve, Schmidt was ready to leave his grandparents and join his mother and brothers in America. He had his American immigration papers, but the German government wouldn't let him go. He had no idea that a war would soon begin.

After the great defeat and 400,000 casualties at Stalingrad in the winter of 1942-43, Germany had to dig deeper for additional troops. On February 15, Hitler Youths aged sixteen and seventeen and still in school were drafted for the flak (*Fliegerabwehrkanone*) defenses or anti-aircraft guns. Schmidt was given a blue *Luftwaffe* (Air Force) uniform, and, after training, sent to the south of France, near Marseilles.[42]

These boys were imbued with patriotism, and Schmidt remembered that they were responding to external threats. But still he wondered if he might be shooting at one of his brothers.

Schmidt's anti-aircraft unit took up stations on the hills surrounding a large airfield where Junker 88's were based. These twin-engine bombers attacked Allied shipping in the Mediterranean. "But we didn't have air cover by German aircraft anymore." American P-47 Thunderbolt fighters often tailed and attacked the returning bombers as their flaps and wheels were lowered to land.

Thunderbolts also came in low, hugging the terrain, bombing the anti-aircraft units around the airfield. Schmidt was assigned to one of the three anti-aircraft guns defending against these attacks. Each gun had four short barrels that could be quickly swung around. One man controlled the aiming and firing, while four fed ammunition.

By the late fall of 1943, American low-level attacks were frequent, resulting in many German casualties. Schmidt recalled: "Every man was ordered to have his own hole where he jumped in and pulled a heavy wood cover over top." They also used their covered holes when attacked by big bombers. These were so high that Schmidt's small gun was of no use.

The German Retreat

German propaganda at this time claimed that their troops pulled back to better positions to wait for the enemy to make costly mistakes in attacking. One of Schmidt's comrades was able to hook up an antenna to receive forbidden short-wave broadcasts by the British Broadcasting Corporation,. "There was nobody in our outfit who would have turned us in. Forget those films you see. There weren't that many Nazi fanatics. When people have to depend on each other to survive, you have to stick together." Schmidt and his friends plotted the BBC reports on their maps and saw that German troops were retreating on all fronts.

The Allies landed in Normandy in June 1944, and pushed inland. Schmidt's unit was ordered to move out. They blew up their guns and radar set. They had no transport. Nor could they move during daylight because of the almost continuous Allied air attacks.[43]

Marching up the Rhone River valley, they were blocked by the French resistance. Americans had also landed at their rear along the Mediterranean, so for three days they seemed blocked on all sides. "It was chaotic. Everybody was on their own, trying to get through." German military police would check identity papers and organize men separated from their units. Schmidt saw some trying to escape. They were shot. "That was when we began to doubt we're going to win."

His group fortunately included a sergeant who could insist that the men were part of a unit going to rendezvous in Germany, so they were able to continue their retreat. "Otherwise they would have just grabbed us and stuck us in the defense line. That was when Hitler declared 'total war' over the radio. If an officer retreats, the lower man can take command. That's how it was explained to us. A private could take over a command if he feels like the officer is not doing his job."

They walked, then hitched a twenty-mile ride with tanks, then took a day-and-a-half ride on a Red Cross train. Then more walking at night, since during the day anything that moved was attacked from the air. As they neared the Swiss border "a lot of guys looked over toward [neutral] Switzerland, but it was sealed off with military police."

Finally they crossed the Rhine River into Germany. In a small village, they were re-outfitted and assigned new men to replace casualties. They were ordered on to Nuremberg, to set up new anti-aircraft positions, as German armies continued to collapse throughout Europe.

Hitler Youths and the Bombing

The Catholic areas of Germany, including the Catholic periphery of Swabia, were generally less enthusiastic about Hitler and the Nazis. Gerhardt Bay remembered that his Hitler Youth service was not militaristic. He was in the drummer corps and marched with the other musicians. During summer vacations, he took many of the special courses offered by the *Hitler Jugend*—skiing, mountain climbing, piloting gliders, and gymnastics. "Even during the war we never had rifles. There was no indoctrination unless somebody came from the outside." Nor had the Nazis penetrated much everyday culture as they had in the rest of Germany. The common greeting was still the South Germans' *Grüss Gott*, not *Heil Hitler,* even though *Heil Hitler* was required by law. Bay recalled that in his Catholic town of 4,000, "you could count the dyed-in-the-wool fanatics on one hand."

Younger members of the Hitler Youth were assigned defense jobs on the home front, including dealing with the almost continuous bombing of cities by American and British planes. The strategic bombing of civilians was first instituted on a mass level with the 1937 raid on Guernica by German and Italian planes during the Spanish Civil War. Germany bombed cities as part of its invasion of Poland at the start of World War II. In September 1940, Germany launched a nine-month blitz to force the British to surrender. Over 40,000 civilians were killed in the United Kingdom. In London alone, more than a million houses were destroyed or damaged.

In reaction, the Royal Air Force in February 1942 officially authorized the bombing of German civilians. The following month, the RAF used phosphorous incendiary bombs in a test attack on Lübeck, a lightly defended cultural center. The British had seen how the German incendiary bombing of Coventry had created destructive fires. The first wave of planes over Lübeck used explosive bombs to shatter roofs in the medieval city center. More bombers dropped incendiaries. The many fires created a huge firestorm that left 25,000 homeless. Incendiaries destroyed six times more area than an equal load of high explosive bombs and killed many more people. German records show that as many as 85 percent of civilian deaths were due to incendiary bombing.[44]

The RAF used incendiaries on other cities in Germany, including Hamburg, where 43,000 died in a firestorm. The winds that were created by the huge fires were so strong that people were thrown to the street, where even the tar was burning. The destruction forced the evacuation of one million people. For the rest of the war, the British bombers flew at night and used mainly incendiaries in indiscriminate saturation bombing of cities.

Initially the American Army Air Force focused on military and industrial targets in "precision bombing" during daylight. But many bombs hit civilian areas. At the beginning of 1944, targeted American bombing of civilians in cities was officially authorized. At war's end, the American Air Force joined the RAF in the 1945 carpet-bombing of Dresden, undefended and crowded with refugees. Estimates of those killed in that single raid range from 35,000 upwards.

A Fire Brigade of Fifteen-Year-Olds

The aim of the carpet-bombing was to destroy the morale of the German people, especially workers. Bay's experience during the war reveals how the German work ethic and gift for organization were used to counter the incendiary attacks. Bay and seven fellow fifteen-year-olds were assigned to a small, three-hose fire brigade. His town's church bells tolled to give the fire alarm. Bay worked seven miles away, so he picked up another boy on his bicycle and went home quickly. A driver hooked up the fire equipment behind his beer truck. They were part of the 150,000 men, from sixty miles around Munich, who were organized to deal with the thousands of fires from a bombing raid.

At the edge of Munich, they were met by a motorcyclist who knew which streets were still free of debris from collapsed buildings. He would lead them to their assigned fire. The seven boys would hook up their portable pump and the hoses to a water main or to a pump truck if a taller building was on fire. Two boys were needed to control the largest hose.

"By the time we got to Munich it was almost one great big fire. So we went to our assigned location and did our job. Soon a small tank would come by, and the hatch would open. The next wave of bombers was approaching." Even if their fire was still burning, they were ordered to load the equipment, drive around the rubble, and get out of the city. Firefighters were deemed critical, and they were the only people permitted to leave. The public was ordered to remain in shelters.

One time, Bay's fire brigade stopped to pick up another crew's hose left behind in the rush. At that moment, a woman with a baby carriage was hurrying to a shelter. The loose hose struck her in the back of the legs, and she fell. Some of the boys helped her up, while others ran to catch the baby carriage rolling down the street.

The woman was hysterical, so they just took her along. "We went out a few miles, where we watched the bombers. She was so happy to get away from the bombs." When they returned to duty in the city, they mercifully left the woman and her baby behind on the outskirts. Munich was bombed that time for three days running.

For Bay, the firefighting in Munich was a great adventure. "I just never gave death a thought." He survived despite the danger of bombs with delayed fuses plus follow-up raids specifically aimed at killing firefighters and rescue workers.

Smaller Towns Were Bombed

A few miles east of Bay's town was the larger town of Donauwörth, with 10,000 people and a major railroad yard. The housings for the V-2 ballistic rocket were built there. At night Bay would see trains with three railcars coupled together holding the long rockets. One night he looked out from the third story of his home to see a *Tannenbaum* (Christmas tree), a set of brightly burning flares dropped to light up the target for bombers. Germans likened the white flares to the German Christmas tree which traditionally had candles.

"That was the British, because they bombed at night. Munich was the Americans, because it was daylight raids." Bay recalled: "You would think they'd bomb the big factory and railroad yards, but they bombed the living daylights out of the town instead. My aunt and uncle died in the attack. The whole city was totally gone."

Later Bay saw hundreds of bombers flying in daylight towards, he thinks, Dresden, to carry out the infamous raid reported firsthand by Kurt Vonnegut in his book *Slaughterhouse Five*. Along with the bomber formations, he saw fighter escorts. "Evidently they didn't have enough fuel to continue on, because they turned around a little past our town, [and] dropped down to strafe everything, especially trains." One Saturday Bay went home from work on "the one train that always took a chance." During Bay's ride home, everybody had to jump out and crawl underneath the train. The windows were shot out, but no one was killed.

Despite the trauma of the bombing and the many casualties, there was little or no public outcry against the war or the Nazis. People grumbled about food shortages and other difficulties they wanted the regime to fix. A Nazi intelligence report early in the war cited some of the negative attitudes in Stuttgart: "Everywhere one finds the opinion that in this war the little people are the losers once more. They must work, do without and keep their mouths shut while others can afford anything with money, connections, license, and ruthlessness. Everything is just like it was before." People decried the "big shots and plutocrats." So much for the community of all German people that the Nazis proclaimed.[30]

After the debacle at Stalingrad, Nazi propaganda minister Joseph Goebbels gave a speech asking the German people to rise up in a storm of total war to defeat the Russians. However, frontline German soldiers complained, "The Russians are conducting total war; we are fighting an elegant war."

Only the White Rose students at the university in Munich dared to overtly criticize the regime early in 1943. They were promptly arrested, sentenced to death, and beheaded. Most Germans continued to accept the propaganda line that secret weapons would turn the war in favor of Germany. The 1944 attempt on Hitler's life was generally condemned. It was seen as a crime and it temporarily bolstered the regime. People continued to believe that Hitler would save them even if the Nazis didn't.[30]

Drafted

In early 1945, even fifteen-year-olds like Bay were drafted into the army. He was called from work and ordered to assemble in a town eighteen miles away. As he and twenty other Hitler Youths were walking, they saw an old soldier, a member of the *Volkssturm* (the home guard of invalids and old men) organized in the winter of 1944-45. The soldier had a captured American flier.

Just looking at the pair, the boys realized who was winning the war. One man was young and healthy, dressed in a new uniform with fancy flying boots, and smoking a cigarette. The other was an old man, in an old uniform, without a cigarette. "Jesus, we kidded that old man." As for the boys themselves, Bay remembers, "In 1945, what kind of uniform could you have? I had a ski outfit on. Just the belt and the rifle were regular army. We looked like losers."

The old man told them, "I'd like to give this guy my rifle and get his cigarette." Then the old man asked, "Why don't you kids go home?" The boys' leader was some four years older and from another town, a stranger. Bay and his friends wondered how he felt about the straight talk of the old *Volksturm*. But they hesitated to say anything themselves.

The boys continued on to their assembly point at a schoolhouse. "There were about a thousand kids there. Rifles were stacked, and there was straw bedding in every room. But there was chaos. You heard all these groups talking, and it was like every man for himself. There were eighteen of us from my town, and not one of us stayed for even one night." They took off for their homes, walking only at night and following the meandering Danube River instead of roads. It took two weeks to reach Dillingen, where they could hide. "Everybody was scared. You heard about deserters and what happened to them. Nobody said a thing, even though by this time, the town's few Nazi fanatics had disappeared."

The Germans did shoot deserters, right up to the formal signing of the declaration of surrender, which occurred eight days after Bay arrived home. In fact, justice in the bigger cities had gotten so severe that, in the last years of the war, even civilians were executed for minor crimes.[45]

Surrender

As American troops approached Dillingen, they sent one soldier ahead to ask whether the town would fight or surrender. No one wanted to take the responsibility of surrendering. The head of a group of French POWs, a captain, asked the town mayor if he could do the negotiating. The American soldiers, of course, were not about to negotiate. They indicated that all German soldiers were to move out or surrender; otherwise they would shell the town. When the French POW reported back, a couple of "hotheads" wanted to defend the town. The POW argued that a few old men couldn't stop the Americans. It would only lead to the town's destruction. So a Frenchman surrendered the town to the Americans.

Bay went up into the tower of the nearby church where he could look out, protected by the thick walls. Later he learned that the mayor and the local chimney sweep were talking near their homes at the edge of town when the Americans arrived. Bay saw the chimney sweep, dressed in his black suit and top hat, carry a white flag into the town's central plaza. The Americans followed, backing their tanks and trucks into parking spots around the plaza and nearby streets.

By the time Bay got down from the church tower, his mother, who could speak English, was talking to the American GIs. Suddenly, a German staff car careened down the narrow street lined with American vehicles. The Americans were relaxing, smoking cigarettes. They couldn't swing their vehicle-mounted machine guns around fast enough to get the car in their sights. By the time the car reached the plaza, they were shooting but missing, blasting holes into walls. The staff car finally stopped at the Germans' own tank traps at the Danube River bridge. They jumped out and got away. "It was funny as all hell."

Next, a German motorcyclist roared by, and as he turned to cross over the bridge he slid out on the cobblestones. He instantly raised his hands before he could be shot. The Americans put him up against a wall and left him there. Bay recalls, "Nobody bothered with him, they just took his rifle and threw it onto a pile with the motorcycle. Then they burned that beautiful motorcycle."

The Americans also ordered every gun in town turned over to them. Bay laments losing the two hunting rifles plus two target rifles his family owned, ball-and-powder guns that were works of art with inlaid wood. Gasoline was poured on the guns, and they were set on fire. But Bay suspects that not all the antique guns were burned. Some of the nice ones probably made it to America as souvenirs.

Bay recalls his family's introduction to the Americans as happy. His young sister was allowed to look inside an American tank, and she and the other kids were given chocolate, something they hadn't had for years. When the tankers learned his mother spoke English, they asked if she could cook some chicken. They returned with chickens, no doubt requisitioned from the local peasants, and she "cooked up a storm for them." The Americans then opened up the supply boxes carried on the backs of their tanks, and out came peanuts, chocolate, cigarettes, and other food. They even gave Bay's family some gasoline, which they needed for cleaning the type in their family printing business.

Bay's mother told the Americans that they had better behave in her house. Bay's older sisters, aged seventeen and twenty-two, didn't have to hide, but they "avoided showing themselves off." The soldiers were mostly well behaved and only came into the house to eat and sleep, although some drank "like there was no tomorrow."

The Americans continued to come and eat at Bay's house even after a field kitchen was set up around the corner. They must have appreciated the fact that Bay's mother had once cooked at Shrafft's, an esteemed New York City restaurant chain.

Bay remembers that after eating and drinking, the Americans were most concerned with finding a field to construct a baseball diamond. Next, they put up a huge bank of showers, using water pumped from the Danube. The Americans knew they wouldn't be fighting any more for a while. The Danube River and a blown-up bridge blocked their path.

Surviving the Bombing

The war experiences of young children varied if they'd lived in a city or in a rural area. In small rural villages, life went on more or less as usual until the approach of the enemy at the very end of the war. But cities were bombed.

Eugen Wahr was five years old in 1944, in the Swabian city of Heilbronn, a rail junction and river port. Until then, much of Swabia had been bombed only lightly and sporadically. Wahr would watch the flares dropped to mark the targets and then look for the fiery glow around the propellers of the following planes.

Wahr's mother would order him into the basement shelter. His two older sisters took down his two-year-old brother, who usually slept in a laundry basket to make it easy to carry him downstairs. There the women and children from families in the building would wait out the raids.

Wahr's father was a World War I veteran. In World War II, he helped work on the railroads and the German supply system in Poland. He was severely injured in an accident and nearly died. After he recovered, the family put on a big welcome-home dinner for his friends after making a special trip to Wahr's grandparents in Upper Swabia to get some chickens. As they were sitting down, the air raid sirens sounded. When they emerged from the shelter, they found the house a shambles. All the windows and much of the interior had been smashed. The dinner was full of glass shards.

That September 1944 attack was the first serious bombing of Heilbronn. There were a number of close calls after that. One raid demolished a building down the street, quarters for Polish workers. In still another raid, a row of bombs straddled Wahr's building. The building behind was hit, destroying one wall. The neighbor's chicken coop between the buildings got a direct hit. In front of his home were unexploded bombs on the sidewalk.

One Saturday afternoon, Wahr's mother let his older sisters take him to a movie in the city center. During the film the sirens went off. His mother rushed to find the children safe in a shelter.

Late in December 1944 Heilbronn was hit by a major incendiary raid, destroying the congested, medieval center of the city and killing 6,000 people. Wahr's parents decided to move immediately to the grandparents' house in a small rural village. Many German children in the cities were evacuated to the countryside. Wahr was luckier than most, since he moved with his whole family.

Stuttgart was another important target in Swabia. A woman who worked at a Red Cross office in the city recalled: "We were bombed eighteen times, and the nineteenth time we had a direct hit. We were okay in the shelter, but all the people in a shelter 300 feet from us were burned up.

"When Stuttgart was burning, there was no daylight for ten days. You had to put a wet towel around your eyes and nose so you could see and breathe. You also had to have your house open when there was a sudden air raid alarm, so that passersby on the street could come in and go to your cellar. You didn't know if it was safe to let others in. But there was a law that if someone steals something, they would get a hearing and then be shot.

"We had to put in so many hours digging to help build shelters. There were no men, so the women had to do that. And then you came home from the shelter to your house, and three walls weren't standing. Then we had to go to a soup kitchen to get our meals. Going to the toilet meant going out in the woods." She finally went to her home in Eybach, a small town. "I worked in a small factory. Nobody was allowed to stay home. You had to work even if you were sick."

Survey research after the war revealed that the British carpet bombing did relatively little to destroy morale.[46] Nor did the aimed, strategic bombing of the Americans hit many industrial targets until late in the war, because of the strength of the German anti-aircraft and fighter defenses. Industrial production of German war material increased up until the very last months of the war. When a city was bombed and destroyed, nonessential workers like clerks and waiters were freed to work in industry. When factories were destroyed, they were moved and then rebuilt. The Allies lost nearly 160,000 aviators in the bombing campaign. Was that cost worthwhile? Perhaps the physical destruction of German cities was psychologically gratifying to those who directed the air assaults.[44, 47, 48]

A Rural Village

Swabians like Walter Kraft (born in 1935), who lived in a small rural village, experienced no bombing. He recalls that people were primarily concerned about working and getting food.

One night after the air raid sirens sounded, Walter and the other children went outside and looked in the direction of Pforzheim, a city eighteen miles away. The sky was as bright as daylight. Walter wasn't concerned about his personal safety. During earlier raids, he had watched enemy bombers and the German fighters attacking them. If bombers were hit, they would jettison their loads harmlessly in the fields.

The air attack on Pforzheim was a successful use of the RAF's combination of explosive and phosphorous incendiary bombs, the firestorm destroying 83 percent of the city's buildings and killing over 17,000, about a quarter of the residents. Firestorms were so deadly because the poisonous phosphorous fumes seeped into the cellar shelters. Some tried to escape by jumping into rivers but were killed by the burning phosphorus floating on the water.

There were seven children in Kraft's poor family, so his father wasn't called up until 1942. His mother and the children were left to run the farm. Townspeople decided which families needed the most help and assigned prisoners and other foreigners to replace missing German workers. By 1943, twelve million foreigners comprised some 40 percent of the workforce. Kraft's family used two forced laborers, a Polish girl of sixteen or seventeen who knew no German, and an older French POW. They taught the Polish girl German by reading with her.[47]

"We treated them all right, and they even visited us later on [after the war]," he recalled. Later the Frenchman was assigned to a large farm, but he escaped and came back to work for them. After the end of the war, Walter's family employed a German refugee who used to own a large estate in the East before he had to flee. Walter's father was missing in action in 1943, but after the war the family learned that he was alive and a prisoner. He was finally freed and allowed to return home three years after the war ended.

Schmidt, the eighteen-year-old anti-aircraft gunner, had a relatively happy experience at the end of the war. As Germany collapsed and American troops approached Nuremberg, Schmidt's unit was ordered to retreat to the Alps in southern Bavaria. He realized he would be heading in the opposite direction from home, so he and two others decided to desert and hide in the woods.

Three days later Nuremberg fell, and the three gave a farmer all their money in exchange for civilian clothes. Schmidt recalled, "He was a good man. I wonder if he realized the money was worthless." Schmidt and his comrades started walking, but after twenty-five miles they were captured by the Americans.

After three days in a POW camp, Schmidt and two others escaped at night. Shots rang out as they went through the fence and disappeared into the woods. One man stayed with Schmidt. His home was in the French Occupation Zone, where POWs were reputed to have a rough time. The two traveled at night and, when stopped, said they were displaced persons from Russia.

After the final surrender of Germany, they tried to find work. At the local employment office, they told two farmers, "We'll do anything to eat." Six months later, in early 1946, the farmer's doorbell rang. Two American soldiers were looking for Schmidt. One was Schmidt's older brother!

Schmid's older brother had been drafted by the American army and was working as an interpreter for a unit selecting German industrial equipment for war reparations. The brother brought him to Heidelberg, where his army unit was stationed, and set him up with a room and a job for the military.

Fraternization

Initially, American troops had been prohibited from fraternizing with Germans, a policy announced by General Eisenhower in September 1944, when American soldiers reached the German border. It was thought that a haughty military aloofness would create respect among the German citizens, while fraternization would trigger an unfavorable reaction among the American public. A common announcement on armed forces radio in the spring and summer of 1945 ran, "If in a German town you bow to a pretty girl or pat a blond child...you bow to Hitler and his reign of blood...you caress the ideology that means death and persecution. Don't fraternize."

Soldiers were prohibited from entertaining Germans, visiting German homes, shaking hands with Germans, giving or accepting gifts, accompanying Germans on the street or to places of entertainment, or conversing with Germans, especially about politics. Most of all, contact with German women was punishable by up to court-martial. Special military police patrols were assigned to parks, woods, and alleys, to prevent such contacts. Most units conducted nightly bed checks. Despite all that, one study estimated that eight out of ten younger GIs consorted in one way or another with German women.[49]

On June 8, 1945, Eisenhower indicated that the rules were not intended to apply to "very small children." About this time, word also went out that a sexually transmitted disease would *not* be used as evidence of fraternization. On July 14, conversations between soldiers and Germans were permitted "on the street and in public places." On August 6, a radio broadcast to the German public indicated that soldiers were now permitted normal contacts with Germans.[50] With the policy at an end, the Schmidt brothers could officially talk to each other.

The Black Market

Contact between Americans and Germans had serious economic effects. Even the lowliest GI possessed what seemed like enormous wealth in food and other items, especially cigarettes, supplied by the military. The German food ration was fixed at 1,500 calories per day, about half of what the occupying soldiers were getting.[51, 52] In addition, Germans had no legal way to obtain tobacco, since it had to be imported, and the occupiers did not permit foreign exchange used for that purpose. Cigarettes were popular since about 60 percent of Germans smoked and smoking was especially valued because it suppressed hunger. Coffee and chocolate were also expensive and heavily taxed imports.

Americans, inspired by the spirit of free-enterprise, and the opportunity for a quick buck, helped the Germans out. They created a black market where goods were illegally sold for exorbitant prices. Some GIs made so much by selling cigarettes and other post-exchange goods that they could more than triple their pay. Soldiers could get a carton of cigarettes for a dollar and trade it for up to $200 of goods from Germans on the black market. It was no wonder that soldiers would order extra cigarettes from the States.[50]

Schmidt got a job as driver for the motor pool. As he drove American soldiers around, he noticed crowds of boys gathered at intersections where American vehicles had to stop momentarily for traffic police. There the American soldiers would casually flick their cigarette butts to the pavement, and the children would dart out to scoop them up. This tobacco would be used to manufacture new cigarettes.

Schmidt also recalled the methods used by the American authorities to halt the black market for army goods. They began confiscating American items in the hands of Germans, such as blankets, soup, toothpaste, whiskey, and cigarettes. Every so often, Schmidt got a phone call from his brother telling him to gather into a blanket everything he had that was American to give to his brother. The military would seal the city and search every building, confiscating American items. Since there was a curfew for German citizens, Rudy Schmidt had no way of getting rid of his American possessions, and it was only his brother's quick action that saved him. If Schmidt had been caught, even his brother couldn't have helped, because the regulations on German possession of black market goods were strictly enforced.

Even so, the occupation administration was never very successful in controlling black market profiteering by American troops. Special currency control books were issued to the troops, but the GIs kept illegal duplicates. Next, official swap shops were set up, but American soldiers then ordered goods, such as coffee, sugar, flour, soap, and cooking oil, from the United States., using cheap military postal rates. Germans were trading porcelain, furniture, jewelry, and art in order to eat.

In the postwar years a German wage earner made perhaps 150 to 250 marks a month. This did not buy much of the very expensive food. A chicken's eggs that were sold on the black market in a large city would fetch twice as much money as a miner could hope to make in the same time. Black market prices in October 1946 were 100-500 marks for two pounds of coffee, 200 for the same amount of sugar, 50 marks for a loaf of bread, 250 marks for a kilogram of butter, and 100 to 200 marks for one pack of cigarettes. Many Germans shamelessly dug into American garbage cans.[53]

Schmidt's brother was transferred back to the States in 1946. In the meantime, his mother started immigration proceedings in the United States. She even went to Washington. Eventually, he was notified to come for an interview by army intelligence. For the first couple years of the occupation, the American military ran everything in Germany; there wasn't even a consulate. He had to say what he did during the war, what outfit he belonged to, where he was stationed, and so on. Schmidt's mother badgered her local congressman for several months, and he was eventually cleared for emigration. On the ship to America, he was one of only fourteen Germans. The other passengers were refugees who had suffered at the hands of the Germans.

The Conquering Army

Another Swabian, Helga Geiser, was horrified when the Americans took her small town along the Danube. The American tanks easily pushed over huge pillars erected to keep them out. Then they "blew half the town down and blew all the kids to bits on the outskirts." The youths had been too young to be drafted, but at war's end they were encouraged to make a last stand. "After the Americans got done, they just dumped their bodies on a wagon."

She already had a negative attitude towards Americans. Low-flying fighter planes would shoot at pedestrians. "They shot at us when we walked to church or worked in the fields. One day my brother said we could go for hazelnuts. The trees were in a woods not far away. Suddenly the planes came from nowhere. My brother just threw me in a ditch and landed right on top of me and covered me. You could recognize that they were American planes."

When the American troops came through her defeated town, there were Blacks in front. "I couldn't believe it. I wondered, are all Americans Black?" Geiser was also shocked by their destructive behavior. The GIs quartered in the farmhouse next door destroyed things and burned the furniture, taking whatever else they wanted at gunpoint. "They went down the cellar, where in Germany you have preserves in jars. They went down with a gun and took everything off the shelves."

Some looting by Americans did occur in Germany, but it could have been worse, given that the Americans had complete power over a defeated people. But unlike victorious troops from other countries once occupied by Germany, American solders did not see themselves as avengers. Later on, when less disciplined GIs arrived, there was more looting.

"While Germans were almost starving, the Americans were putting their food in the garbage and then burning it. Would they give it to us? No. I stood in line for an hour once for used coffee grounds so my mother had some coffee. They still had flavor in them. A second time, third, and fourth time, it was still good coffee."

Geiser's younger brother got the family into trouble when the Americans learned he had a BB gun. During the war, the family had kept about seventy rabbits for food, and he'd hidden the gun behind the rabbit hutches. The soldiers went through the entire house and barn, harassing the family until the BB gun was found.

One day Geiser's father was away, leaving her and her mother home alone with her young brother. Soldiers barged in and started looking through the house. Her mother quickly sent her away to a neighbor. She was only eleven but might still be a target. There were stories about gang-rapes in the Russian Zone. Another time, an American vehicle hit an electrical wire near their house. "They held my mother responsible and almost shot her."

On the other hand, the family was aided by a Black soldier who spoke some German. Geiser's mother had told him of a sister in Buffalo, New York, and a few weeks later, they got a letter from the sister. They couldn't believe it. Geiser recalls, "After that, I figured there were good guys, too."

Postwar Hardships

Other Swabians, like Hans and Emma Schmitz, two children from the Black Forest, came under French occupation. Although some Swabians, like Helga's family, learned to accept dark-skinned Americans, many Germans in the French Zone of Occupation feared the dark Moroccan troops. There was much talk of rape by the Moroccans. Fortunately Emma's father had earlier been stationed in a French hospital, and he had learned how very afraid

French troops were of catching tuberculosis. So he created a haven for the women of the town by saying their house was quarantined for tuberculosis.

Eventually the French requisitioned part of their home for three officers. Two officers slept in their parents' bed, and another in the living room. The five family members were relegated to a single room, and the two grandparents slept below the stairs. Their mother also cooked for the French. "They were friendly towards us, and after they moved on, they came back and visited. They knew we were just people, not Nazis."

The period after war's end was economically much harder than the war itself. Germans called it "Time Zero." The great destruction and scarcities made it seem that they were starting again from nothing.[51,54,55] Because there were food shortages, townspeople went into the countryside to help the peasants harvest. Nor was heating fuel available, since the coal mines were mostly destroyed and few miners available. People had to forage for firewood and collect debris to rebuild their homes.[51]

Life in Germany could have been even harder. At first Treasury Secretary Henry Morgenthau proposed removing all industry and making Germany simply a gigantic farm.[56] But, the Western Allies were convinced that the punitive Versailles Peace Treaty after Germany's defeat in World War I had been a mistake. The best way to avoid again arousing thoughts of revenge would be by helping Germans to their feet, not pushing them down.

Practical considerations also came to the fore. There were millions of refugees who had to be fed. Millions of Germans had come from areas annexed by Poland and the Soviet Union, and twelve million more ethnic Germans were driven out of Eastern Europe, with additional millions of other Eastern Europeans fleeing the Soviets. In addition, there were six million to eleven million POWs, concentration camp survivors, slave laborers, and foreigners who had volunteered to work in Germany. Would all these people be able to support themselves in the farming economy envisioned by Morgenthau? America and the other occupying forces would have had to support the refugees indefinitely. It was in the Allies' best interests to help Germany.[26, 57, 58]

Getting Fuel and Food

Despite the softening of Allied attitudes, Germans like Hans still recall the great difficulties of the postwar period. At fifteen, Hans lost his apprenticeship on the railroad after the war ended, so he got a job making cinder blocks. "It took a couple of hours to hand-mix slag, cement, and sand for ten or fifteen blocks, stamp them in the forms, take the forms off carefully, and the next day they were ready. It took all summer long to make enough for a house." Housing was a priority; a majority of German cities were at least half destroyed. Some twenty million West Germans were homeless.

People also had to search for fuel. During the war, Hans had brought home from his job a rucksack full of coal taken from a locomotive. Now he had to gather coals one by one from along the track-bed or find fallen wood in the forests. Emma helped pull the cart to the forest every weekend. People weren't allowed to bring hatchets along but only gather dead wood.

Emma remembered, "If the forester found we had green wood, we'd get a big fine. We had to look for dead trees and push them back and forth until they gave way. We took them, roots and all. We also gathered pinecones for burning. But the best way to get stuff was with the hatchet. One person was the lookout while the other chopped. If anyone came, the youngest of us would run off with the hatchet. Those years, the woods were spotless. No dead wood was lying around."

Food was also scarce for a number of years. Farmers were reluctant to sell because they didn't trust the old German currency. Hans recalls having nothing to eat or drink. His family even ate clover: "It was juicy." His grandfather had a couple of cows, and he'd fetch milk for his family. He recalled, "I'd go in the kitchen and stick my finger in the butter. Oh, was that good! Then I made it smooth with my finger again, so no one could tell. When my younger brother found out, he wanted to get milk from grandpa so he could taste some butter, too."

The postwar inflation was also a serious problem. One immigrant recalled, "There was big inflation in 1946 and 1947. I was walking so I could save ten cents on the streetcar, but afterwards the savings were worth nothing. I could have bought two houses with the money I had saved before the war, but then after the war, because of the inflation, I could just buy my suitcases."

In 1948, Deutsche Marks were issued to replace the old Reichsmarks. Each German could exchange only sixty of the old Reichsmarks into sixty new Deutsche Marks. Years later people would get back a total of just ten percent of their savings. Most of their savings was lost.

Conflict

During this time, there was a lot of animosity between Germans and the *Volksdeutsch*, people of German descent who had flocked into Germany at war's end. They had been driven out from places where their families had lived for centuries—the Ukraine, Romania, Hungary, Yugoslavia, Czechoslovakia, and Poland. These ethnic Germans had acquired many foreign customs from living with Eastern European neighbors. In addition, Germans living in the East, in Prussia, Pomerania, and Silesia, areas that had been German territory since the tenth century, were forced to flee by Polish and Russian annexation. Altogether perhaps a million died in the flight, but some ten million survived and crowded into the new, smaller Germany.[54]

Rudy Bay recalls the refugees with some remorse. "I never knew these people were told by the German army to leave and come to Germany. They had no choice about it. But once they got into Germany, you know how they got treated–like shit." For many Germans, *Flüchtling* or refugee was a curse word.

Bay recalls another side of the refugee problem. "Guys in our town were going out with their good-looking women. Parents would scream bloody murder. Those women wouldn't bring anything [land] into a marriage. The young people accepted the refugees, but not the older ones."

Most of the refugees had lost everything, and they felt people in Germany should help them. Fortunately, there was a long tradition of paternalistic governmental concern for citizens. Germany had instituted old-age pensions in 1889, the first nation to do so. Continuing in this tradition, the German government passed various "equalization of burdens" laws after World War II, taxing Germans who were not refugees to support those who had lost their homes and lands.[59] With this cash, the refugees seemed to live better than many Germans, in the opinion of Hans. He felt, "If the refugees lost all the farms they said they had, they would have owned all of Russia."

Settlement policies also created animosity. Social differences were not taken into account. City people were settled among rural people, Protestants among Catholics, and *vice versa*. The refugees living near Hans "had big mouths—always a lot of big talk. Those Prussians weren't quiet like us Swabians. We didn't like them." Emma recalled, "They spoke faster than us. In the time we said a word, they said a book already. And they showed off and took advantage of people. They thought we owed them. We had houses, and they didn't, so the government gave them money and made us feel guilty."

America

Many younger Swabians like Hans and Emma wanted to escape to America. The Rhineland, the Ruhr, Hamburg, and Berlin were in shambles. In addition, Swabians in America were sending packages of food and clothing, reminders that people in the United States. were much better off.

Helga Geiser had a close connection to America. Three years after the war, her American uncle visited and wanted to sponsor her whole family. She was fourteen, finished with school, and working. Her brother, older by three years, was doing his apprenticeship. However, clearance problems for the rest of the family prevented Helga from emigrating until 1951, when she was seventeen.

Occupation authorities had planned a de-Nazification process to prevent former Nazis from taking important positions. But the plan was ineffective and then dumped after the Cold War developed with the Soviet Union. Even though her father had been a member of the Nazi Party with an important job at the local factory, the whole family was eventually cleared.

In America, seventeen-year-old Geiser found a job as a nanny. She knew no English, but her employer spoke German. And the four girls under her charge helped her quickly learn English. The family was Jewish, and Geiser knew what had happened to Jews during the war. As a child, Geiser had seen trains going through her town towards the concentration camp at Dachau. One day in 1944, when she was ten, a neighbor hid three escapees in his barn. She questioned why, but her parents claimed not to know. "But that neighbor knew. The Jews came to him and his house next to the woods."

Geiser's Jewish employer in America learned that she had many skills besides babysitting. She started cooking and baking, including traditional Jewish dishes. Next, the maid who did the washing was let go, and she did everything, even the ironing. "But they were very good to me," Geiser recalls. "The family didn't hold it against me that I was German. I don't know if they lost anyone over there. I never heard anything about it."

Another post-World War II escapee, Andrea Clark, came to America as a preteen and had some adjustment problems as a refuge. Puberty is a particularly stressful time in a person's life, especially in America, where great freedom leads teenagers to group together for mutual support. Woe to those who are outsiders, such as immigrants. It is difficult for them to belong and get the self-esteem that belonging provides. Partly because of difficulties in seeing herself as an American, Clark would later return to spend a year in Germany at the end of her teen years. Unfortunately, she then learned that she was a misfit and was rejected there, too, as not completely German.

Kinderfeindlichkeit

Clark's story highlights an aspect of German culture that some Germans are themselves sensitive about—*Kinderfeindlichkeit*, literally, treating children as enemies, or, more loosely, child abuse. Her early experience of this made her later appreciate America and its more positive attitudes toward children.

She was born in Stuttgart right after the war, the child of refugees. Her mother was of Danish and North German peasant stock. Her father was a German-Polish aristocrat who had spent some time in a German concentration camp. After the war, he worked in France for the American military, and she saw him only a couple of times a year. Most of the adults in her world were females. "There were boys my age, of course, but there were fathers only here and there." In fact, the 1946 census in Germany showed thirty-six million females and only twenty-eight million males.[60]

Clark lived with her mother in a room on the second floor of a house, sharing a bath and kitchen with another woman. The woman's sister lived on the ground floor with her husband and five daughters. Clark and her mother were fortunate because the sister on their floor "sort of adopted" them. Refugees, or anybody different, often had a hard time being accepted by the local people. Her father, when he visited, was called a "Polack," and the family downstairs would refer to a half-black, half-German boy as a "nigger boy."

While German children liked American soldiers, adults would point out the GIs' lack of culture. When Clark brought home Christmas angels made at a youth center run by the Americans, the woman downstairs criticized them. "How tasteless." According to Clark, "They had this thing about Americans being very uncultured." She told me that this attitude still persisted when her German family later visited her in America, and they often displayed a superior attitude. They were critical because American houses are often built of wood, and because even brick houses are often just facades of brick over wood. Germans, in contrast, will build their houses to last. They go for "quality." Helga wondered whether this superior attitude might come from feelings of insecurity and inferiority.

Even though Clark was born after the war, she still experienced its lingering effects. When she started school in 1953, it was in a bombed-out restaurant with a tar-paper roof and a defused bomb in the basement.

Harshness

Most of all, Clark recalled the harshness of the people in her early life. Her father was away much of the time when she was small, so she wasn't subject to the classic authoritarian and punitive German father. It was her mother and the other females around who were hard on her. Clark never suffered severe physical punishment. At most, her mother might angrily make her braids real tight. The harshness was psychological.

Despite most of Clark's authority figures being female, or perhaps because of it, they made a point of fostering great shame and guilt. She could shudder when she recalled the women looking at her and saying, "How could you have done that..." or "How could you have forgotten...*Schäme dich* [Shame yourself]!" They were negative rather than positive. One time, she scratched her behind while out on the street. They told her, "You're going to turn into an ape." She was so young that later she couldn't remember the incident, but it was always brought up when she did something wrong.

Perhaps if there had been male as well as female authorities in her life, she could have gotten more positive strokes. If the men were punitive, the women could have been protective, or *vice versa*. The authorities in Clark's life, the women in her home and, later, the teachers in the school, were essentially "good people," according to Clark. "They meant well. Maybe they were just following how their own parents and teachers had behaved toward them."

Perhaps the harshness of adults had something to do with the difficult times after the war. Like after World War I, many people were smarting from defeat and, at first, inflation and then later simply from continued scarcity due to all the destruction from the war.

Clark's story helps one understand how Freud, who based his theories primarily on the Germanic culture around him, devised the concept of the "superego," the internalization of the strict parent. Children would then control their behavior along the lines desired by the parents. Children would feel anxious and guilty when they thought of doing something "bad." She internalized all the critical things that her mother and, especially, the other women in the house, had to say about her.

The upshot of this sort of training is that a German child may grow up to internalize what Clark terms a "strict regimentation." There is a feeling that one just "has to do it." For example, the cleaning of the stairs had to be done every Saturday, on the knees and using steel-wool, whether the stairs were dirty or not. "This feeling sticks with you. It's inflexible. Growing up you learn you have certain tasks that have to be done at certain times, no matter what."

Clark found these long-ago feelings of shame and guilt reactivated when her mother later visited from Swabia. Clark had to have the house very clean. Otherwise she would feel bad. But shame and guilt were worse for her mother. When her mother had visitors, she couldn't relax enough to entertain them. She had to busy herself out in the kitchen doing cleaning. She, too, must have been punished when she failed to take care of her work. Only punishment would seem to create such inflexibility in behavior.

Anxiety

Perhaps this kind of behavior is what people mean when they refer to the "*Angst*" (anxiety) of the Germans. They are driven by anxiety that they will be punished if things are not done, and done right. Punishment may have come originally from outside, but it has long since been internalized. Their superego tells them, "Do it—or else!" Unfortunately this feeling of being driven, of being serious and strict, can extend to petty matters. Clark noted that "Germans can make a big thing out of a little thing."

The stereotypical German traits of compulsiveness and thoroughness, as well as the need for order, may have some of their roots in anxiety inculcated very early in life, even before the child can understand shame and guilt. Freudians refer to these traits as the "anal character" that arises during the time when the child is toilet-trained, first encountering the imposed requirements of the parent, and first encountering punishment. Not surprisingly, Clark was toilet trained at ten months. Rather, they tried to toilet-train her then. Naturally, it didn't work. An infant has no voluntary control over the sphincter so early. She was even taken to a doctor who "gave her shots" to aid in her toilet training.

When psychologists speak of an "anal" character, they have in mind compulsive cleanliness and orderliness, common in German culture.[61] Clark remembered how these traits were emphasized at school. There was a story "about King Solomon, how he kept everything clean and then he saw someone who was dirty. Of course, that was very, very bad." Clark showed me her elementary school math book, with its protective paper cover that all the children had to make. She had also saved her art work, but "is it really art, it's so meticulous, not expressive like the art my children do here in school in America."

Clark felt that the compulsiveness about cleanliness was not all bad. When she returned to spend a year in Germany, the nuns where she worked at a hospital took great pains to show her how to do things like washing down a wall. She wished she had taught some of these techniques to her own children. It would have made life easier for her. She also recalled how good feelings could be part of compulsiveness in Germany: "As children, we learned to be proud of the good job we did cleaning."

When Clark arrived in America as a ten-year-old, she spent a year in a special class for foreigners. It provided social support as children puzzled out the English language together. "You could understand your feelings of being different, of being seen as stupid by Americans. You learned that other kids had the same feelings as you did." After that year, she took regular classes with no problems. Her vocabulary wasn't quite as big as that of American students, but that problem passed with time. However, she never did feel fully part of American life.

Homesick

Despite Clark's traumatic German upbringing, she was homesick. At age seventeen, she went back to "get a sense of belonging." She wanted to experience a year at a German *Oberschule*, or high school. Unfortunately, the message she got there was, "What a freak you are, you've picked up a new culture, you're not German!" Once, when a teacher dropped his keys, she picked them up and tossed them on his desk, rather than walking over and handing them to him. "Your manners are American," she was told. They were critical about everything: "Your pronunciation of German is so American that it is really poor." When she wrote a paper in music theory, the teacher read it aloud, saying, "If I had written this, I would have been too ashamed to turn it in." According to Clark, they did this to all the students, "but I guess everyone else sort of got used to it."

Clark liked the students at the school, believing that the real problem was in the German system itself. It had been the same in much of her German elementary school. She recalled a friend who was so unathletic, so impaired, that she could hardly walk. "She cried and cried in physical education class, but they were so regimented, they could only tell her to try as hard as you can."

Clark eventually dropped out of the German high school because of all the insults and humiliations. She then got a job in a hospital. There they complained, too, "I worked ten hours a day, and they said what I did, a German could do in four hours." She contrasted America with Germany, "Here people respect you for what you can do, while in Germany they humiliate you for not living up to standards."

When she returned to America, she went to college and got a degree in literature and social science and a teaching certificate, but she never used it. "I didn't feel like a person; I just wanted to find a secure place to hide and be a nobody. I never had any sense of security." Since then, she married, raised two children, and worked at a variety of jobs, finally becoming a nurse. It took her a long time to overcome her disastrous early life and the resulting inhibitions, but she finally felt she was "a person" with a sense of self-worth.

9: SONIA CIRESA: WARBRIDE

Like most Swabians, Sonia Ciresa loved music. Nazi Party statistics showed that the Swabians excelled only as musicians.[62] Ciresa's story illustrates the failure of the Allied strategy of area bombing to end the war by destroying civilian morale. Postwar surveys showed that the initial bombing raids reduced morale, but subsequent raids had little additional effect.[46] People like Ciresa continued working conscientiously. Ciresa's story also shows why some marriages between American soldiers and German women could be difficult.

****

Music

I learned to play the piano when I was nine years old. My mother would work a whole day to pay for my lesson. We were a musical family, always singing in the evening. We didn't turn on the lights. We just sat there in the dark, my parents, my two brothers, and me, and we played our instruments and sang folk songs.

I was born in 1923 and grew up in Wangen near Stuttgart. I went to school there for the first two grades. Then I walked two miles over the Neckar River bridge to Untertürkheim for school. Also across the river my family had a little garden of about five acres. We had all kinds of fruits and berries. After school we worked there till nine or ten in the evening. It was the highest place around, so during the war most of the fruit trees were cut down and anti-aircraft guns put up.

Next, I went two years to a girls' middle school in Stuttgart. Most people in Germany were done with school after the eighth grade. But my mother said, "You're going to work in the office, so you have to learn typing, stenography, filing, and bookkeeping." In Germany your mother or father pushed you into some kind of job, so I had three more years of school. I also had to learn a language there. I chose English because I had two uncles and an aunt in America.

After war broke out in 1939, I worked at a factory making machine tools for other countries. I remember the Russians because they came beautifully dressed in dark blue suits. They took the machines apart to see that everything was okay, and then they stamped the machines with the hammer and sickle.

Bombing

In 1941 bombs fell in our town during *Kirchweih* [the church's anniversary fair]. The siren sounded, but we didn't get out of bed. Why should we? Surely there was no danger. Suddenly there was a big noise, and out we got! About 600 yards away bombs had blasted a couple of huge craters. We walked out to look. We had no fear. It was all new. People hoped that the bombers were confused by the fair's lights and were intending to bomb somewhere else. We soon learned differently.

Then bombs hit close. My goodness, it looked like you could put a house in those craters. The dirt blown from our garden knocked our outhouse door off its hinges. From then on, when we heard sirens we always got out of bed.

In Germany, house cellars have ceilings with thick stone arches, like wine cellars. We kept wine and cider barrels down there. At the beginning of the war, we were required to install a sturdy cellar door made of metal with big latches on top and bottom. This door was at the very bottom of the steps to the cellar. There was another door at the top of the stairs. Then there was a little space and then our front door.

The government also made us install an underground gangway between our house and neighboring houses. One neighbor's house was right next to us, wall to wall, so my father cut a hole in the wall. It was covered with flimsy lattice, so you could easily climb through. On the other side of our cellar we took bricks out of the wall and dug a crawl tunnel to the next house. The whole block of houses was connected. If our house were hit and we couldn't go up through the cellar door, we could probably go through to one of the neighbors' houses.

In the cellar, my family had bunk beds and a pail always full of water. We made masks out of gauze and a rubber strap. You can't survive if you inhale too much dust. So you just dip the gauze in water and use it as a mask. We had gas masks, too. There was always food down there. Even before the war, my mother stored our bread there and potatoes for the whole winter. We also had jellies, preserves, and apples and other fruits as well as coal briquettes.

There was an air raid shelter about 200 yards away, a bunker built right into the side of the hill. You weren't supposed to stay in your house during the big raids. The bunker was safer. It went down about twenty steps into the hill. It also had bunk beds. My mother had a suitcase packed with her valuables, silverware, papers, and so on. It was always at the ready to take to the bunker.

The radio would give a special "beep" and interrupt the regular program. "Enemy planes approaching..." Immediately you'd see people running past the house to the shelter. People started when the planes were far away in France, even when they didn't know where the planes were heading. Just the idea that planes were approaching would scare people. My mother would run, too.

Nazis

My father was a special security guard at the Kodak plant. Hitler said, "If the enemy comes, burn your papers; don't let the enemy get anything." My father was not a member of the Nazi Party, and that was dangerous for him. Sometimes one of his friends in the office would say, "*Heil Hitler*, Wilhelm," and my father would just answer him, "Good morning." Fortunately, he had a very good relationship with his bosses. We raised rabbits, and when my father butchered one he'd keep the pelt and say, "Just in case they send me to fight the Russians, I'll need some warm clothes.

When I was in school about 1936 or so, they had a Nazi girls' organization, but my father didn't want me to join. Then my schoolteacher became involved with the Nazis. I used to be his favorite pupil, and suddenly I wasn't anymore.

My father decided I could join, but I was eventually thrown out because I was too much of a disturbance. The teacher also slapped me and called me a Commie. They told me that my name, Sonia, was a Russian name. But my mother named me that because the sun

[*Sonne*] was shining when I was born.

My father went to the school and said he'd kill this teacher, but he was restrained by the director. The teacher was supposed to be reprimanded, but it never happened. They were all government employees and belonged to the Nazi Party. You had absolutely no rights.

My father had to serve in the town's civil defense. He was lucky he didn't have to fight. One of my brothers had to go in 1944 when he was seventeen. My younger brother had been evacuated with other schoolchildren. They lived in the smaller villages, which usually weren't bombed. He got draft papers in February of 1945 when he was fourteen. My father tore them up. Girls were supposed to serve in the *Arbeitdienst* [National Work Service Corps], but I didn't have to go, maybe because I was working in an office. I guess we had God watching over us. My brother came back alive in 1945, and we all survived.

More Bombs

At the first wail of the air-raid siren, my father had to run to Kodak and guard the factory. My mother and I listened for the enemy planes coming over. We'd knit or crochet or darn socks. We had to keep busy.

There was a complete blackout before the raid. It was so pitch black on the street you couldn't see your hand in front of your face. People would run through the street with children, wagons full with belongings or old people. You could get hit by a wagon or baby carriage. Or a kid might be lying on the street where he fell. People would bring him to the bunker and describe him, "Who lost a kid?" There was lots of confusion. Mother would take her suitcase and run to the bunker. I'd take things and go to the cellar, but sometimes I'd say, "I'll be there a little later," and later I did go to the bunker. It depended on how I felt.

Just before the raid, an enemy plane would drop the "Christmas Trees" that would light up the town so brightly you could read a newspaper. Then there were two different kinds of bombs. The first kind, a *Luft* [air] bomb, would explode above the houses, and they would collapse. You would be safe because of the way the cellars were built. The other kind was worse. It went straight through the house into the cellar and then exploded. That was the end.

Next were the incendiary bombs to start fires. They came down in bunches. We were told to pick them up and carry them out of the house. But we never knew when they might explode. If some of the chemicals got on our skin, we were supposed to take a knife and cut the area out. It just eats you up, like the napalm America used in Vietnam.

More Destruction

One day my older brother and I were in the cellar when a *Luft* bomb hit real close. It tore the cellar door off its hinges, and we could open it only a few inches. There was rubble on the other side. I looked up the steps, and the outside door was gone. I could see just dust and the glow of fire reflecting off the dust. Right away we crawled through to the next house. But we didn't feel safe, so we came back again. We didn't know what to do.

Then we heard our father call, "Are you all right?" He knew a bomb had hit someplace close, and he had come running from work to check. He climbed over the rubble and cleared the way to get us out. We saw the streets were full of rubble from houses. The *Luft* bomb had exploded up high, and the houses had just fallen apart.

First we went across the street. Half of the house there was gone. I knew that somebody was in the cellar. The old man would never leave for the bunker. There was also a lodger who worked at Kodak. I saw him lying in what used to be the kitchen. I learned later he'd come up from the cellar because he thought he heard one of those incendiaries. Then the *Luft* bomb hit. So we freed him, carried him to the restaurant, and laid him on top of a table.

Then we called for the old man. When he answered, we cleared a way and hauled him out. Then I walked him down a couple of blocks into a house that wasn't damaged. The man's wife was OK—in the bunker. From then on, when there was an air raid, I put the old man in my wagon and raced up to that bunker. Then I would come back. I felt safer in the cellar at home.

In another raid, the front wall of our house fell out into the street. We had a Tudor-style house built with strong masonry, but the walls just collapsed. Masonry fell onto my bed from an interior wall. I could have been buried if I was sleeping. We had to move to my grandma's house.

My grandmother was in her seventies, and her house was a quarter mile further from the bunker. Often we just stayed down in the cellar. Other times I took my grandmother's hand, and we ran to the bunker. We would listen to the bombs. People always used to tell us then we had nothing to be afraid of. Once we didn't hear them anymore that's it. My mother would bury her head in my father's lap.

A lot of times, a squadron of planes would come from the north, passing over us and going on to Göppingen. We thought, "Fine, what do we care?" All right, we have to take shelter, but that's all. But the planes turned around and flew right along the Murr River valley. That's when we got it. I think they were aiming for the Mercedes factory.

The English planes came during the night and American planes during the day. It wasn't as frightening during the day, because you could see them. In fact they looked beautiful, like silver birds.

At work the most important papers had to be put in special wooden crates and taken down to the basement. Sometimes we would go outside to look at the airplanes. We could see when the bombs would drop and know which way to go. Don't ever run away from a bomb. Run more or less towards it. Otherwise it catches up with you. Better to lie down than run away from it.

On a clear day, you could see the railroad get hit. Those bombs were sure. Days, they were targeted raids. At night the bombs were dropped all over. It was especially senseless when those incendiaries burned the tar on the street. People got tar stuck on them and ran burning into the river.

After a while there were so many air raids that I was up all night—air raids, air raids, one right after the other. I didn't undress anymore. I went to bed with my clothes on. At 6 o'clock in the morning, I would be at work. My boss would dictate a whole steno book full, and I'd keep falling asleep, I was so tired. He was talking, so he stayed awake.

Then, of course, during the day there would be air raids, too, so we were constantly on the run, back and forth. Sometimes I used to take my typewriter home and work between the air raids in order to get stuff done. We had to work even though we felt worn out all the time.

Fixing Things

The bombs broke the office windows, and it was cold. We hung burlap until we got new glass. The glaziers showed us how to install it. Everybody worked installing the windows because the glaziers couldn't keep up with the work anymore. Whether you were a white-collar worker or not, it didn't make a difference. We all worked at everything.

At home there was more work rebuilding our house. We collected the bricks that could be saved. We cleaned them, and father mixed the cement. We kids had to help at whatever had to be done. We had to carry cement. I even worked up on the roof fixing the shingles. We had to carry wood down the cobblestone path from the top of the hill using wicker baskets on top of our heads. Grandma was very good at balancing those fifty-pound baskets on her head—like in the movies—without holding on. I had to use my hands.

Another job we had was taking care of the toilet in the outhouse. We used to cut up the newspaper for toilet paper. We'd use a bucket of water to flush everything down into a cesspool. Once a month, the cesspool had to be emptied into a big barrel. It was good manure. We put it on a wooden farm wagon and pulled it all the way up the hill. No horse. One brother was in front, the other brother and me in the back, or *vice versa*. The back was the worst, because the stuff slopped over you. On top of the hill we filled *Butten* [large backpacks] with the manure and carried them into the garden. My father had no trouble emptying his by leaning over sideways. But I bent the wrong way to empty mine, forward. It emptied on me. But those were, all the same, good times. We kids had to work hard, but there was discipline.

What was bad was the war. When people in America talk about war, they have no idea what it is. They think maybe there is a shortage of this or that, some inconveniences. Otherwise, they know nothing. You have to go through a war in order to understand it. And if Americans talk about crimes committed by the Germans, then I say the Allies destroyed a lot of human lives, too, unnecessarily.

My father helped build shelters in the hillside behind Kodak for the employees. We had a lot of forced laborers. Hitler got them from Holland, from France, and, of course from 1941 on, from Russia. They lived all together nearby and were transported to the factory. There were Russian girls and boys, thirteen or fourteen years old. I was in charge of food for them, so I always gave more than they were supposed to get. My employers were very good to them.

In fact, some of the forced laborers were in the band we formed there at Kodak. We used to play music in the cafeteria, Germans and foreigners together. We didn't have them under lock and key. When our cafeteria was bombed, I got permission so they could come to my home to play. They had no reason to run away. They were nice people. In fact, after the war, my mother would write me in America how some came to visit and reminisce. My father was good to those forced laborers when he was a foreman, and they liked him. That probably saved our lives later, during the French occupation.

Occupation

The American soldiers arrived first, across the river from us [on the east side of the Neckar]. We heard orders, "Destroy the bridges so the Americans can't cross." My father wanted to get a group together to overpower the guards, dismantle the explosives, and save the bridge. He always said it was nonsense to demolish a bridge. Later on you have to build it again, but he couldn't stop them. The bridge was blown up. That's why we had the French occupation on our side of the river and the Americans on the other side. Of course the French hated Germans more, because they had suffered under them. The Americans never had war in their country, and they didn't know what it was. The French did.

One day my father announced, "The French are coming. The family will stay together." We went up to the factory. The first shots were fired from a hill about a quarter of a mile away, and they hit our building. A man with a high position in the company walked out carrying a white flag. He told the French, "You don't have to shoot anymore. Come on down." But they beat him bloody.

The French told us, "Anybody caught with firearms will be shot." Of course, my father still carried his revolver. He slipped it down between his legs and got rid of it. We had our family papers and valuables with us. I also had my brother's leather motorcycle gloves and leather jacket. The French soldiers took everything. Later on, my father spoke to one of the forced laborers and told him what happened. He told the French commandant that my father was always good to him. We got our stuff back.

All in all, the French were nice. One time I was at home playing the piano when there was a knock at the door. It was three French soldiers. My mother was scared. They had their guns, and they came right into the living room. I stopped playing, but they said I should keep on. They sat down and leaned their guns against the table. My mother wanted to move the guns away. She didn't like guns, but she was told by gestures to leave them right where they were. All the soldiers wanted was that I should keep playing. I remember how their white teeth shone because their faces were so dark.

The French set up a headquarters at Kodak, and I was invited to play the piano for their entertainment. I said I would accept only if my parents would be allowed to go with me. I knew what would happen otherwise. When we arrived, there were already girls from town. They were quite embarrassed when we saw them. The girls went there on their own. They were hungry, and the French gave them something to eat, and then...and then... Even old women got VD [venereal disease]. People said, "Shame on you." But what would you do? Go hungry?

During the occupation there was a curfew. Germans were allowed out only one or two hours a day. But I had a special pass because I did some work at the police station. The police found a list of members at Nazi Party headquarters. These people were asked to supply a bed, linens, and furniture for those who were bombed out. I had to record the things people brought. An aunt came to me and tried to get out of it. I told her, "I'm sorry, but it's my job." She had the pleasure before of a better life, and she now had to take the consequences.

Orders were issued, "Anybody having a gun at home, bring it to the police station." People brought them, a whole mountain of guns. The French let some of the forced laborers come and take their pick. One of the laborers took a pistol and walked up and down the street with it. Once he stuck his gun in my back, even though I had a special pass to be out. I reported him. He had no right to do that, to be a menace to society. A couple of days later one of his own people shot him in the leg.

He truly wasn't treated badly by us. People had been good to him. But I can't blame him. If somebody takes you away from your home, you will have hate. It's natural. And there is no way to make up for it. But you can make people feel a little better by being nice to them and showing them that it's not you—it's the system. It's the government that's doing it, not the individual.

I had gotten engaged in 1943, but Martin was killed in Russia in 1944. One day after the war, I went to visit his parents with a bouquet of flowers. They lived across the Neckar River, but only half of the bridge was left. To cross, you had to go onto the fallen masonry and use the cables and boards to go from one rock to the other, then climb a ladder up to where the rest of the bridge still stood.

The current was very strong there. So I waited to see if anybody made it over. When some did, I thought, "I can make it, too." The first board was easy, but not the second one. It slid, and I fell in the water. Luckily there was a cable I could hold onto. Some men came running to pull me out. My clothes were soaking wet, and water was coming out of my shoes, but I still had my flowers!

Playing the Piano

After the war, our little band of musicians split up. The foreigners were leaving. So I started playing piano for the French in Stuttgart. I couldn't play dinner music, nothing by heart, only with the notes. But they didn't care as long as there was soothing music. I played all kinds of things, semi-classical, dance music, whatever I had the music for. In exchange, I would get some food, a can of coffee, a bag of flour or sugar.

Then I played the piano for Polish forced laborers, and soldiers, too, at a New Year's celebration. The hall was so cold, they had fires inside big metal drums, and I wore a fur coat while I played. We had to play from 8 p.m. until 6 a.m. They brought us stacks of sandwiches and drinks, but we couldn't stop playing. They were so happy there, and we had to play and play. There was no time to tell my mother I wouldn't be home. But at 6 a.m. came the reward. A whole bag of food—butter, coffee beans, flour, sugar, you name it. You should have seen my mother's face when I came home with that bag of food.

In 1946, I met my husband, Jim, while I was playing piano at the

American Army barracks in Bad Cannstatt. He was a chaplain's assistant, and he played the piano at services. The Americans had USO [United Service Organization] people—singers, comedians, dancers, jugglers, who'd come and entertain the troops. They'd tell me what music they wanted played. Jim also played the piano for them.

There was something special about Jim, I don't know what it was. He didn't have a German background; the family name was English, but I didn't care one way or the other.

America

When Jim was shipped back to America, he sent for me. I came to America in 1947, and we married eight days later. I didn't have a penny in my pocket when I came. Germans were not allowed to bring any money out. I later learned that my first American clothes, from my mother-in-law, were secondhand from church bazaars. I was happy because clothes were scarce in Germany. There I had one knit dress that used to grow with me, hem after hem added on the bottom. To buy anything you needed ration stamps.

It was a small Illinois town, population 600. The people were nice, but I always had the feeling that they looked down on me. I worked first in a bobby-pin factory. I didn't know the language well enough to work in an office. In the factory they brought me pails full of bobby pins, and I had to put them onto pieces of cardboard.

My father-in-law was a butcher, and he owned a food locker plant, too. Jim showed me a picture while I was still in Germany. Farmers would bring cattle, and my father-in-law would butcher them and package the meat for their lockers, but in 1948 my father-in-law died. My mother-in-law sold the house, and all three of us moved to Chicago.

There I worked at Motorola soldering the wiring for TV sets. In a short while I became the key operator, the one who has to be able to do all the jobs on the line. If someone had to go to the toilet they couldn't leave until I took over for them. After a year I became forelady.

But I had trouble at home. My husband did not like to work. He had a headache during the day. But it went away in the evening, so he could go out. I tried everything to make the marriage work. Then I was pregnant. I was tired all the time, and I had to quit working. After our son John was born, I had to go back to work. We still lived with Jim's mother. My husband did not believe in having his own home. My uncle even gave him a loan for the down payment, but Jim figured it was cheaper to live with his mother.

I always got along with my in-laws. My mother-in-law and I still write. She took care of the baby, and I went back to work. My husband stayed in bed. Evenings, he went out.

One day, I got a phone call from home. Jim was supposed to be babysitting, but our son John had swallowed a pocket knife! He was two years old, and his intestines were small, so he couldn't pass the knife. The surgeon told me I should separate from my husband. I thought for the sake of the child I stay. A child needs two parents, but a year later I got a divorce.

Single Parent

I moved East, and John and I lived with my aunt until I could rent an apartment. Then my girlfriend came from Germany and shared the rent. Eventually I got a place of my own. When my mother saw only my name on the back of letters, she knew something was wrong. When she found out, she tried to talk me into going back to Germany. She would take care of John.

But I wanted to make it on my own. I didn't want to go back. I didn't want anybody to laugh at me. Over there they would say, "Didn't I tell you it wouldn't work out?" and "Now she comes back because she can't make a go of it." The neighbors in Germany used to tell me I shouldn't get involved with an enemy of ours, and they'd look at me coldly. That's why I wouldn't go back. In a small town like Wangen it would be bad. My mother was born in the house she lived in, and all the old people knew each other.

My mother came to the United States in 1953 and insisted I go visit Germany. She paid for the ticket. When my father had a heart attack, I decided to stay in Germany and get work. I had no more money, and I didn't want to leave Germany while my father was sick.

Then my ex-husband decided he needed me, so he came to Germany. John hadn't seen his father for a couple of years. When John would ask about him, I used to say, "He's working in Chicago like a lot of other fathers." That's all he knew.

John couldn't speak any German when he went to Germany, but

within a few months he had learned it perfectly. But when his father came, he couldn't talk English to him anymore!

Jim wanted us back and tried everything in his power to get us back. I said, "We might consider it if you come East and work there, if you can make a living there for us." Well, my father got better, and I came back to America in 1956. My son had been all enthused when he saw his father in Germany. He had a father after all! But when we came back to America, there was no father. Jim didn't leave Chicago to live with us.

I found secretarial work. I worked and helped John go to university. He has a bachelor's degree in marketing, and he works as a manager for a department store in Delaware now.

It was many years before I was able to play music again. I had to support my son first. Then I joined a Swabian singing group. When they couldn't afford to pay a conductor any more, I started directing. I'm now music director for three different choruses and sometimes even a fourth.

But the singing societies are fading away. The old singers are dying off, and the young ones are not interested in singing German songs. Young men visit a time or two and say right out, "Do you have any young women?" Young women also come and ask about men, but none of them stay because younger people are not interested in German folk songs.[63]

You know, if I hadn't been playing at the American barracks and met Jim, I might have married a German. I wasn't looking for an American. I just got attracted to him. But a lot of German girls back then were looking for Americans. They had nobody in Germany. They became involved with Americans, thinking they were going to the United States to live a good life.

A lot of girls met soldiers over there and knew nothing about their background. I'm sure many soldiers were nice people. Back in America, one works as a fisherman, another as a policeman, but maybe another doesn't work at all. When they are in the army, you can't tell the difference.

Work

I tried to make a go of my marriage. See, in Germany we were brought up to work. When you came home from school, you worked in the garden turning over the soil. Whatever had to be done, you did it. If there was a bit of time, you'd darn the socks, even cotton stockings. I darned them so many times I don't think there was an original heel in there anymore. Reading was allowed only on a Sunday. During the week you worked. No novels or stories. "What, are you reading again? Do something constructive." So I'd do whatever had to be done. We Germans were brought up to work, no matter what kind of work. No excuses.

Jim didn't like to work. He felt there was more to life than working. Of course, there is more. I enjoy life, too, but work comes first—and money, you must have money to live. I said to myself, you go to America and you both work together, husband and wife, and in no time you can have a house. But we never talked about it in Germany. Jim just said to come to America, and I just figured he goes to work. I just took it for granted. I never got any financial support from my husband. I had a child to raise, and I had to put him through school, get him clothes and everything. I did it all on my own. I'm proud of that.

10: THE FLIGHT OF THE *VOLKSDEUTSCH*

Sathmar Swabians

At the end of the seventeenth century, the Ottoman Turks were retreating from their empire that once covered much of the Balkans. The Emperor of the Holy Roman Empire awarded rights to some of the new lands to Hungarian Prince Alexander Karolyi.[64-66] Prince Karolyi decided to import 14,000 Catholic peasants from Swabia.

Over the course of the eighteenth century and into the early nineteenth century, other immigrants from southwest Germany took up invitations from the Karolyi family. They settled in a wide arc some twenty to thirty miles south of the city of Satu Mare (Sathmar in English) in present-day Romania. Many came from Upper Swabia, where the land was poor and living hard. Undivided inheritance was practiced there, and the children who did not inherit found the opportunity to become a farmer in Hungary a great incentive.

These Sathmar Swabians were one small part of several centuries of emigration by Germans to Eastern Europe and to Russia. The nobility of these countries wanted to improve agricultural practices and make their lands more productive. Poor Germans were offered land and other incentives such as freedom from military service and no taxes until they were established. These *Volksdeutsch*, or ethnic Germans, kept their language and culture. They remained Germans but became citizens of the nations where they settled. Many Germans settled close to the

Danube River, and they became known as *Donauschwaben*, or Danube Swabians. Most were not actually Swabians, but came from further afield in Germany, from places such as Hessen. They were called Danube Swabians because they travelled through Swabia on the Danube River to get to their new homes.

Compared to the local Hungarian and Romanian peasants, the German settlers were privileged. They had a contractual relationship with their lord, who owned the land where they worked. They paid rent to the lord—like most peasants in Germany. But they were not slaves, as was common in Eastern Europe, where the lord could demand services, including even the "right of the first night" with new brides. Besides rent, the Sathmar Swabians had to provide only very limited contractual services. Rights and obligations were hereditary, so the special status of the Sathmar Swabians was passed to subsequent generations.

The peasants' first contract promised enough land and woods plus adequate plow animals and feed, so that farming could begin right away. For the first years, there would be no taxes or personal servitude obligations. After that, the peasants had to pay five Gulden and one- to two-tenths of all produce for the use of the lord's land, plus fifteen days' personal labor service a year. Also expected were the traditional gifts of hens, eggs, butter, and the like on the major holidays.

By the twentieth century, the Sathmar Swabians were a small group of ethnic Germans surrounded mainly by Hungarians. They numbered 40,000 in some thirty villages at the eastern edge of the great Hungarian plain, the Puzta, in present-day northwestern Romania.

Life in Sathmar

Bill Leili, today a New York City resident, was born in 1935 in the village of Scheindorf. He described a life not too different from that lived by his ancestors who first came to the area 250 years earlier. "We were about 150 families altogether. Our farmlands were spread out for an hour to two hours [by horse] from the village. The main crops were wheat, potatoes, beets, sunflowers, and corn. But wine was the most important crop. Everybody had vineyards that produced thousands of gallons of wine. Some was used to pay our farm laborers, the Romanians, who were also paid with bread, bacon, whiskey, and so on. No money was exchanged.

"Almost everybody in the village was a farmer, and we had to do almost everything ourselves. For example, all the houses and barns were built by village people helping each other. We did basket-weaving from willow branches. Everybody grew flax to make their own clothes and textiles during the winter when there was no farm work. My father would weave carpets from six o'clock in the morning till eight o'clock at night. The only things we traded for were suet, sugar, coffee, and kerosene. A grocer, blacksmith, shoemaker, and butcher were the only non-farmers. Two of these businesses were Jewish. The rest of us were very religious and very superstitious Catholics."

A typical tale told by the Sathmar Swabians is about a very diligent boy, Stefan, who worked from early in the morning till late at night. He fed the animals, cleaned out the manure, and cut weeds in the vineyard or in the fields. He had to do it all because his father had been in ill health for some years.

Once he let the manure build up for a few days, and he felt he had to clear it all out and spread fresh bedding, but his sister came from the house to tell him, "You better come, father doesn't look well. I think he's dying."

"Tell him to take it easy," Stefan replied. "I have to finish this job and then I'll come."

When Stefan finished, he ran to the house, but it was too late.

Stefan cried out, "Couldn't he have waited just a little bit, until I was done with the work?"

Fleeing the Red Army

Working and keeping up their farms was a high priority for the Sathmar Swabians. However, late in September 1944, miles-long columns of wagons drawn by horses and oxen passed through their villages. Saxon Germans from Transylvania, just to the east, were fleeing their homeland of some seven centuries. They would not be leaving without good reason. The Red Army must be coming. Just a month earlier, the Romanian regime that ruled Transylvania had switched sides and was now helping the Red Army clear German troops out of Romania.

Stefan Brendli, a priest in Sathmar, noted that some people were stingy when the Saxon refugees asked for hay for their animals. He heard the Saxons warn that soon the Swabians would have to follow and leave their hay behind.

Two weeks later, they did. Leili recalls, "I usually took care of the livestock at home, since I was still a kid at the time. One afternoon, a troop of German soldiers came on horses and told us to have our horses and wagon ready in the farmyard by six o'clock in the morning. We could take only what we could load on the wagon. The Russians were about eighteen miles off. Whoever was not ready at six would be shot."

People were so reluctant to leave their homes, farms, and belongings behind that the German military had to resort to threats to get people to leave.

"Everybody was ready. We moved mostly by day. Nights, my mother, younger brother, and sister slept in a tent on top of the wagon. I slept with my older brother and my father under the wagon, sometimes in the snow. We had no sleeping bags. Whatever blankets we had were used to cover the horses."

The wagon train covered 250 miles in eighteen days to reach the relative safety of western Hungary. But the Red Army continued to advance. The refugees in the slower-moving wagons, pulled by cows and oxen, were put on trains for Thuringia, Germany. The wagons pulled by horses continued westward for thirteen days and 156 miles more to the Austrian part of Germany and then another thirteen days and 190 miles to the ultimate refuge of Altmünster on the Traunsee in Austria.

Refugees in Austria

Leili recalls what happened when his wagon train reached the German refugee camp in Austria. "My father worked for a farmer, getting just what he could eat or steal, mainly dried bread and potato skins, the kinds of stuff they feed to the pigs. We were hated. We were *Flüchtlinge* [refugees]. The Austrians felt we were taking jobs and food away from them.

"We lived in a wooden barracks, our family of six in one room, eight by eighteen feet. It was kitchen, living room, and bedroom, all in one. We were lucky. We had plywood walls to separate us from other families. Some people didn't. There was no running water. You had to walk three-quarters of a mile and carry the full pails back. The outhouses were far away, too.

"We were always hungry. My father kept the food in a foot locker—the flour, butter, and so on. Once, my older brother and I broke the lock and ate all the bread and crackers. When Father saw what happened, our behinds were so sore we couldn't sit for a week, and we didn't get our regular share of the food, either."

At the end of the war in 1945, the American Army came and occupied a hotel in Altmünster. Leili recalled, "By then we had nothing to eat, so ten of us kids used to dive into the garbage cans after the soldiers emptied their mess kits. The soldiers also played with us by flipping a cigarette and watching us jump for it. Or they'd drop a butt on the floor, and, when we reached for it, stamp on it.

"In 1946, things got better. The farmers started to hire some of our people. They knew we did good work. They paid mainly in bread, potatoes, and flour. We also got government rations. Our family of six got two quarts of milk a day and two pounds of butter a month."

"Luckily, my uncles in America sent food packages. We lived off the cigarettes and coffee sewed into the linings of clothes. We traded them in the black market. I used to go out at night by bicycle to a place five miles away and trade cigarettes for bread. Quite a few people got caught and put in jail, but not me."

New York City

An uncle who'd been in the United States since 1929 was able to help Leili and his family escape in 1950. Leili was fifteen years old. "We went on deck when the ship reached New York Harbor. My father saw the cars bumper to bumper along the West Side Highway, and he said that they have more cars over here than we have flies on the other side."

It was hard for Leili at first. "In high school, the kids called me a 'Nazi.' Then a teacher asked whether anyone knew something about communism. I didn't know all that much, but I had heard from relatives visiting from Romania, so I told the kids how lucky they were. They started to look at me differently. And then I got to be number one in my plumbing class, because I worked hard.

"In New York City, a lot of Sathmar Swabians became superintendents of buildings. At first, they lived with relatives and took care of a building part time while working at some other menial job full time. While the men were at that job, the wife and kids pulled the garbage, hauled out the ashes, filled the coal bins, cleaned and swept. In my father's building, we three boys knew there was no play if there was any work to be done. On the weekends and at night, the supers did maintenance and repairs—plumbing, plastering, electric work. Officially, they weren't skilled repairmen, but in terms of what they did, they were.

"We lived in one of my uncle's buildings for three months. Then my father was a super for four years while he had an outside job, first as a dishwasher in a country club in Mamaroneck, then in a textile factory as a maintenance man. Finally he got a job as elevator operator.

"My mother made her own noodles, bread, preserves, pickles, and so on. We had a little garden, just eight by twenty feet. From an uncle in New Jersey, we'd buy our meat, alive. We'd make ham, bacon, and wurst and store it in the basement. We'd buy grapes and make our own wine, 250 gallons a year.

"The Swabians would usually try to better themselves by learning a trade, like construction, carpentry, or masonry, and after five or ten years they'd go into business for themselves."

A Refugee in Germany

Some of the Sathmar Swabians were able to move from Austria to Germany a few years after the war. A German professor who had researched the Sathmar Swabians helped them. They settled in Upper Swabia. Stefan Brendli recalled, "The German government gave us everything: rooms, clothing, a stove, and enough to eat. But the local people were the same as in Austria. They didn't like us. When some firewood was stolen in the town, the town crier said, 'When you see a *Flüchtling* [refugee], if you kill him, it's just gonna be one less.' He said it even though we were standing there and listening to him."

After Stefan Brendli finished his schooling, he got a job as an auto mechanic. "You signed a contract for three years, but the first month you're on trial. I was there almost four weeks, and I liked it. But when the boss read the contract and saw I was born in Romania, he told me, 'verfluchte Flüchtling, hau ab! [Damned refugee, get out of here!].' He thought I was local because the dialect I spoke was almost the same as his, and I'd been living there for two years already, too. And he said it to me just like to a dog. I went home crying. I was just fourteen years old.

Fortunately the professor friend found Brendli a place as an apprentice in a larger firm located near Stuttgart. "I lived in a home they had for forty other boys, mostly refugees from all over, and they treated us good." Brendli came to America with his family a year later. "I was interested in ceramics. The church in our village had real nice tiling. So I went to a ceramics business. The guy I worked for was a *Dummkopf* [idiot]. He just didn't get ahead in the business, and I left after a while for a big tiling company. I worked there for eight years, and I stole knowledge from them. Then I went into business for myself."

He is grateful for life in America and disparaging towards American youths. "They have the schooling for eight years and then four years in high school, they have the library, they have so much. But they have no trade. I get so angry." Brendli adds, "Go look, it's there in front of your eyes. Go pick it up, anything you want to do."

Later Escapees

Some Sathmar Swabians didn't escape to America until years after the first postwar refugees from Germany or Austria. These people had assimilated to the dominant Hungarian culture around them. The newly independent Hungarian state and its Catholic hierarchy felt minorities should become Hungarian, unlike the more liberal attitude toward minorities when the Sathmar Swabians had earlier been under the Romanians. In the census of 1930, people were asked about their ethnicity, and 31,000 in the Sathmar area said German. But when asked the language spoken at home, less than 22,000 said it was German.

Maria Brendli from the village of Hamroth, just a couple of miles away from Leili's Scheindorf, recalled the earlier assimilation to the Hungarian language. She also described how more recent Sathmar emigrants, such as her grandchildren, came to America.

"When I was born in 1908, Sathmar was Hungarian, and it stayed that way until 1919. When I went to school, we spoke Hungarian. We were not allowed to talk Swabian. Outside the school, we talked Swabian, but if we weren't careful and someone heard, there was trouble.

"My parents were Swabian, but we were *Magyariziert*

[Hungarianized]. The Hungarians pressured us so much in so many ways that at the end we were three-quarters Hungarian. But because we were not completely Hungarian, they considered us *Volksdeutsch* [ethnic Germans]. For example, you couldn't hold a government position like policeman or teacher if you had a German name. Everybody in the village, including my husband, was a farmer, but if you wanted to go higher, you would have to change your name to a Hungarian one, say, from Klein to Kish.

"In 1919, the Romanians took Sathmar away from Hungary, and they let us talk German again. Then the school only had one hour of Hungarian language. But then it changed back again in 1940. The Hungarians took Sathmar away from Romania until the end of the war in 1945, when Romania took it again."

To Escape or Not

Brendli's husband fought in World War II as a Hungarian soldier. When the Germans were retreating, people told her, "You are Hungarians, and if you leave now you're never going to see your husband again. You should just stay home."

Brendli recalls, "Some Swabs volunteered for the *Waffen* SS [SS part of the German Army]. Otherwise they had to go to the Hungarian Army. We lived in Hungary after all, and when men were twenty-one they had to go into our country's army. Whoever didn't volunteer for the SS, then the Hungarians would call them in.

"The German army told everybody in Hamroth to leave, and about half did, but I stayed. The next day, the Russian guns shot from the woods down on the German soldiers in the middle of the town. Then Russian soldiers came. Everything was burning. Then the Germans pushed the Russians out with much shooting. Again the Germans told everybody to leave, and I took my boy on one of the buses they had for us. But the Russians caught up with us in Czechoslovakia. At the end of the war, they sent us back to Romania."

Upon her return to Hamroth, now Romanian territory, she found most of the town's 200 houses burned to the ground. "Romanians were in the four or five houses still standing. Everything useful was stolen—bricks, wood, everything. And they told us that Germans were not permitted there anymore. So we went to friends or relatives in other towns. After a year, the

Romanian government said we had rights just like the Romanians and we could go back to our town and build.

"But my husband didn't come home from the war. I didn't know if he was alive or not. Finally, after five years, he came back from being a Russian prisoner. He started to build a house, and I was allowed back in the town with my boy and allowed to get a job. I worked on the collective farm hoeing corn and potatoes. Because they only had four school grades in the village, I put my boy in the city schools. I worked for the priest, doing cooking, cleaning—everything, to help pay.

"My husband didn't live much longer. He died in a couple of years. It was hard working on the collective farm. We women used to go out in the fields, hoeing corn and potatoes. That's when I came to America because I have a sister here. I worked and stayed for seven years. In the meantime, my son got married and had a family, so he didn't want to come to America. Times were all right then in Romania, so I went back to live with him and stayed in Romania five years."

Bad Times

Communist Nicolae Ceausescu became president of Romania in 1965 and embarked on disastrous economic programs. With the goal of paying off the county's foreign debt, he forced the export of most of the country's agricultural and industrial products, resulting in serious shortages of food and other necessities. Romania's standard of living dropped to near the bottom in Europe.[67]

Brendli recalls, "When times got bad in Romania, people left the collective farms. All the young people left for the city, for factories, where they could get a salary. Only a few of the old people [Germans] and the Romanians stayed on the collective farm. In our village, they opened the saloon at three o'clock in the afternoon. People would say 'why care for tomorrow, what's the use?'

"People worked hard only when the corn was ripe. Everybody went home at least twice a day so they could take some corn along in their pockets. That way they got more from the work than what they were paid. Everybody was stealing, whether they were German or not. They even took home clover for their rabbits. The older people could hardly stand it, having to steal to be able to live. I asked my brother how he could go to confession. But the priest told him that he was just stealing from his own land.

"Everybody had to have a ration ticket then in Romania to buy food. They measured out everything according to the tickets: sugar, flour, oil, milk, butter, everything. You could go to the store and see it there, but you can't touch it. You could get just what is on the ticket."

According to Brendli, all the German families wanted to leave. "They were called the 'Black Swabs,' the ones who became Hungarianized, changed their names to Hungarian ones and couldn't even speak German anymore. Some went to Germany—some legally, others illegally, maybe just on vacation—and then they'd stay. If a man went, after a year he could bring out his wife."

To America

Brendli returned to America, bringing her son's two girls. "I came back to America because the girls were grown up, fourteen and seventeen years old, and because the living in Romania was terrible. The girls were lucky here because they went to a German school in Romania. They speak and write four languages: German, Romanian, Hungarian, and now English. The girls stayed in America because of the discrimination against the Swabians in Romania. They just don't like the Swabs there, because the Swabs are smarter and do better.

"Even the Hungarianized Swabs got it bad after the war. They said they didn't know how to speak Schwab, but the Romanians pointed out who they were to the Russians. They were sent to Russia for five years and many died. But I think that's all over now. They discriminate now because the Germans are doing better.

"Germans are supposed to have the same rights legally in Romania, but the girls found it was not so when they went to school. Eva, who was older than the others in her class, was a good learner, but her Romanian or Hungarian friends got better grades. She used to come home and cry. She did her homework well, but a Hungarian or Romanian girl copied it from her and got a better grade. That's why she likes it now in America. When the girls went to high school here, they got As in American History, and the teacher said to the others, 'Shame on you!'"

11: GUNTHER LEILI'S STORY

Leili was another unlucky Sathmar Swabian. His October 1945 wagon train went to Budapest, Hungary, where his family was put on a train for Thuringia, in what would become Communist East Germany.

****

In Germany a farmer took us in. He was well off, with eight cows and a tractor. I was treated like a son. I was just four years old. But in August 1945, the Russians transported us back to Romania.

My father was in the German army and captured by the Americans. But we didn't know whether he was dead or alive. So there was just my mother and the three of us children. I was the youngest.

Back to Sathmar

There was nothing left when we got back home. All the land was colonized by the Romanians. They came from fifty miles away, lumberjacks who didn't know anything about farming.

At first we lived in the priest's house. He hadn't come back after he fled. We were two or three families in each room, and there were five rooms, so we were twelve or thirteen families altogether. Three or four people slept together in each bed. My bed was boards on blocks, with some straw and a cover over the straw. Everyone in the house had to share the single stove. Other people lived in the schoolhouse, while still others lived with Romanians in other towns.

I used to ask my grandma, "How come things are so bad for us?" She would say, "We can't do anything about it. Maybe when you grow up things will be different." She would tell me about America. She had a son and daughter who went there in the 1930s. "That country is rich," she said. "Here we have to suffer."

A lot of times I would go to bed after eating just cornmeal boiled in water. I'd put some salt on it, that's all. Maybe there'd be a crust of bread, too. That was a good meal. Other times there was just a potato as the whole meal. At three o'clock in the morning, I used to wake up and holler at my mother, "I'm hungry. I want a piece of cornbread." Lots of times there was nothing.

I went to school in 1948. You had to be eight years old to start. They let us have a German school, where everything was in German. But we were good in other languages. From the third grade on we had Romanian and Russian classes. I spoke Romanian when I played with the other kids. Of course, some would say, "Go to Hitler. Don't stay here."

Some of the Romanians came from the woods, and they used to be like wild animals. They'd fight with axes and knives. These were the strangers that took our farms away. The old Romanian families, the ones that always lived in our town, were OK to us. They would give us help—a piece of bread, or a couple of potatoes.

Surviving

In 1950, we were permitted to move back to part of our own house. It had two big rooms, one on each side of the kitchen, so we had one room, and a Romanian family had the other. We shared the kitchen. But we couldn't use our garden or the barns.

My mother worked during the summer for that family, and my twelve-year-old brother, too. He used to lead the horses while the man plowed or used the cultivator. We had to work for the Romanians who owned our land now.

They gave us jobs because we knew about farming. Besides, the Romanian man in our house needed help. He only had a fifteen-year-old daughter to help. They were not bad people. They were reasonable. A lot of times they used to bring us a piece of cornbread or some cornmeal.

Even though things got a little better, we were still living from one day to another. We could only survive over the winter on the little that my mother earned in the summer. We got no help from my father. We didn't know if he was even alive. A lot of times I used to go to school without breakfast. Only at night would I get some cornmeal and a potato.

My mother used to go for months to a neighboring village and work there. They had a grain like wheat, only it grows higher and is darker. She would work at threshing it. They'd grab the big, long stalks—they were close to six feet long—and hit the heads against the table to get the grain off. Then the stalks were used to build roofs on houses. Once she got sick, so then we didn't get any food. She was paid only from what she threshed.

Begging

When my mother was away working, I lived with my grandmother and brother. Me and my grandmother would go around to all the Romanian villages and beg for food. We asked for cornbread or a potato or maybe bean soup. A lot of times the Romanians would throw stones at us. We had no shame. When you are hungry, you are not ashamed to beg.

So we survived. Little by little, things got better. The Romanians needed help running the farms. My mother used to help hoeing the corn and sunflowers. My sister used to babysit for the Romanians. Then my sister went to live with an aunt over the mountain. The aunt was married to a Romanian, so her farm hadn't been taken away.

Around 1955, we were able to save enough to buy a pig so we could fatten it and have meat later on. Also in 1955, we had to join the collective farm if we wanted our house back. In the space behind the house we started to raise little pigs and chickens, and we also grew potatoes, pumpkins, and corn for them. We got our vegetables from the garden and also got some grain as payment for working for the commune.

There was a market six miles away where we would go to buy pigs. For chickens, we had to go all the way to Sathmar. Vegetables we used to grow ourselves. For onions, every September 14th I went about twelve miles over the mountain on the day when there was a special market. I used to get maybe ten or twelve braids of onions—as many as I could lay over my shoulder, and then walk home.

The Collective Farms

A lot of the *Schwaben* joined the commune to get their houses back. The commune was smart. They knew the *Schwaben* were hard workers. The Romanians used to leave the oxen in the barn and not go to work. They'd just not do things. The commune really appreciated the *Schwaben*; otherwise, it couldn't have survived. On the commune we had cattle, pigs, sheep, oxen, and a few horses. Oxen were used for most of the work. For harvesting we still used the scythe.

In 1955, we learned for the first time that our father was alive in Germany, and so my brother was able to go to school for an apprenticeship. It worked this way: We had an uncle working on a commune, a blacksmith, so he was earning money and could help us. My father in Germany would send money to the uncle's family in Austria in exchange for the uncle's paying for my brother to learn being a bookkeeper. In 1957, he became bookkeeper on the commune in Scheindorf. So everything began to get better. My sister used to help with babysitting, and she supported herself. My grandmother had died in 1952, so there was only my mother and me.

I finished school when I was fifteen years old. My mother couldn't send me to learn a trade. She said, "Your older brother is going, and I can't afford to send you." So I worked in the vineyard for a year or two. I'd hoe, prune, tie up the vines, spray, then hoe again. It was a state farm made up of only the German farms. The Romanians were able to keep their own vineyards.

Starting when I was seventeen, I worked as an oxen driver for the commune, for four or five years altogether. I used to call all the oxen by their names and tell them to go *'cha'* or *'hois'*—that's Swabian for right or left.

There was always some work for the oxen. In the springtime, we would get loads of bushes and put them in piles for fence-making. We also spread manure. There were big barns with cattle, horses, sheep, and we would take wagonloads of manure out to the fields. We used to plow with the oxen, too. Then there was hay time, and so it went all year long. Oxen were used for almost everything. The three or four horses we had on the commune were used to pull the carriage to the city.

The commune figured your work according to norms. For hauling manure with a wagon and oxen, the norm might equal three loads in a day. They were even weighing the loads to make sure people weren't cheating. Sometimes you made one-and-a-quarter or one-and-a- half norms a day, more than was expected in a day.

Twice a year they added it up so you could be paid.

But first the commune had to calculate the costs—how much the machinery from the state cost, how much for the seeds, the feed for the animals, and so on. The commune had to pay grain to the state to cover those costs. The rest was ours. They would add up how many norms everybody in the commune worked and then figure there was so much grain for each norm. What you got paid would depend on how good the harvest was and also on the costs paid to the state. That's how we got our grain. Some years, the commune raised sunflower seeds or hay, and we got some of that, too.

Of course, you weren't independent on the commune. You had to do what they said. Each day, you had to ask for a job, and then they told you they needed this or that done. It was like a factory. The foreman would also mark out the fields of corn or sunflowers or potatoes. He would tie rags to sticks to mark off maybe an acre. Your family would take care of this from the spring to the harvest time–the planting, the hoeing, and so on. With this system, the foreman would know who was responsible if the work wasn't done right, who to penalize. On the wheat and the hay, it was different. They just needed planting and harvesting, so it was up to the people how much they wanted to do, how much they would plant or harvest. After you worked, the foreman measured the area and calculated how many norms it was.

When the state set up the collective farms, they took land from everybody, *Schwaben* and Romanians. But Romanian people got all the animals and wagons and other things. They had so much, but they lost them, so they had to join the commune. Instead, the *Schwaben* were growing more and more things at home and getting better and better off. First, they would buy a calf, then a second, next a cow or two, and even a wagon. See, the *Schwaben* were saving and working harder than the Romanians.

America

My father was able to leave Germany for America in 1956. After six years, he was able to start trying to bring us over. But it took three more years, until 1965. We were twice rejected, but America finally consented that families could be together. Since I was unmarried, I could come over as part of my mother's family. My brother couldn't come since he was already married, and so was my sister.

After I came over, the only work I could find was building houses. I worked at that for close to a month. It was very hard, and I was weak and thin when I came from the other side. I was only 130 pounds, and I had to carry heavy lumber. I couldn't do it. I said, 'Father, if you don't get me another job, send me back to the other side.' So my father got me a job where he worked in a sheet metal shop, and I've been there ever since. I learned welding, and I make metal frames and cabinets. I weld all kinds of metal, like aluminum and stainless steel.

I met my wife at a dance at the *Sathmar Verein* [Sathmar social club]. She left Romania as a six-month-old child with the wagon train that got to Austria near the end of the war. In 1955, she left Austria and came to America as a eleven-year-old.

So we started our family, three children in three years. It was rough at first, living in a small apartment for two years. Then we got a loan from our parents, and we bought an old house in Paterson, New Jersey. Two years later, we moved to Clifton where the neighborhood is better, the schools are better.

I like America. You can be independent here and say nothing, just go to work and take care of your family and yard. Maybe once or twice a year we go out; the rest of the time is spent at home. We are taking care of the family and saving what we can.

I am not into politics. Well, the government is OK, but I'm not for other people getting welfare money for not working. Well, every country has something wrong. But otherwise, for working people, America is the best country.

12: THE CHILDREN OF THE IMMIGRANTS

The difficulties of those who escaped to America sometimes continued for their children. The immigrants usually continued to speak German at home, and it often became the first language of their children.

Children are quick to adapt, and they eventually learned English and seemed quite American. However, there is often some carryover of the immigrant mentality. For the children of the Swabian immigrants, individualism and conscientiousness, even stubbornness, are part of their cultural heritage.

Rudy Steinthal's father, Werner, had to leave Swabia because he wasn't Jewish enough. One of Werner's grandfathers had been baptized Christian at six months. If this ancestor had been circumcised at birth according to Jewish custom, the 1935 Nazi race law would have allowed Werner to marry Lotte, a full-blooded Jewess. But there was no record of a circumcision. Lotte and Werner couldn't marry in Germany, so they left and eventually settled in the Bronx in a Jewish community, where Rudy was born at the end of 1936.

Rudy Steinthal had an uncle and aunt who were both doctors, and, despite their problematic parent, the Nazis considered them full Jewish, so they were prevented from practicing as doctors. The Nazis were not consistent in certifying Jewishness, in this case probably because they wanted to eliminate the two from competing with "Aryan" doctors.

Language Trauma

Rudy Steinthal's childhood years coincided with the beginning of World War II, when a German heritage could create difficulties in America. He grew up speaking German with his parents and his maternal grandparents, who had also left Germany in 1941. After World War II broke out, the family tried to switch to speaking English with Rudy. But the kids in the all-Jewish neighborhood (mostly Eastern European Jews) continued to call him "Kraut" or "Nazi." He was furious. Finally Rudy decided, "I'm never going to say another word of German."

In 1942, the family moved to a small Connecticut town in order to get away from the anti-German discrimination, but there they suffered anti-Semitic discrimination. An old lady once saw Lotte Steinthal going into one of the Jewish shops in town. The woman asked, "You're not shopping with those dirty Jews, are you?" Steinthal told her, "What's worse, I'm a dirty Jew myself."

The FBI investigated Lotte Steinthal's father after he was reported speaking German on the street with his wife. The FBI inquired at Werner Steinthal's office, "Why does your father-in-law speak German?" Steinthal explained: "The man is seventy five years old. How can you expect him to speak English after only one year here?" The family was forced to give up speaking German.

One day in 1942, when Rudy Steinthal was six, the FBI came to confiscate the family's camera and address book. This happened to all German aliens during World War II. Rudy had his toys in a little cabinet, so he blocked access and told the agents, "You can't go in there. I'm an American citizen."

When Rudy was eight, his mother visited an old lady who spoke only German. Rudy couldn't understand his mother and her friend. He was furious. He repeated every German word they spoke, but he didn't know what the words meant. He had forgotten German completely in the two years since he'd vowed never again to have anything to do with it.

An Easy Americanization

Some children of immigrants were able to assimilate in less traumatic ways. Lily Schlimmeyer, born in 1929, had time before World War II to drop her German identification. She initially grew up in Bay Ridge, Brooklyn, where there were many Germans. She went to German Sunday school classes and was fluent in German by five or six. Then her parents moved to Jersey City to be closer to her father's job. She recalled, "It was very American there and also by our bungalow in the mountains where we spent every summer." Her peers were almost wholly American, not German. "I belonged to lots of clubs in high school, and also through the church I met lots of different people."

She eventually married the son of Italian immigrants. "His parents didn't Americanize like my parents because they lived in a small town that was almost completely Italian." In contrast, Lily's mother (Lena Schlimmeyer from Chapter 1) had become fluent in English from working as a maid in American households. There was no stigma among German immigrants if a woman worked outside the home as there was for Italians and other more traditional immigrant groups.[68]

A Conservative German American

Another child of immigrants, Marie Wiesenmayer (daughter of Bob Wiesenmayer in Chapter 1) was born in 1943. She was the only child of two 1920s immigrants who held lifelong memberships in several German social clubs. Survey data show that only two percent of all German immigrants were members of a German social organization. These people often centered their lives on the activities of other German immigrants. Marie followed her parents' lead and also joined several German clubs, where she eventually met her second husband.

While Wiesenmayer grew up with German culture all around her, she worked at being American. She made a point of observing American children. "My parents ate the German way, with the knife and fork in the wrong hands. I was always nervous, because I didn't learn at home what other kids did. I felt very out of it. I had to learn American etiquette and how to dress like other kids, not in German ways. In the seventh grade, when I started to wear a bra, my mother wanted me to wear an undershirt with it, so I'd be warm. Another thing I had to learn is that earthy German humor is inappropriate for most Americans. I had to learn a lot of things about being American that my parents couldn't teach me.

"My parents were strict. They didn't allow me to go to anything other than a church function or a school function My best girlfriend's parents were German, too, and also strict. So we went to a lot of functions together.

"I always wondered how I was different. I suppose it was because I was the only kid in the neighborhood with two foreign parents. It was a German area, but the kids were second- and third-generation already.

"The big change for me was when I got married, to a Catholic who had converted to Judaism. At that point I had too many questions about the divinity of Christ. I believed Christ was a great philosopher, if you look into his words and not the interpretation of his words by some people. He said things like 'You are the son of God...' He did not put himself on a pedestal.

"I go to church, but I won't take communion. I think it's hypocritical. I don't think you need a wafer and a drink of wine in order to be cleansed of your sins, and I just don't think stuff like that matters to God. Why should anybody be cleansed? God knows if you did something wrong or not. I think sins are between me and my maker, not me and the minister. I also don't believe in crosses. If somebody whose philosophy you appreciate was murdered by a hacksaw, would you worship a hacksaw?

"I do pray, I meditate, I read the Bible, and I read other inspirational things. I financially support the church, but I really prefer not to attend. I support the church because the opportunities I had available there as a child–to sing in the choir, be in plays, go to square dances–should be available to other kids if they want to partake.

"The denomination of my church is the United Church of Christ, a very liberal church. I was totally incensed when they started to have altar boys dressed in vestments, with candles and all that. Up until recently there were few dogmas. There was none of the 'if you've done this you're saved, and if you've done that you've sinned.' I think we were fortunate to have excellent Bible readings and then discussions. The minister would go over what each individual thought the reading meant, and then you could make up your mind. Nobody ever said this is the way it is because I'm telling you the way it is."

After her parents died, Wiesenmayer was able to set her own course in earnest. One time, Wiesenmayer went to a Scottish festival, and she enjoyed seeing the various demonstrations, including sheep herding, bagpiping, and tossing the caber. She compared it with the typical German festival where "the focus is beer, and there is an oom-pa-pa band, which you have to be drunk to enjoy. It's a shame Germans can't present a more positive picture of their culture than beer, beer, and more beer." She stopped volunteering at the local German festivals, even though it was expected of her as the child of German club members. The boozy festivals embarrassed her.

However, Wiesenmayer continued to be German, specifically Swabian, in her mentality, such as valuing conscientiousness. It also appeared in her choice of friends and her politics. She grew up in a neighborhood where perhaps half of the people were German, and she continued being friends with people from that neighborhood even after she moved away. She felt more comfortable with friends who had a German heritage, because they were "sensible" people. And whatever they did, "they did a good job." Like her, they couldn't leave work until they finished what they set out to do. When she hired a craftsman to work on her house, she looked for someone with a German name.

She got a job working for a rehabilitation organization that works with people with mild handicaps. "I am a patient person," she explains. She organizes the work of the clients, does public relations, and writes grant proposals. She prides herself on her Germanic ability to be organized.

Wiesenmayer's preference for Germans applied when she voted. "My town here now is run by conservative Republican Germans. The taxes are the lowest around, and yet the garbage is picked up and the streets swept. Where I grew up and where I rent out my old house, the Germans aren't in power. There, I had to beg and beg just to get a tree planted out by the sidewalk. Recently, a scandal came out where the garbage crews were working only two hours a day while they were collecting the highest pay around. That's not likely to happen in my town."

For a long time, Wiesenmayer saw her German background as a central part of her identity. When she met people, she made a point of telling them her name was German and translating its meaning into English. She was proud of being German. Having a German background has "always been a plus," she says. Now she is outwardly American in most respects. However, she is still German in her social relations and attitudes.

Confusions

Another child of immigrants, Ken Ludwig, was born in New York City in 1944. Growing up in two cultures was hard. Ludwig's immigrant parents wanted him to fit in as American, but they didn't know how to help him do that. They told him to do whatever he was told in school and church. "That didn't always feel right to me," he recalled, "because it wasn't always compatible with what my parents emphasized."

The children of the Swabian immigrants eventually replaced much of the culture of their parents with American ways. They didn't want to eat a sandwich with blood sausage or tongue when other kids were eating peanut butter, or to say "Oma" when nobody understood it meant "Grandma," or participate in the youth activities of the German club or listen to "oom-pa-pa" music. It would be embarrassing to be seen going to such a club wearing leather short pants.

These children mostly retained only what sociologists call "symbolic" culture, such as ethnic foods eaten during holidays.[69, 70] Even that died out in time. Reginald Finkbeiner and his wife, Georgia, are fourth-generation Swabian and Ukrainian, respectively, living in a small town. They tried to maintain symbols of their heritage like the German advent calendar and Ukrainian Easter eggs, but after a while these faded away. "We know about them, but we don't do them every year anymore," Reginald said. "Now our son doesn't do anything, but we hope to pass on some traditions to his two children."

The children and grandchildren of immigrants often exercise their American freedom to choose their own mates. Census data show about two-thirds of German Americans have mixed, ethnically diverse backgrounds as a result of marriages between Germans and British, Irish, Italians, or others.

The children of such marriages may prefer one heritage and ignore the other. For example, Sharon Wiel, with one German parent and the other Anglo and Irish, feels closest to her Irish heritage. Her view of Germans is that "they're always either at your feet or at your throat."

Mentality

What often does persist in the children of immigrants and even in generations beyond is mentality and character: values and attitudes such as a focus on spirituality and individual freedom, conscientiousness, and frugality, sometimes in contrast to the American way.

Individualism can persist in the children of immigrants who are otherwise very "American." Rudy Steinthal, whom we met earlier, is a loner and introvert. He has just a couple of close friends. He doesn't care for parties, going out at night, or entertaining company. He'd rather be home: "Maybe I'll read a book or watch television." Steinthal is also a private person like his parents and other Germans. "I don't open up until I know you. I sort of hold back until then."

Often being a loner is expressed by working with machinery and other things instead of people. Steinthal joined the Air National Guard when he was seventeen and subsequently worked with airplanes. He got a multi-engine license, so "I'm qualified to sit in the extra seats behind the captain on a Boeing 747."

Initially Steinthal worked for an airline in load control. "An airplane can weigh just so much at takeoff, and it can't be too tail-heavy or nose-heavy. You have to know how the passenger load is developing, and also make sure the cargo, baggage, and fuel are loaded properly. Each airplane is a little different, and you also have to make sure the airplane is fueled just right for the flight and weather conditions." Steinthal found the job very satisfying because he was essentially his own boss.

Subsequently, Steinthal managed operations at a small airport, where he also enjoyed a great deal of autonomy. "I'm happy in a job where I'm left alone, working on my own, no subordinates or supervisors. Give me a job, let me do it my way, and don't bother me. I don't like subordinates because I'm too much of a perfectionist. I do not have patience."

Lily Schlimmeyer, like many children of Swabians, had a lot of independence as a teen. She remembered going in her early high school years to visit a cousin in Bay Ridge, taking the trolley, the Hudson tube, two subways, and walking to his house, all by herself. Nor did her parents help with her schoolwork; they were both working. Often unsupervised, she was free to craft her own individual life.

She was a housewife all of her married life, even after her children left home. She never looked for work. She didn't feel the need to get out of the home and be with people. Like Rudy Steinthal, she was comfortable being a loner. "I only socialized here [in suburban Washington, D.C.] if it was someone with whom I had a common interest. I never started with the coffee klatch. First of all, you should know somebody before you get involved. I've seen people that have gotten close to others, and then they've gotten angry and had fights. I always went slow and careful with friends and neighbors. I wanted to know somebody, and I didn't want this running in and out of each other's houses. I wanted to control it."

Part of Schlimmeyer's individualism was her love of do-it-yourself projects. "I laid the kitchen floor, and I've even done a little brickwork. At my mother's cottage, I did the two-by-fours and paneling in the living room and bathroom. I'm not real good with a saw. But it's the *desire* that makes you handy. If you have that desire, then you can learn by observing someone else or by getting a book, like one I just got on upholstering furniture." Even though her husband earned good money as an advertising executive, she kept at these projects, such as extensive landscaping and reupholstering the furniture.

Ken Ludwig was similarly very much a Swabian individual. He recalled his childhood as "a continual fight for survival as an individual and preservation of self." He saw authorities like the pastor, teachers, and parents as "trying to damage me and turn me into something I'm not." He particularly revolted against religious authority when he discovered the hypocrisy of a pastor, preaching peace but supporting the Vietnam War.

Ludwig's jobs over the years were ones where he could be independent and also help others become independent. His first job was as a counselor at a camp for disturbed kids, where he used unstructured situations to teach them how to find the inner resources to deal with their feelings. He has also worked as a craftsman repairing and refinishing furniture, fixing up a house and selling it, raising rabbits on his own farm in Nova Scotia, advising small farmers as a county extension agent, and most recently, teaching entrepreneurship to engineering students in college.

Conscientiousness

The children of the immigrants were conscientious like their parents. Rudy Steinthal had the Protestant work ethic: "Even if I'm not happy with my employer, as long as he's my employer, I do my very best for him. I'd rather quit instead of not doing a good job. I've got to do a proper job, or I don't feel right."

Steinthal was also frugal. "I rebuilt my washing machine three times—the switches, programmer, everything but the motor. Why should I call a repairman?" He does almost all the repair work on his car, including the brakes. When his wife didn't drive, he did the grocery shopping. "I usually bought the cheapest brand I could find. I got twice as much food as she did for the same amount of money. I'm not a fussy eater. I can get by on anything that's on sale. I'm also quite thrifty in that I cannot tolerate wasted food or wasted anything. I'll eat things up rather than let them go to waste."

Lily Schlimmeyer also was thrifty even though her husband earned a good income. Her mother taught her how to shop, "buying cheap but smart." She would wear a blouse from Kmart, because "some things have classic lines, and you can hardly tell the difference in price. Of course, on tailored things, people can see if it's cheap. So you pay more, but buy it on sale at the end of the season." She also did a lot of sewing and mending. "I don't throw away clothing that needs to be fixed. I alter. I buy things that are the wrong size and cut them down and alter them."

She learned from her mother to buy reduced fruit that might have a few soft spots that could be cut out. "I am definitely more thrifty than my Italian husband. Very seldom do I pay regular prices."

Spirituality

The children of Swabian immigrants often have strong spiritual feelings expressed outside of organized religion. Steinthal said: "I've gone my own way with religion." He attended services at the temple where his Boy Scout troop met and also at a nearby Dutch Reformed church. He decided he liked the latter more. As a youth, he also enjoyed the Christian services at summer camp because they were outside on a hill: "When the Bible says you should worship in the Lord's house, that's really the whole outdoors."

He felt that following the Ten Commandments was key, in

contrast to the "people who mouth the words in the service and then do their own thing. The way you live says what your religion is. I feel my beliefs are my own, and I don't have to share them with anyone. I can keep them to myself. I don't think going to a church makes you religious. It might help some people, but I don't think it's really required."

Schlimmeyer didn't strike out to find her own religious path, but she did jettison her Lutheran upbringing. Despite the strong opposition of her parents to marrying a Catholic, she accepted his faith. "In order to marry, I had to talk to the priest and get permission from different people. Then I had to promise to raise the children as Catholics. Then we could marry in the church in front of the altar. I converted to Catholicism later. It was no big deal.

"I don't believe that the people who are born Protestant or in other religions are not going to go to heaven. I believe you've got to live a good life and be good to people. Some people are very religious, but they don't do [good things] for other people. For example, my mother-in-law is very religious and a very good woman, but only within the family." Ludwig reveals his spiritual side when he admits, "Trees and the power in a seed impress and wonder me. I don't require more than a sense of my insignificance in relation to these things." In this religious expression he echoes Swabian Albert Einstein who insisted, "The most beautiful thing we can experience is the sense of the mysterious."

The children of Swabian immigrants find many ways to express their conscientiousness. Dorothy Bucher, a police department clerk in suburban Washington, D.C., was very troubled about a boy her teenaged daughter was dating. So she peeked at the computerized system at work to see if he had any police record.

There is some evidence that basic character traits such as conscientiousness and independent-mindedness can persist for several generations. Psychologists say that roughly half of the variation in such basic personality traits is controlled by genetics. Parents and grandparents can also guide the development of character by supervising a child's friends or selecting a particular kind of community to live in.[71]

Ludwig sees his son, the grandson of immigrants, as "...independent, strong-willed, stubborn. He has high standards and a strong work ethic. He's got that from me and from my parents." But his son thinks of it as his personal character, not as being connected to his German heritage.

Technical Interests

Ana Hurm exemplifies how German traits can persist over several generations, even though her Latina heritage is more recent and stronger. She has a slight accent. On visits to Mexico, people think she was born in Veracruz like her mother, but she feels more at home in Chicago, her birthplace.

Hurm's surname goes back to a great-grandfather who came to America from Swabia. But that's her only apparent Swabian influence. Her father, John, felt he had lost whatever foreign culture his immigrant grandfather had passed on. John's father married a Southerner, a teacher, who helped him eliminate his German accent.

As a child, John Hurm left the German settlement around Jasper, Indiana, and moved across the Ohio River to Kentucky, where he grew up among southerners with Anglo-Saxon forebearers. He had to turn to genealogy to illuminate his German and Swabian connections.

Early in life, Hurm did manual labor, hauling bricks and working a jackhammer. He moved to Chicago in 1954 and started working as a shipping clerk and then took other similar jobs. He went to school to learn to work IBM machines, but at the end he wasn't hired because he was too old, thirty-two. He went to work for Bally Manufacturing, first assembling pinball machines, then being a tester and finally a troubleshooter for electrical and mechanical problems in the pinball machines. Hurm recalled, "Many times my boss asked me if I knew how to do this job or that job." His answer was often, "No, but I can learn it."

Ana Hurm is technically inclined, too. Her college major was communications, but she was not interested in performing but rather in operating the equipment. This interest in technical matters is a family tradition on her father's side.

Neither Ana Hurm nor John Hurm nor his father were technical wizards. They share an attitude that technical and mechanical things are interesting and they have a "can-do" attitude. Surveys show that German Americans are overrepresented in technical occupations for at least their first three generations in America.[72]

While the customs of Ana Hurm's German forbearers have died out, a little of the psychology apparently still remains. But as she sees it, her interest in mechanical things is just part of her personality.

Maintaining Cultural Diversity

Hurm retains much of her mother's Mexican culture. In contrast, the children and grandchildren of German immigrants have assimilated so quickly that some now regret their loss of ethnic heritage. It now can be a desirable part of America's "diversity."

Keith Graves is the child of a German Jew and an American with a Scots background. He thinks of himself as "seventy percent Anglo," with the rest German.

"I'm quite willing to be Jewish," he notes, "but German Jews, I understand, always considered themselves German first, then Jewish. So I've probably been influenced somewhat by German culture. While I might tell people I have some German Jewish background, it's probably German."

But his ethnic background isn't important to him. He identifies with the Quakers as a liberal, a pacifist, and as a socially concerned person. Nor does his ethnicity impact on everyday life. His name is not Jewish or German—and he doesn't make a point of telling people he is German or Jewish.

He has maintained little of his mother's particular Swabian heritage. He didn't learn German. His ethnicity is only symbolic, consisting mainly of eating ethnic foods. From his grandparents he learned about German wines, although he doesn't like them. He appreciates German foods like *Sauerbraten* and *Spaetzle* noodles but doesn't eat them because they're so "heavy." He indulges more in his mother's Christmas baking, *Stollen* bread and *Springerle* anise cookies, and he'd like to pass on that part of his heritage to his children. When they get older, he'd also like to foster in them a love of German beer, but that's about the extent of Graves' German heritage.

Graves is aware that losing your ethnic heritage has a cost. "Ethnicity is fun, it's colorful. It's the spice in a meal. I don't want it to disappear from our lives, and I hope people will be more tolerant of the ethnicity that exists. I'd be depressed if America became nothing but McDonald's.

"People should be allowed to retain their cultures. I wouldn't want the 1950s to come back, where American white bread was the ideal, and descendants of immigrants were not allowed to retain their cultures. A lot was lost when people were forced to assimilate. You know, maybe Spanish should be made one of the official languages in America."

Immigrants' customs make America a more colorful, nicer place to live—not just wearing green on St. Patrick's Day or eating brats at a German festival, but being able to follow the Tibetan devotees of the Buddha or earn a Black Belt in Korean Tae Kwon Do. Ethnic diversity enriches lives. It gives people more choices.

German Contributions

Nineteenth-century German Americans brought elements of cultural diversity to America that have since become so commonplace they are no longer considered foreign. They fought against puritanical Yankees for the right to drink alcohol, and they finally won after nearly a century of conflict. They also brought the custom of music and fun on Sunday afternoons—a time that the Yankees felt should be solemn and quiet. Kindergarten, Christmas with a tree and gifts, and the Easter Bunny are all German contributions that are now seen as American as apple pie.[1, 73]

Other German customs, such as eating blood sausage or pig's feet, have largely died out. The German language is hardly ever heard in America, despite the presence of fifty million German Americans, but German Americans provide important elements of cultural diversity today through their values and attitudes.

The German religious sects of Pennsylvania and other nearby states are a vivid example. The Amish and Mennonites are not important because they speak German, use horses to plow, or wear plain black clothing. It's their beliefs in material simplicity and the importance of the spiritual as well as their emphasis on frugality and family closeness that have an impact. Their distinctive lifestyle can remind other Americans that they don't have to "keep up with the Joneses." The Amish also practiced conservation and environmental protection long before other Americans were aware of these issues.

Most descendants of German immigrants do not use Amish

farm methods or wear Amish clothing, but some do exemplify the Amish belief in living a relatively simple and frugal life.

Diversity can make America a more interesting and effective country. There is more to diversity than racial differences. More important than skin color is the psychology of individuals. The frugality and conscientiousness of the Amish can be a complement to other Americans who are free-spirited and willing to take risks. Studies show that America has an extrovert culture, so German introverts who can work by themselves can complement other Americans who are extroverts. America needs both.

13: WALTER LUIKART'S STORY

Luikart (1926-2011) practiced psychiatry in Manhattan for many years. Despite the usual German preference for privacy, he gave me a detailed portrait of his mentality.

****

Background
Back in the 1920s when my father came over, it was understood that if you were serious enough to have a relationship with a woman, and you got her pregnant, you would marry her. Well, my mother found out she was pregnant. In the meantime, my father had gone on to Philadelphia, and there he found another woman, the owner's daughter at the butcher shop where he worked, and she wanted to marry him. My mother went down to Philadelphia and confronted him, and they got married and came back to New York City to live. That's how I appeared on the scene.

My father came from a very small village south of Stuttgart, near Kirchheim on the Teck, where the Swabian Alps begin. Because the family farm wasn't big enough, he and the other middle boy were both apprenticed out. The oldest one of the four boys eventually got the farm, while the youngest boy got money to buy his own farm. The two middle boys sort of got the short end of the stick.

Food was always scarce while they were growing up even though it was a farm. The best food was sold. They never got an egg unless they stole it. But during the First World War they were able to make some money when people came out from the cities to buy food that was rationed. When he was a teenager, my father was a black marketer, leading cattle over the mountains at night down to a hotel where he was paid handsomely. By the end of the war he had enough money to buy one of the best hotels in Stuttgart, but the economy collapsed, and the money was worthless.

So he went to New York City, where he met my mother. She came from Stuttgart and had also been sent away by her parents. Her father worked in a shoe factory, and there were half a dozen kids. She had no skills; she'd only worked in a cigarette factory for a while. In America she worked as a maid.

Standards

The family is very important to Swabians, so if there is an extramarital affair the family may not break up, unless it comes into the open and exposes one or the other to ridicule. Otherwise a partner doesn't want to know about it, since the family is more important.

The worst thing that could happen to you was that you would be made a fool of in public or look disgraceful in some way. Death doesn't hold a touch of fear for me. And physical pain or discomfort I can handle. But to be trotted out in public in some disgraceful way would be absolutely terrifying for me.

It has a lot to do with a sense of privacy you grow up with. My house, for example, should be private. My wife keeps it an open place and doesn't care how it looks. My background tells me it should be completely locked up, curtains on all the windows.

I have a real sense of "inside" against the "outside." There are layers and layers. There's an inner you. Then comes the family with the home, very separate from the street. If you go out somewhere, you make a special effort to get dressed. Then there's the neighbors and immediate outside, and beyond that, there's politics, the police, and the social order, all things that are totally foreign. You stay away from them as much as you can.

We never had strangers come to visit when I was growing up, just relatives and close friends who were from the Other Side. No Americans. When I brought another kid home, it was extremely awkward. Now, I'm that way still.

My parents didn't live in German sections. They were independent and moved away. We lived mostly in Jewish neighborhoods because my parents appreciated that there was good food and good merchandise in the stores. My impression is that, prior to the Nazis taking power in Germany, the Germans who immigrated to this country didn't have any anti-Semitic feelings.

The Authorities

I have a very deep suspicion of religion and of religious folks. I react very strongly to the ritualistic aspect. When I was preparing for my confirmation, the pastor asked me about the commandment, "Thou shalt not kill." When is it permissible to kill? I knew the answer he wanted, so I gave it to him: "Well, when the government tells you it's alright to kill, then it's OK." He was so enthusiastic and so overjoyed that one of his students would know that. I thought to myself, "you goddamn hypocrite." At that moment I broke any real connection I had with the church. I went through the confirmation, but after that I was finished with religion.

I went for a couple of weeks to the summer camp run by the *Bund* [German American Nazis]. It was the same thing, just worse. They were militaristic and macho, marching around all the time. All those Germans lined up in formations. When my father found out, he hauled me home.

I didn't find the Boy Scouts appealing either. They had the same thing: celebrating false values. It was not in my nature to submit to those things. I tried the Boy Scouts, the *Bund*, and the Lutheran Church, and I quit all three organizations.

I volunteered for the Navy in 1944, and I got in trouble there because I couldn't say "Yes, sir." They would call out the roll, a hundred names. Everybody would say "Yes, sir," and I'd say "Yes."

Becoming a Doctor

After the Navy, I went to college. Because of my background I didn't know what options were open to me. I knew butchers, and I also knew doctors—my own pediatrician, a Jewish man who had been trained in Heidelberg, a very good man. I sort of identified with him, and my parents did too. So it was being a butcher or a doctor!

I went into medicine hoping I would do some biological research. Once I got into it, research became less appealing. It became clearer to me that I could not work for anyone or become part of an organization. So I went into practicing medicine, and, eventually, in order to separate myself from some structure, I became a psychiatrist. Now I do psychotherapy. I'm totally independent in my practice. I started very slowly, built it up from patient referrals–not agency referrals, just my own patients' word-of-mouth to their relatives or friends or whatever. I'm totally unassociated with any organization.

I help people to cope. A lot of my patients have an artistic potential, but they grew up where this potential was responded to in a way detrimental to the development of it. They need someone to reinforce and support them against all the conventional standards. I'll recognize the artistic potential and help them develop it.

Swabians and the War

The Swabians over here, including my parents, were emotionally pro-German during the Second World War. They felt that Germany had some laws, some rights for the individual. They only knew pre-Nazi Germany. They weren't in touch with the ultimate truth of the Nazi system. And they could not recognize Nazis as they were described in the news media here. They assumed that the propaganda put out about the Nazis was equivalent to what was put out in the First World War–German soldiers eating Belgian children, and so on.

If the Germans achieved a victory in Russia and moved ahead a couple of hundred miles, they would get some gratification from that: "That's what Germans do." At the same time, they were still very much American. Like other Americans, they worked very hard for the war cause. They worked like fiends. They were definitely Americanized and liked living here.

So there was a split in their thinking. They had a positive emotional response to Germany, to the idea of Germany. It must be a good place, good things were going on–but on the other hand, they identified with America as a good place to make a living, to be free and independent. Whatever the German army achieved was a sort of expression of what they, as hardworking Germans, were achieving over here.

It wasn't until my parents went back to Germany that they finally understood what Nazis were all about. They had to go to the concentration camp and they had to speak to their own people to be convinced that Nazism was beastly. They learned what had happened to relatives, to their family doctors, and so on. They finally were convinced that the propaganda was true, and they were very, very ashamed.

The relatives in Germany that I've asked about the Holocaust only had a vague idea of it at the time. Like an uncle, for example, who happened on a freight train loaded with people who were obviously going to die in the cold. He was told by a guard to forget what he saw.

I get the impression that, in the beginning, some relatives had a certain pride about being anti-Nazi. But once the war started, they wanted to help win the war. They were very pro-German, whether it was Nazi or not. They did not find it possible to distinguish between a Nazi regime and the goal of winning the war till the very end or even after the end of the war.

Anti-Semitism

The anti-Semitism I did find among my relatives over in Germany was in people who felt downtrodden, left out, or left behind. They were the less successful, the less self-confident. The more confident family members were Marxists or Social Democrats. Now there aren't many Jews over there, so the less successful people are blaming the Catholics.

It all goes back to the extremely high standards that are part of the culture. If someone is inadequate, they have to find an explanation, but instead of blaming themselves or attacking the source of the standards, they blamed the Jews.

My uncle, my father's brother, was a highly intelligent person, but his father told him he was a failure in terms of the father's standards. The father was very hostile and brutalized him—physically and in other ways, and my uncle couldn't confront that hostility. He was coerced by fear into identifying with his father, to believe in him and what he said. He accepted that he himself was to blame for his failure, and then he shifted the blame onto the Jews.

My own father handled the same problem by confronting his father and the authority that was putting him in the position of being a failure. My father didn't blame himself for coming up short, and he didn't blame the Jews. He just rejected the standards. He told his father to go to hell.

It's not that German fathers are brutal. It's the high standards, and it's the lack of forgiveness in the culture. It is so closed in, it leaves the individual so little room to maneuver. Everything has to go in such narrow channels.

Some cultures, like in Latin America, may have high standards, but if someone doesn't do the job on time, there is forgiveness. It must have to do with the Catholicism there. Nobody really expects you to achieve all the great things you dream.

In fact, the German nation became Nazi at a time of great failure. The Germans were defeated in war and also economically. They had just recently, at the end of the nineteenth century, come together and developed this sense of being one people. They thought of themselves as being number one in a lot of ways, and then there was this sudden sense of failing and falling way down.

My Germaness

I grew up German, I spoke Swabian at home, and I learned regular [High] German, including reading, at a *Turnverein* school in New York. So I was pretty German until the fourth or fifth grade. Then I remember a school program where they asked all the children what their parents' origins were. First, the teacher asked about my father, so I had to say "Germany." Then my mother—"Germany" again. The whole class got very quiet. They just stopped talking.

After that, the Jewish kids took out on me what was happening in Europe. About 90 percent of the kids were Jewish, 10 percent non-Jewish, and maybe only 1 percent German. They'd call me "Nazi, Nazi," so I was forced to be a German and fight back. I had to fight every day. In junior high school, in 1938, most of the kids left me feeling that I was anti-American, a German. It was easy for them to take out all their frustrations on me. But in the Bronx High School of Science, they made a point of not discriminating on account of race or religion. It was all on the basis of what you could achieve.

When I was finishing high school, in 1943-44, we lived in Yorkville, on 86th Street [a German area of Manhattan]. We used to hear screams and yelling at night. Of course, it was the FBI raiding apartments, separating the adults from the children and questioning them about Nazis.

Oh, if I had been in Germany, given my personality, I think I would have been a Nazi. Hitler was going to free all the workers from the industrialists, that's why it was a National Socialist party, or at least that was the propaganda. I would have been a Nazi for a while anyway–not forever. Even in the United States, being under attack as a Nazi, it took me a while to catch on to what it meant–

being told what to do, what to think. Over there, either I would have been shot very quickly or I might have gone along with it, up to a point, and then gotten into the war, and gone along with the fighting, because when you're in the service, you have to fight to save your neck.

14: RUTH GOLDSTEIN'S STORY

Goldstein's ancestry in the small towns of Swabia goes back at least to 1820. Her parents fled Germany for New York City in 1939. Ruth carries their Swabian individualism, frugality, and religious independence.

****

I married "out."[74] I married to escape my parents and their German Jewish friends. My husband is "Standard American Jewish." Two of his grandparents were of Polish Jewish descent and the other two, Russian Jewish. Those are different from each other, but not as different as both are from German Jewish.

German Jews often look down on Jews from the East, and none of my parents' generation married an Eastern European Jew. None. How could they marry a Yiddish-speaking Jew?

In looking for a mate, I looked for someone different from my brothers and father. They are go-getters. They do things. My father is a definite Type A person. None of his friends just sit. They're always purposeful, even in recreation. I'm like them. I didn't want more by marrying a spouse like that, too.

Carrying on Some Customs

I guess I still follow my parents in a lot of ways. The foods we eat are the same—the crepe soup, for example, and the *Spätzle* dumplings. I used to have a machine to make them, but my family said they didn't taste like my mother's. So I went back to the old way of making them with the board and the knife. Once a year in the winter, I make *Hutzelbrot* [fruit bread] from figs, prunes, and nuts. And I also make *rüble* from flour, eggs, and grease, which you grate and cook in a soup, and lots of other things that I learned from my mother.

I save things like my parents, too. You never know when they'll come in handy. But I do have a box for certain kinds of clutter, and when it gets full I throw things out to make room for more clutter. That's how my husband has influenced me. Otherwise I would keep everything, like things that don't work anymore but which I might fix, old materials that I might have a use for some time, or a book that I might just read again. I should say we have a lot less stuff than anybody else in the family. My father is constantly saving every screw, nut, and bolt, and he carefully catalogs them. And he can find all of them!

My big thing is independence. I can't stand it if somebody is going to tell me what to do, if I have to do the same job every day, if I'm completely obligated to somebody else, or if somebody else is making my schedule. I'd feel like the walls are closing in. I've got to be free. I used to work for a lawyer, but I wrote up things on my own. Just tell me generally what you want, I'll write it up, and you revise it. That's fine. I just can't work from direct orders.

Differences

I'm different from my parents, who require routine, tradition, and precedent. For example, they have a definite routine at mealtimes, and even their cup of coffee is made at the same time every day. They also have tea at eleven o'clock every night. Maybe it's a search for security, I don't know.

My parents attended services at a German Jewish congregation in Manhattan primarily because of the traditional music. There was comfort for them in the ritual that they did as a child. But their observance outside the temple was not at all traditional. They didn't keep kosher, for example. They are sort of a combination of Conservative and Reform Jew.

I think I'm about as religious as my parents. We go to a Reform temple, but I would be just as happy going to a Conservative one, except they would bother me about some things I don't believe in, like keeping kosher. Kosher foods are very available, easy to buy here. And keeping kosher is not hard. You really don't need two separate sinks, only separate dishes and utensils. A lot of people are going back to it today, just not me.

Eastern European Jews

I grew up with a sense of being different from Eastern European Jews. Their family structure was different. They emphasize the extended family—aunts, uncles, cousins, second cousins, and so on. We had so few, because my parents were the immigrants. We couldn't pick and choose among relatives. Those we had we held onto. And we made honorary cousins from friends and friends of friends.

Eastern European Jews also had a lot of language and foods that were different. When I got to college, there were a couple of guys who told me, "You're not Jewish."

I told them, "Of course I'm Jewish. I go to temple, I'm Jewish."

They said "How come you don't know what "boobie" and all those other words mean?" So they sat me down, and they gave me a list of Yiddish words and Yiddish foods I was supposed to know.

A really big difference between German and Eastern European Jews is in the showing of emotions. Germans don't. Crying and laughing and hugging are not done.

My husband's relatives carry on all the time. They have this loudness and nervousness. People seem to say, "See how nervous I am. Look at me, I'm shaking." That includes the men, too. "Look at what you're doing to me," a man might say in business or in family relations. They carry on and scream about things that happened forty years ago.

If German Jews are nervous, they are not permitted to show it. They have a certain proud stoicism and impatience with things like illness or self-limitations. When my uncle died, my aunt was dry-eyed at the funeral. She was sad, but very, very controlled. We don't wear our hearts on our sleeves. We're very German in that way.

Being Different

I spoke only German until I was five years old. I was born in 1941, and at that time in the 1940s we got a lot of flak, both because we were Jewish and because we were German. It was very difficult because we lived in a very prejudiced neighborhood, Jackson

Heights. The Irish were very down on us.

I think I can take more risks now than other people because my parents supported me. Having immigrant parents and being alienated when you're young makes you a lot more comfortable when you're older because you know who you are and what you are. My children didn't have that. There were many ways that I was different, and it's difficult for kids to be different. But from something like that, you understand what's important, how you want to fit in, and how you don't want to.

Independent Children

Rearing the children is very important to me. It's my business. That's what I do. I read a lot about it. I'm very aware about childrearing. For example, I don't stand behind the children and pick them up when they fall down. I explain to the child what is happening, but I won't interfere.

A lot of parents do it the other way, making sure their children go to nice playschools, taking them on educational outings, doing things with and for their children. My husband calls it "nudging," protective hovering. I don't buy into that.

My husband's mother is a real Jewish mother yet. She'll tell him, "It's cold outside, be sure you wear a hat," or, "My son, the professor, see how he behaves."

We took our nephew, who's definitely Eastern European Jewish, along on vacation. It was cool in California, and I said to Philip, "It's a little cool, do you think you might want to put a jacket on?" And he almost fell over, because he was expecting, "Philip, put a jacket on." I would never say that.

My teenaged girls can do things on their own, and they can do what they want to do, but I do try to get them to want to do some things that have value. I try to make it known that watching music videos on television for six hours a day is not necessarily the best thing for their social development. I want them to learn to be independent, and you can't "nudge" independence. I ask them, "How do you think you're going to handle that?" and I get them to think. If somebody beat them up or was nasty, I'll say, "What are you going to do about it? You want my help?" rather than, "I'm going to do something about that for you."

Different Cultures

The girls know from our "rogues gallery," the pictures we have up in the dining room, that they have ancestors who came from two completely different cultures. Unfortunately, Hebrew school didn't help the girls much in getting culture. It's a turn-off for most kids. They start as eight-year-olds and learn the letters so they can sound words out. Then they can read the prayers, and they know what the prayers mean because there is the English translation. But the Hebrew language is just not taught.

My children learned about another culture from my immigrant parents. My father was constantly telling stories about what life was like when he was a boy in Swabia. And I tell my stories to the children, too, about growing up in New York City.

Next summer, my father and mother are going to take our girls to Germany. My parents have been over there twice since the war. They have school chums they visit, so the girls will see Swabian culture firsthand. They won't just be tourists.

They already know a lot about Swabian values, like being thrifty and careful about things. Fixing things is not an American thing to do, but my family follows the old way. My brother did the brakes on his car. It took him a whole week. His time cost him three times more than he would have paid for a brake job. But he gets a feeling of self-reliance, and my other brothers do the same. They tinker constantly, always fixing something. All three of them are PhDs, but fixing things is what they do in the evening.

Sure, it's not always smart to be frugal, especially if there is inflation. People say it's smarter to be a debtor, but if it's risky it will be bad for your gut. If it's going to make you insecure, it's not worth it. Do without—that's the answer.

Israel

My opinion about Israel is not the standard view within the Jewish community. I consider Israel a foreign country where a lot of my cousins live. They're there, and I'm here, and I'm American. I haven't been to visit Israel, but I would if I had the money and if it weren't automatically considered a political gesture of support for Israel—that no matter what Israel does, you automatically like it. I can't stand that, so I'm not going.

In terms of the Holocaust, we are at least as safe here as we are in Israel. The United States is not Germany. It's a wonderful place, and it deserves all my energy and anything I have to give to it because it welcomed us, and it gave us a very nice life.

I believe I'm more Jewish than those people who are so positive about Israel. A lot of people use the support of the state of Israel as an excuse not to consider the more difficult questions, like watching what goes on in your own backyard, watching for discrimination and seeing other things that Jewish Law teaches us. I believe that you can be a perfectly wonderful, ethical Diaspora Jew [living outside of Israel]. This is the crux of the arguments among Jews these days. Some are big on Israel, but not good Jews, not religious Jews.

Intermarriage

In the past several years, my husband and I have become centers of controversy over intermarriage [between Jews and non-Jews] as well as the question of Israel and Jewish identity. We see intermarriage as perfectly acceptable. You bring up the kids, you do what you can, you give them the values that you have to give them, and if they marry out and that causes them to fall away from the religion, so be it.

If your kids decide not to take the values you have to give them, maybe there's something wrong with your values. Of course, if you didn't give your kids any kind of values or training or appreciation for what they are, and then they marry out, don't come crying to me. Not when you never even sent your kid to Hebrew school or when you thought living in a Jewish neighborhood was enough to make them Jewish.

It's not that I'm willing to live with my children's decisions. I just don't think we have any choice about it. You do what you can, but your job as a parent ends at some point. You can't do more than that. As long as you did it conscientiously, you can look back with satisfaction that you did your job.

15: CONCLUSIONS

Today's Germany is very different from the Germany that forced so many to escape to America. Swabia is no longer a rural economy with small farms of five or ten acres. It has eclipsed the former seat of industrial power in the Ruhr. In fact, Swabia is by some measures the most prosperous region of Germany due to the growth of modern industry that has surpassed the power of the coal and steel industries of the north. Baden-Württemberg is ahead of even Japan and the United States in per-capita exports,` and it leads the rest of Europe in patents per capita. It is also second behind Silicon Valley in world sales of business software and computer services. It also has the greatest number of research institutes in all of Europe.[75]

Because Swabia is so prosperous, it has become a magnet for immigration instead of pushing its people to escape. In the closing decades of the twentieth century Swabia attracted many European immigrants such as Italians and Yugoslavs as well as Turks. Such immigrants initially came as "guest workers," expected to return to their countries after working in Germany for a time.

German attitudes then changed. There was recognition of a serious need for workers as birthrates dropped and Germans aged. German laws were also changed, no longer restricting citizenship based solely on blood. Starting in 2000, children born in Germany became citizens at birth if at least one parent had a permanent residence permit and had resided in Germany at least eight years. Evidence of the changed attitude towards non-Germans is Chancellor Merkel's invitation to over one million refugees in 2015.

Modern German attitudes towards Jews are reversed from those of the Nazi years. Germany has been a staunch supporter of Israel, and it has welcomed Jews from Russia and Eastern Europe. The terrible deeds of the Holocaust cannot be undone, but there is no longer a threat of similar actions in modern Germany.

Finally, the legacy of World War II has meant a change in German attitudes towards military adventures. Germany did not join the United States in actions against Iraq, Libya, and Syria. Such pacifist attitudes suggest that Germany will not readily become aggressive and start wars that would again impoverish their own country.

For all these reasons, there is no longer a need to escape the hell that used to be Germany in much of the twentieth century. Today, Germany is for many a goal to reach, not a place to escape from.

REFERENCES

1. Wieland, G.F., *Celtic Germans: The rise and fall of Ann Arbor's Swabians*. 2014, Ann Arbor, MI: George F. Wieland. 406 p.
2. Wieland, G.F., *Stubborn & liking it: Einstein & other Germans in America*. 2016, Ann Arbor, Michigan: George F. Wieland. 312 p.
3. Rivers, T.J., *Laws of the Alamans and Bavarians*. 1977, Philadelphia: University of Pennsylvania Press. xi, 208 p.
4. Moeller, R.G., *Dimensions of social conflict in the Great War: The view from the German countryside*. Central European History, 1981. **14**(2): p. 142-168.
5. Scheff, T.J., *Bloody revenge : emotions, nationalism, and war*. 1994, Boulder: Westview Press. xi, 162 p.
6. Scheff, T.J. and S.M. Retzinger, *Emotions and violence: shame and rage in destructive conflicts*. 2002: Backinprint. Com.
7. Scheff, T.J., *Runaway nationalism: Alienation, shame, and anger*. Understanding terrorism: Building on the sociological imagination, 2007: p. 93-114.
8. Hamilton, R.F., *Who voted for Hitler?* 1982, Princeton, N.J.: Princeton University Press. xv, 664 p.
9. De Jonge, A., *The Weimar chronicle : prelude to Hitler*. 1978, New York: Paddington Press : distributed by Grosset & Dunlap. 256 p.
10. Diamond, S.A., *The Nazi movement in the United States, 1924-1941*. 1974, Ithaca, N.Y. ;: Cornell University Press. 380 p.
11. Miller, M.D., *Wunderlich's salute*. 1983, Smithtown, N.Y.: Malamud-Rose. xi, 336 p.
12. Kammer, A., *Undue process: The untold story of America's German alien internees*. 1997, London: Rowaman & Littlefield. 224 p.
13. Holian, T.J., *The German-Americans and World War II : an ethnic experience*. 1996, New York: P. Lang. xii, 243 p.
14. Tolzmann, D.H., *The World War Two experience--the internment of German-Americans*, in *German-Americans in the world wars*, D.H. Tolzmann, Editor. 1995, KG Saur: Munich. p. 1418.

15. Gannon, M., *Operation Drumbeat : the dramatic true story of Germany's first U-boat attacks along the American coast in World War II*. 1990, New York: Harper & Row. xxii, 490 p.
16. Schoenbaum, D., *Hitler's social revolution : class and status in Nazi Germany, 1933-1939*. 1967, Garden City, N.Y.: Doubleday. 324 p.
17. Tänzer, A., *Die Geschichter der Juden in Württemberg*. 1937, Frankfurt: J. Kaufmann. xv, 190 p.
18. Jeggle, U., *Judendörfer in Württemberg*. 1969, Tübingen: :Tübingen Vereinigung für Volkskunde. 361 p.
19. Dicker, H., *Creativity, Holocaust, reconstruction: Jewish life in Wuerttemberg, past and present*. 1984, Brooklyn: Sepher Hermon Press. 234 p.
20. Barkai, A., *German-Jewish Migrations in the Nineteenth Century, 1830–1910*. The Leo Baeck Institute Yearbook, 1985. 30(1): p. 301-318.
21. Gordon, S.A., *Hitler, Germans, and the "Jewish question"*. 1984, Princeton, N.J.: Princeton University Press. xiv, 412 p.
22. Sauer, P. and Dokumentationsstelle zur Erforschung der Schicksale der Jüdischen Bürger in Baden-Württemberg 1933-1945., *Die Schicksale der jüdischen Bürger Badem-Württembergs während der nationalsozialistischen Verfolgungszeit 1933-1945; statistische Ergebnisse der Erhebungen der Dokumentationsstelle bei der Archivdirektion Stuttgart und zusammenfassende Darstellung*. 1969, Stuttgart,: W. Kohlhammer. xvi, 468 p.
23. Sauer, P., *Die Schichksale der jüdischen Bürger Baden-Württembergs während der nationalsozialistischen Verfolgungszeit 1933-1945*. 1969, Stuttgart: W. Kohlhammer. 468 p.
24. Brickman, P., A. Abbey, and J.L. Halman, *Commitment, conflict, and caring*. 1987, Engleweood Cliff, NJ: Prentice-Hall. 317 p.
25. Rhodes, J.M., *The Hitler movement : a modern millenarian revolution*. 1980, Stanford, Calif.: Hoover Institution Press. 253 p.
26. Marrus, M.R., *The unwanted : european refugees in the twentieth century*. 1985, New York: Oxford University Press. xii, 414 p.
27. Bard, M.G., *48 hours of Kristallnacht : night of destruction/dawn of the Holocaust : an oral history*. 2008, Guilford, Conn.: Lyons Press. xiv, 240 p.
28. Johnson, E.A., *What we knew : terror, mass murder, and everyday life in Nazi Germany : an oral history*. 2005, United States: Basic Books. 434 p.
29. Schadt, J., *Verfolgung und Widerstand*, in *Das Dritte Reich in Baden und Württemberg, hg. v. Otto Borst*, Stuttgart. 1988. p. 96-120.

REFERENCES

30. Steinert, M.G., *Hitler's war and the Germans ; public mood and attitude during the Second World War*. 1977, Athens: Ohio University Press. x, 387 p.
31. Drinkwater, J., *The life and adventures of Carl Laemmle 1931*, New York: G. P. Putnam's Sons. xii, 288 p.
32. Hinck, W., *Leben im Exil: Probleme der Integration deutscher Flüchtlinge im Ausland, 1933-1945*. Vol. 18. 1981: Hoffmann u. Campe.
33. Dubrovsky, G.W., *The land was theirs: Jewish farmers in the Garden State*. 1992: University of Alabama Press. 272 p.
34. Maier, C.S. and American Council of Learned Societies., *The unmasterable past history, Holocaust, and German national identity*. 1997, Harvard University Press: Cambridge, Mass. p. xix, 227 p.
35. Horowitz, I.L., *Counting bodies: The dismal science of authorized terror*. Patterns of Prejudice, 1989. **23**(2): p. 4-15.
36. Hoess, R., *Commandant of Auschwitz: the autobiography of Rudolf Hoess*. 1974: Pan Books Ltd.
37. Fein, H., *Accounting for genocide : national responses and Jewish victimization during the Holocaust*. 1979, New York: Free Press. xxi, 468 p.
38. Katz, J., *One who came back : the diary of a Jewish survivor*. New ed. 2006, Takoma Park, Md.: Dryad Press in association with the University of Wisconsin Press. xvi, 231 p.
39. Yeshiva University. Museum., *The German Jews of Washington Heights : an oral history project*. 1987, New York, N.Y.: Yeshiva University Museum. 60 p.
40. Eaton, W.W., J.J. Sigal, and M. Weinfeld, *Impairment in Holocaust survivors after 33 years: Data from an unbiased community struggle*. The American Journal of Psychiatry, 1982. **139**((6), June): p. 773-777
41. Koch, H.W., *The Hitler Youth : origins and development 1922-45*. 1976, New York: Stein and Day. ix, 348 p.
42. Lang, D., *A backward look : Germans remember*. 1979, New York: McGraw-Hill. 112
43. Ludewig, J., *Rückzug : the German retreat from France, 1944*. 2012, Lexington: University Press of Kentucky. xviii, 435 p.
44. Rumpf, H., *The bombing of Germany*. New York. 1962: Rinehart and Winston. 256 p.
45. Sauer, P., *Württemberg in der Zeit des Nationalsozialismus*. 1975, Ulm: Süddeutsche Verlagsgesellschaft. 519 p.
46. United States Strategic Bombing Survey., *The effects of strategic bombing on German morale*. 1947, Washington,. 2 v.
47. Whiting, C., *The home front: Germany*. Vol. 32. 1982, Chicago: Time Life.

48. Beck, E.R., *The Allied Bombing of Germany, 1942-1945, and the German Response: Dilemmas of Judgment*. German Studies Review, 1982. **5**(3): p. 325-337.
49. Zink, H., *The United States in Germany, 1944-1955*. 1957, Princeton, N.J.,: Van Nostrand. 374 p.
50. Davis, F.M., *Come as a conqueror; the United States Army's occupation of Germany, 1945-1949*. 1967, New York,: Macmillan. xvi, 271 p.
51. Botting, D. and T.-L. Books, *The aftermath: Europe*. 1983, Alexandria, VA; Morristown, NJ: Time-Life Books.
52. Bach, J.S., *America's Germany, an account of the occupation*. 1946, New York,: Random house. x, 310 p.
53. Boelcke, W.A., *Der Schwarzmarkt 1945-1948: vom Überleben nach dem Kriege*. 1986: Georg Westermann Verlag.
54. Botting, D., *From the ruins of the Reich : Germany, 1945-1949*. 1985, New York: Crown. 341 p.
55. Enssle, M.J., *The harsh discipline of food scarcity in postwar Stuttgart, 1945-1948*. German Studies Review, 1987. **10**(3): p. 481-502.
56. Mayne, R., *Postwar, the dawn of today's Europe*. 1983, New York: Schocken Books. 336 p.
57. Dinnerstein, L., *Who were the displaced persons?*, in *Immigration and ethnicity*, M. D'Innocenzo, Editor. 1992, Greenwood Press: Westport, CT. p. 247-256.
58. Douglas, R.M., *Orderly and humane : the expulsion of the Germans after the Second World War*. 2012, New Haven [Conn.]: Yale University Press. xii, 486 p.
59. Dow, J.E., *The German Nation: Displacement and Resettlement*. 1968, New York: American Press. 194.
60. Sorge, M.K., *The other price of Hitler's war : German military and civilian losses resulting from World War II*. 1986, New York: Greenwood Press. xx, 175 p., .
61. Dundes, A., *Life is like a chicken coop ladder : a portrait of German culture through folklore*. 1984, New York: Columbia University Press. xi, 174 p.
62. Nationalsozialistische Deutsche Arbeiter-Partei. Reichsorganisationsamt., *Partei-Statistik, Stand 1. Januar 1935*. 1935, [München? 3 v.
63. Hinkle, L.B., *Meaning of choral experience to the adult membership of the German singing societies comprising the United Singers Federation of Pennsyvania*, in *School of Music*. 1987, Pennsylvania State University: State College.
64. Schmied, S., *Scheindorf 1780-1970*. 1970, Leubas/Kempten: Self published. 36.
65. Weidlein, J., *Geschichte der Ungarndeutschen in Dokumenten, 1930-1950*. 1958, Schorndorf,. 408 p.

REFERENCES

66. Weidlein, J., *Schicksalsjahre der Ungarndeutschen : die ungarische Wendung*. Ostdeutsche Beiträge aus dem Göttinger Arbeitskreis. 1957, Würzburg: Holzner-Verlag. vi, 164 p.
67. Georgescu, V. and M. Calinescu, *The Romanians : a history*. 1991, London ; New York: I.B. Tauris. xiv, 357 p.
68. Steinberg, S., *Why Irish became domestics and Italians and Jews did not*, in *The ethnic myth: race, ethnicity, and class in America* 1989, Beacon: Boston. p. 151-66.
69. Gans, H.J., *Symbolic ethnicity: the future of ethnic groups and cultures in America*. Ethnic and racial studies, 1979. **2**(1): p. 1-20.
70. Waters, M.C., *Ethnic options: choosing identities in America*. 1990: Univ of California Press. 224 p.
71. Harris, J.R., *The nurture assumption : why children turn out the way they do*. 1998, New York: Free Press. xviii, 462 p.
72. Greeley, A.M., *Ethnicity in the United States: a preliminary reconnaissance*. 1974, New York: Wiley. 347 p.
73. Wust, K., et al., *Span 200 : a companion piece to the Span 200 exhibit, the story of German-American involvement in the founding and development of America*. 1976, Philadelphia: Published in behalf of Institut für Auslandsbeziehungen, Stuttgart by National Carl Schurz Association. 95 p.
74. Cerroni-Long, E.L., *Marrying out: socio-cultural and psychological implications of intermarriage*. Journal of Comparative Family Studies, 1985: p. 25-46.
75. Trübenbach, M., *Die Superlative der Region Stuttgart und Baden-Württemberg*. n.d., Ostfildern: Matthias Trübenbach.

INDEX

abortions, 55, 108
abuse, child, 136
affidavits, 17, 37; accumulating 107; children make difficult, 94; during Great Depression, 67; hard for families, 81; not sufficient, 90
airmen, Allied losses, 126
alcohol, 15, 26, 33; permitted, 185; taxed, 30
alcoholics, 29
Alien Registration Act, 49
aliens, German, 49-51, 174
Alps, 127
altar boys, 25, 176
Amish, 185
anal character, 139
annexations, 2, 132; refugees from, 134
anti-Semitism: due to high standards, 191; in Connecticut, 174; in Germany, 188. See also Nazis
anxieties, 139
appreciations, for America, 3, 172
apprenticeships, 11, 23, 34, 47, 162, 170, 187

Arbeitdienst, 146
assimilation, 3; name change, 164; not necessary, 184, 185; to Americans, 174, 175, 178; to Hungarians, 163
Austria, 160-61
atuhority, problems with, 5, 10, 20, 138, 180, 189
autonomy, 179. See also indpendence
Baden-Württemberg, 60, 66, 67, 201
bakeries, 36-42, 48
bankruptcies, 23
Bartenbach, 8, 9
basket making, 32
Bay (Gerhardt's mother), 123-24
Bay, Gerhardt, 117-124, 134
Bay Ridge, 174
beds, bunk, 92, 145
beer, 15, 28, 75, 77, 176, 184
begging, 169
Berlin, 45, 59 68, 100
Bible, 10, 14, 15, 49, 176, 181
Biddle, Francis, 51
birthrates, German, 201
Black Forest, 48, 61, 71, 95
black markets, 49, 128, 129, 161, 187

blackouts, 146
Blacks, 130, 131, 137
Black Swabs, 166
bombings: carpet, 2, 118, 119, 125; days, 148;initial, 144;bombings nights, 148; strategic, inaccurate, 125
bombs, air, 146, 147
bombs: defused, 137; incendiary, 118-19, 125-26, 146
Brazil, 12
Brendli, Marie, 163-166
Brendli, Stefan, 159, 162
bricks, 13, 144, 149, 164
Bronx, 173
Brownshirts. See Strom Troopers
Bucher, Dorothy, 182
Bucher, Ferdl, 25-42
Buffalo NY, 21, 131
Bund deutsche Mädchen, 63, 115, 145
Bund, German American, 46, 47, 189
bunkers, air raid, 145-48
burdens, equalized, 134
butchering, 23, 77, 79, 83, 91, 102, 104, 145, 162, 189
cigarettes, 121, 123, 128-130, 161
camps, internment, 50. See also concentration camps
Catholics, 22, 45, 135, 157, 159, 182, 191
Ceausescu, Nicolae, 165
Celts, 5
character, maintaining, 73, 179, 182
Chicago, 153-55, 183
children, 9-12, 15; of immigrants, 173-186; work, 8, 161
choral groups, 49, 78, 155
cider, 7, 11, 30
cigarettes, 121, 123, 128-30, 161
circumcisions, 173

Ciresa, Sonia, 143-156
citizens, American, 50, 52, 174
citizenship, German, gaining, 201
civil liberties, 45
Clark, Andrea, 136-141
cleanliness, 139
Clifton NJ, 172
clubs, 14, 49, 175
coffee, 89, 129, 131, 152, 161
collective farms, 165, 169-171
Communists, 13, 14, 43, 44, 45, 53
complexions, Swabian, 5
concentration camps, 56, 65-66, 75, 77, 84, 90, 92-99, 102-104, 108-111, 190
conflicts, sibling, 16
Connecticut, anti-Semitism in, 174
conscientiousness 3, 6, 7, 173, 177, 178, 182
conscientious objector, 50
consent, parental, 35
conservation, land, 185
consulates, 17, 64, 94, 130. See also affidavits
Corpus Christi, 26
courts, 6, 44
Crailsheim, 14
criticisms, 140
Crystal City TX, 51
Crystal Night, 2, 64-66, 77, 90, 94
culture, American lack of, 137
culture, symbolic, 178
cultures, Jewish, German and Eastern European, 198
curfews, 89, 129, 151
customs, maintaining, 195
Dachau, 65-66, 67, 94, 135
Danube River, 122-24, 130, 157
Danube Swabians, 157
Democrats, 23
de-Nazification, 135
deserters, 122, 127

210

INDEX

Deutsche Marks, 134
Dillingen, 122-24
discrimination, 200; by Germans, 61, by Jews, 174; by Romanians, 166-68
diversity, cultural, 184
divorce, 154
Donauschwaben, 157
draft, 2, 27, 50, 70, 98, 146
East Germany, 167
eggs, 24, 68, 129
Einstein, Albert, 2, 49, 182
Eisenhower, General Ike, 127, 128
elections, 44, 45
Ellis Island, 36, 51
Emergency Detention Program, 49
emigration, from America, 23, 36, 48, 154
emotions, display of, 197
employment agencies, 38-39
enemies, Sonia warned of, 154
engagements, 152
English, learning, 18, 37, 102, 135, 140, 143, 173-175
entrepreneurs, 21-23, 40, 162, 163, 180
ethnic Germans, 99, 132, 134, 157, 163. See also Sathmar Germans and Leili, Gunther
evacuations, 118, 146
executions, civilian, 122
Eybach, 125
factory work, 13, 21, 37, 153
fares, ship, 14
farmers, preferences, 17
farms, urban, 21
farm work, 12-18, 75, 93, 94, 97, 109, 126, 127. See also Bucher, Ferdinand, Sathmar Swabians, and Leili, Gunther

FBI, 49-52, 174, 192
fear, 34
festivals, 176
Finkbeiner, Reginald and Georgia, 178
Fischer, Hermann, 43
First World War, 5, 9, 26
flails, 6, 31
flares, 146
Fleischer, Richard, 107-113
Flüchtlinge. See refugees
food 5, 11, 27, 36, 66, 71, 89, 98, 109, 112, 120, 123, 126, 128-29, 131-32, 135, 145, 152, 160-61, 165, 169, 181, 184, 187, 195-97
forgiveness, in culture, 191
fraternization, 70, 127-28
frugality, 7, 36, 37, 73, 178, 181, 185-86, 196
garbage cans, 129, 161
gas, poison, 27
gas masks, 145
Geiser, Helga, 130-31, 135-36
German (language), 154, 173, 197
German, remaining, 177. See also assimilation
German Americans: contribution of, 185; mechanical aptitudes of, 183; pro-German, 190
Germans, ethnic, 99, 132, 134, 157, 163
Germany: emigration to, 166; no need to escape, 202
Gideon, Max, 75-85
girls, German, and soldiers, 155
Goebbels, Joseph, 67, 121
Goering, Hermann, 45
Goldstein, Ruth, 195-200
Graeber, Gunther, 51-52
grafting, 31
Graves, Keith, 184-85

211

Great Depression, 20, 36, 39, 45, 48, 56, 67
greehnorns, 35, 38-40
Gruber, Hilda, 22
Gruber, Karl, 22
Gruber, Louis, 9, 10, 50
grumbling, about war, 120-21
guest workers, 201
guilt, 44, 50, 135, 137-39
gun cotton, 37
guns: BB, 131; confiscated, 123, 150-51
half-brothers, 34
Hamroth, 163-66
hard work. See work ethic
harshness, 137
hatreds, anti-German, 27, 48. See also anti-Semitism
hay, 8, 33, 75, 159, 171
heaven, 41
Hebrew schools, 84, 198, 199, 200
Heidelberg, 127
Heilbronn, 58, 59, 60, 124-25
Heil Hitlers, 10, 46, 47, 48, 118, 145
heritage, Swabian, 178, 184, 195, 199
Hindenberg, 45
Hitler, Adolf, 43, 44, 45; attempts on life, 121; praised, 52, 54
Hitler parties, 50
Hockele, Walter, 46-48
Höfer, Henry, 17, 22
Hohnweiler, 27
Holocaust, 87-113; danger in america, 199; knowledge of, 190
homeguards, 121-122
Hoover, J. Edgar, 49-50
houses, repairing, 149
houses, building, 39
houses, burned, 164

houses, open, 125
House Un-American Activities Committee, 47
housewives, 19, 179
housing, scarce, 133
humiliations, 44, 65
Hungary, 157-160, 163-64, 166
Hurm, Ana, 183
Hurm, John, 183
identity, immigrant status fosters, 197
illegitimacy, 17
Illinois, 153
immigrants, German attitudes towards, 201
incendiaries, 118-19, 125-26, 146, 148
independence, 7, 21, 179, 189, 195-96, 198
individualism, 1, 3, 5, 7, 173, 179, 180, 195
inflation, 11, 12, 14, 133-34, 199
inflexibility, from punishment, 138
inheritances, 1, 5, 6, 15, 16, 17, 35, 42, 187
interviews, 3
introverts, 186
invalids, 9, 27, 52
Irish, 197
Italians, 175
Jackson Heights, 197
Japanese Americans, 52
Jasper, IN, 183
Jersey City, 174
Jesus, 41, 176
Jews: anti-German, 192; attitudes towards Israel, 199; attitudes towards intermarriage, 200; as cattle dealers, 29; Conservative and Reform, 196; in diaspora,

INDEX

200; as doctors, 173; Eastern European, 197; emancipation of, 1, 57; as employers, 18; fired, 2; hated by farmers, 53; in New York City, 18, 102; as peddlers, 29; in Pforzheim, 48; Polish, 82, 195; Russian, 195; in Weimar Republic, 44; visit Germany, 71, 112, 199; Yiddish-speaking, 82, 195, 197
Jim, husband, 152-56
John (son), 153-56
Kaiser, 28
Karolyi, Prince, 157
Kirchberg/Murr, 6
Kirchheim, 187
Kirchweih, 144
Kodak factory, 145-150
kosher, keeping, 196
Kraft, Walter, 126
leather, 12
Lebensraum, 47
Leili, Bill, 158
Leili, Gunther, 167
leisure, 13
literacy tests, 17
loners, 60, 97, 113, 179, 189
looting, 130, 131
lords, of peasants, 158
Ludwig, Ken, 177, 180, 182
Luikart, Walter, 187-193
Lutherans, 5, 10, 11, 41, 189
machine tools, 144
maids, 3, 18, 19, 56, 62, 68, 102, 112, 136, 175, 188
manure, 7, 8, 13, 26, 31, 75, 149, 159, 170
marketing, 32
marriages, 3, 35, 38, 59, 134, 143, 153, 155, 178, 200,
mass media, 44. See also Goebbels
master, *Meister*, 11. See also apprentice-ships
Mauser, Ernst, 50
Mayday, 47, 67
mechanical aptitudes, 179, 183
Mein Kampf, 44
men, scarcity of, 111, 136
Mennonites, 185
mentality, German, 173; maintaining, 178
Mercedes factory, 148
Merkel, Chancellor, 201
Methodists, 11, 22
military adventures, German, 202
morale, and carpet bombing, 125
Morganthau, Henry 132
Moroccans, 131
Motorola, 153
Munich, 43, 119-20, 121
music, 11; in Swabia, 143
napalm, 147
Nationalist Party, 44
Nazis, 13, 43-54; attitude towards, 190; capitalized on failure, 192; going along with, 192; labeled, 161; provide supplies, 151. See also anti-Semitism, Jews
Neckar River, 143, 152
nervousness, 197
nigger boy, 137
norms, on collective, 170
nudging, 198
Nuremberg, 60, 70, 117, 127
obedience, 9, 10, 89. See also independence
occupations (military): American, 100-01, 122-24, 127-31, 137, 150, 152-53, 160-61; French, 43, 127, 131-32,

150-51
office work, 143, 148
orderliness, 139
organization (trait), 119, 177
Ottoman Turks, 157
outhouses, 149
oxen, 34, 159, 160, 169, 170
packages, from America, 135
parliament, 44-45
Paterson NJ, 172
peasants, 5-20, 46, 52, 56, 57, 59, 75, 132, 157-58
pensions, 134
Pforzheim, 46, 48, 126
Philadelphia, 11, 18, 23, 34-35, 48-50
pianos, playing, 143, 151-53
Polack, 137
Poland, 48, 64, 77, 81-82, 88, 92, 97, 99-100, 112, 118, 132, 134
poverty, 7- 21, 30-31
POWs, 26-27, 51, 99, 113, 122, 124, 128, 129, 164
pregnancies, 33, 55, 108, 153, 187
pretzels, 31
pride, 156, 139, 177
priests, 10, 25-26, 31, 159, 165
privacy, 3, 179, 187-88
problem solvers, 20
Prussia, 44, 45, 135
psychiatrists, 187
puberty, 136
punishments, physical, 9, 10, 25, 28, 137
Putza, 158
quotas, 2, 17, 66, 67, 71, 88, 92, 94, 96,
rabbits, 131, 145, 165
radios, 48, 98, 117, 127-28
rapes, 131
rationing, 27, 89, 91, 94, 109, 153,

161, 165
recipes 40
Red Army, 88, 159, 160. See also Russians
refugees, 2-3, 49, 51, 57, 60, 63, 68-69, 71, 94, 102, 119, 126, 130, 132, 134-37, 159-60, 162, 201
regimentation, 138, 140
Reichsmarks, 111, 134
Reichstag, 44-45
religiosity, 6, 7, 25, 41, 176, 178, 182, 189
reparations, 43, 44, 112, 127
Republicans, 23, 177
requisitioning, 123, 132
resentments, 53
Rhineland, 43
Romania, 87, 157, 159, 163-72
Roosevelt, Pres. Franklin D., 47, 49, 52, 84
routines, preference for, 196
Ruhr, 43
Russians, 47, 100, 144. See also Red Army
Sabbath, 13, 58, 61, 81, 82, 103
Sathmar Swabians, 157-66
Satu Mare. *See* Sathmar Swabians
sauerkraut, 31
savings, 134
Saxon Germans, 159
Scheindorf, 158-60
Schleissweiler, 5, 6
Schlimmeyer, Lena, 5, 13, 17, 18, 52, 175
Schlimmeyer, Lily, 174, 175, 179-81, 182
Schmidt, 115-17, 127-30,
Schmitz, 132-33
schnapps, 15, 26-27, 30-31
scrennings, consulate 17
Seagoville TX, 51

INDEX

sects, 10, 11, 22
self-sufficiency, 7, 158
sewing, 19, 33, 39, 63, 102, 103
sex, 32, 33, 44, 55, 60, 62, 128, 151
shame, 1, 27, 53, 64, 130, 137, 138
shelters, 124, 125, 126, 144-48
ship fares, 14
Shrafft's, 124
simplicity, material, 185
single parents, 154
slave drivers, 22
Social Democrats, 44, 59, 191
soldiers: American, 69-71, 100-101, 122-24, 127-53, 160-61; English, 97; French, 27, 43, 150-52; German, 9, 69, 99, 121, 159, 164; Hungarian, 164; Polish, 100; Russian, 98, 99, 100, 108-110, 160, 164
Sonia, as Russian, 145
Spanish (language), 185
spirituality, 5, 10, 25, 41, 178, 181, 182, 185
sprees, alcoholic, 33,34
SS, 47, 65-66, 88, 96, 99, 108-109, 112
stab in back, 44
starvation, 110, 167-68, 169. See also rationing
stature, Swabian, 5
status, 29, 32, 44, 73, 158
Steinthal, Lotte, 173, 174
Steinthal, Rudy, 173, 174, 179, 180-81
Steinthal, Werner, 173
stepbrothers, 34
stepfathers, 29, 30-31, 33, 34, 35
stigma, 15, 175
Storm Troopers, 45, 59, 60, 78-79
strafing, 120, 130
strictness, 10, 28, 104, 138-39, 175

stubbornness, 16, 173
Stuttgart, 2, 12, 34, 35, 56, 58, 61, 64, 65, 81, 82, 90, 91, 95, 101, 107, 121, 125, 136-138, 143, 152,
submarines, 51, 52, 110
suicides, 16, 56
Sulzbach, 7
superegos, 138
Super Germans, 1
superintendents (building), 20-21, 161-162
support, from other immigrants, 140
tanks, 123
taxes, 16, 30, 31, 34, 57, 69, 157, 158, 177
teachers, 2, 9, 10, 31, 76, 78, 138, 140, 145, 163, 180, 192
teenagers, 2, 103, 115, 136
threshing, 31
Time Zero, 2, 132
tobacco, 128-29
toilets, 125, 139, 149, 160
total war, 117, 121
Trailhof, 5
Transylvania, 159
tuberculosis, 132
Turners, *Turnverein*, 13, 192
Type A person, 195
U-boats, 51, 52, 110
Ukrainians, 112, 178
unions, labor, 20
United Church of Christ, 176
Untertürkheim, 143
Upper Swabia, 162
Veracruz, 183
Versailles Treaty, 44, 132
victimization, 53
vineyards, 30, 158
Volksdeutsch. See ethnic Germans
wagon trains, 160, 172

215

Wahr, Eugene, 124-25
Wangen, 143, 154
wars, having to fight, 192, 193
war brides, looked down on, 153
wartime, German Americans as
    pro-German, 191
Weber, Ernst, 17, 21, 22, 24, 46
Weber, Louise, 19
welfare, 12, 17, 74, 172
White Rose, 121
Wiel, Gottlieb, 7, 12, 16, 20, 21, 24,
    46, 52
Wiel, Sharon, 178
Wieland, Gene, 8, 9, 11, 15, 18, 23,
    48, 49
Wieland, Paula, 14, 23, 24
Wiesenmayer, Bob, 6, 8, 10, 12, 14,
    15, 16, 21, 24, 53
Wiesenmayer, Marie, 175-78
Wilhelm, King, 28
windows, broken, 148
wine, 25, 30, 101, 144, 158, 162,
    176, 184
women, 8, 14, 17, 109, 110, 111,
    125, 128, 132, 133, 137-
    38, 165
wood, gathering, 31, 133
work, buiding houses, 172
work on Sabbath, 13, 38, 81, 103,
    155,
workers: forced, 149, 150; foreign,
    126; nonessential 126
work ethic, 13, 22-23, 28, 68, 74,
    119, 155-56, 159, 171,
    180, 182, 190
World War I, 5, 9, 26
Württemberg, 9, 28, 57, 67, 75, 77,
    91, 92
Yiddish 68, 82, 195, 197
Yorkville, 19, 192
Youngstown OH 17, 21, 46

THE AUTHOR

George F. Wieland holds a B.A. in psychology from Stanford and a Ph.D. in sociology and psychology from the University of Michigan, Ann Arbor. He has taught and conducted research at Michigan, Vanderbilt, and Guy's Hospital Medical School in London, England. He has written several books on hospital and organizational cultures. His latest books on German immigrants are *Celtic Germans: The Rise and Fall of Ann Arbor's Swabians* and *Stubborn & Liking It: Einstein & Other Germans in America*. A native of New York City, he currently lives in Ann Arbor, Michigan.

Made in the USA
Charleston, SC
06 February 2017